LUTHERAN QUARTERLY BOOKS

Editor

Paul Rorem, Princeton Theological Seminary

Associate Editors

Timothy J. Wengert, The Lutheran Theological Seminary at Philadelphia, and Steven Paulson, Luther Seminary, St. Paul

Lutheran Quarterly Books will advance the same aims as *Lutheran Quarterly* itself, aims repeated by Theodore G. Tappert when he was editor fifty years ago and renewed by Oliver K. Olson when he revived the publication in 1987. The original four aims continue to grace the front matter and to guide the contents of every issue, and can now also indicate the goals of *Lutheran Quarterly Books:* "to provide a forum (1) for the discussion of Christian faith and life on the basis of the Lutheran confessions; (2) for the application of the principles of the Lutheran church to the changing problems of religion and society; (3) for the fostering of world Lutheranism; and (4) for the promotion of understanding between Lutherans and other Christians."

For further information, see www.lutheranquarterly.com.

The symbol and motto of *Lutheran Quarterly,* VDMA for *Verbum Domini Manet in Aeternum* (1 Peter 1:25), was adopted as a motto by Luther's sovereign, Frederick the Wise, and his successors. The original "Protestant" princes walking out of the imperial Diet of Speyer 1529, unruly peasants following Thomas Muentzer, and from 1531 to 1547 the coins, medals, flags, and guns of the Smalcaldic League all bore the most famous Reformation slogan, the first Evangelical confession: the Word of the Lord remains forever.

V|D
M|A   *Lutheran Quarterly Books*

TITLES

Living by Faith: Justification and Sanctification by Oswald Bayer (2003).

Harvesting Martin Luther's Reflections on Theology, Ethics, and the Church, essays from *Lutheran Quarterly* edited by Timothy J. Wengert, with foreword by David C. Steinmetz (2004).

A More Radical Gospel: Essays on Eschatology, Authority, Atonement, and Ecumenism by Gerhard O. Forde, edited by Mark Mattes and Steven Paulson (2004).

The Role of Justification in Contemporary Theology by Mark C. Mattes (2004).

The Captivation of the Will: Luther vs. Erasmus on Freedom and Bondage by Gerhard O. Forde (2005).

Bound Choice, Election, and Wittenberg Theological Method: From Martin Luther to the Formula of Concord by Robert Kolb (2005).

A Formula for Parish Practice: Using the Formula of Concord in Congregations by Timothy J. Wengert (2006).

A FORMULA FOR PARISH PRACTICE

Using the Formula of Concord in Congregations

Timothy J. Wengert

WILLIAM B. EERDMANS PUBLISHING COMPANY

GRAND RAPIDS, MICHIGAN / CAMBRIDGE, U.K.

© 2006 Wm. B. Eerdmans Publishing Co.
All rights reserved

Wm. B. Eerdmans Publishing Co.
2140 Oak Industrial Drive N.E., Grand Rapids, Michigan 49505 /
P.O. Box 163, Cambridge CB3 9PU U.K.
www.eerdmans.com

Printed in the United States of America

12 11 10 09 08 07   8 7 6 5 4 3 2

Library of Congress Cataloging-in-Publication Data

Wengert, Timothy J.
    A formula for parish practice: using the Formula of Concord in
congregations / Timothy J. Wengert.
        p.   cm.
    ISBN 978-0-8028-3026-5 (pbk. : alk. paper)
    1. Formula Concordiae. 2. Theology, Practical.
3. Lutheran Church — Doctrines. I. Title.

BX8069.4.W46 2006
238′.41 — dc22

                                         2005034329

Contents

Contents

Foreword

People have described the *Book of Concord* in many ways during the past four hundred years, but it has seldom been labeled a handbook of pastoral care or a guide to parish practice. In fact, however, each of its documents indicates the way of thinking that the Wittenberg professors of the second quarter of the sixteenth century tried to cultivate in their students, a way of thinking that proceeded out of concerns for proper pastoral care of sinners being turned into saints. Philip Melanchthon could not separate his public teaching from the practice of the church when he composed the Augsburg Confession. Its first twenty-one articles affirm the biblical foundation and catholic tradition upon which the theologians of Wittenberg confessed their faith, and its final seven articles applied their teaching to the critical practices of the regular life of congregations, practices that had fallen under the condemnation of the reformers. Melanchthon's Apology deepens his pastoral critique and his suggestions for solutions to problems and abuses connected with the usages and practices of the people of God.

The Smalcald Articles lay down the foundations of Wittenberg teaching in the affirmation of the ancient creeds in part I, and the confession of the "first and chief article: that Jesus Christ, our God and Lord, 'was handed over to death for our trespasses and was raised for our justification' . . ." in the second part, article I. Luther's elaboration of the chief article addressed the crisis of pastoral care that beset the late medieval church and had evoked his call for reform. He criticized, for instance, practices connected with belief in purgatory, the Mass, pilgrimages, and other customs of contemporary piety. In the third section, on topics to be discussed at council, the reformer first treated sin, law, and repentance, all topics that reflected his concern for sinners at a practical level. He ended the document with brief formulations of teaching on the life of the church (excommunication, ordination and vocation, marriage of priests, monastic vows, worship practices) and the good works that flow from faith. For the Wittenberg reformers the burning issues that needed to be addressed by the council were all of a practical, pastoral nature. The Small Catechism, Luther's confession of faith to Germany's young people, their parents, and their pastors, was dropped down right in the middle of congregational life. Its first part, anchored in law (the Ten Commandments) and gospel (the creed) flowing into life in conversation with God in prayer and meditation, provides the foundation for the proper conduct of daily life. The second and third parts of the Small Catechism lead young learners into the practice of the faith through Luther's program for daily prayer — morning, evening, and at mealtime — and his program for service in vocation, the Table of Christian Callings. Each of these confessions of faith reflects a mind-set focused on pastoral care and parish practice.

So, too, the Formula of Concord wrestled with controversies among the Lutherans of the third quarter of the sixteenth century that the disputing participants viewed as matters affecting the spiritual care of the people of God. Particularly its tenth article, dealing with *adiaphora,* or neutral matters, arose out of concerns about how laypeople would perceive changes in the conduct of worship life. It also sprang from fears that the religious policies of Elector Moritz of Saxony threatened the integrity of the church in relation to the power structures of society. This article sought to give guidance on the public confession and practice of the faith for pastors and laypeople alike. Other articles also reflect the fundamental concern for pastoral care of beleaguered sinners. The range of problems that beset Luther's and Melanchthon's heirs in relation to defining the justification of the sinner in God's sight through Christ arose out of the challenge of how best to proclaim salvation in Christ and apply it properly to consciences in need of comfort. That range of problems embraced everything from original sin (article 1) to the uses of the law (article 6) and God's election of his own (article 11). The authors of the Formula regarded the proper understanding of the Lord's Supper (articles 7-9) important because the sacrament served as a means of providing comfort and hope to troubled minds and hearts. Indeed, the Formula of Concord was necessary, in the view of its authors and the secular governments that funded their efforts, because of the offense given pious consciences by continuing controversy.

This focus on pastoral care and parish practice grew smoothly out of the very nature of the Wittenberg Reformation itself. For Luther had addressed first of all the crisis of pastoral care that was plaguing the late medieval church. He directed God's Word to defiant hearts in need of repentance and to repentant hearts in need of the consolation that Christ alone can give. In this volume Timothy Wengert has recognized this context of parish practice and how it shaped this formula for concord among the heirs of the Wittenberg call for the return of the church to the foot of the cross. He perceptively guides readers into the Lutheran way of posing questions and identifying the biblical framework for reality.

In the process of leading us to the right questions, Wengert lays down a hermeneutical foundation for the study of Scripture and the implementation of spiritual care among the people of God. He effectively uses vignettes for conveying how the Word of God actually works in people's lives. Like the biblical writers, Luther and his colleagues and students were concerned with the story of human life, with principles that are played out in daily living and cannot be understood apart from human flesh and blood, human emotions, human thought. That is God's way of interacting with us, as a God of and in human history, and it is the way his revelation works among us. For God reveals himself in person, not in principle. Lutheran theology confesses the conversing God, who creates and restores human life by talking, and through his talk by acting as the Lord who judges and who saves.

It is this God who stands at the center of Wengert's discussion because this God stands at the center of the concordists' effort. Wengert effectively pulls their text into twenty-first-century contexts. He takes the text of the Epitome of the Formula and shows how this summary by Jakob Andreae of the larger work of his five colleagues in concord, the Solid Declaration, cuts through the smoke and mirrors of contemporary Western culture. Wengert shows how Andreae's words can aid Christians today in delivering God's judgment and mercy in our world.

Andreae and his colleagues knew that to confess what God says involves saying no to alternatives formulated by other voices. Following the text of the Formula, Wengert helps contemporary readers see how to evaluate deceptive and misleading elements in our culture as well as the message of forgiveness, liberation, and new life in Christ, a message that restores those who have strayed from trusting in God to true human living in him.

This book captures the way the Wittenberg circle practiced theology. Thus, it does not point us back into the sophisticated structures of medieval theologies, based on insightful epistemological constructions of the path to knowledge of spiritual things, nor does it mire us in postmodern reflection on how to overcome the false dichotomy of objective and subjective left behind by the Enlightenment. Instead, it applies the direct address that the Wittenberg reformers took from Scripture and hurled at their hearers and readers. They believed that God acts in his law when judgment is proclaimed and that God acts in his gospel when the death and resurrection of Christ are pronounced upon sinners longing for a Savior. Wengert uses the twelve articles of the Formula of Concord to illustrate how this theological method works.

In place of the medieval *via moderna* and *via antiqua,* Luther and Melanchthon and the Wittenberg team surrounding them constructed a *via Wittebergensis* that differed from its predecessors not only in its content (its formulation of certain doctrines, including grace, faith, and the way God's Word functions) and in its point of departure (the relationship of the sinner to God rather than questions of authority in the church), but also in its method. The Wittenberg way of practicing and exercising the Word of God proceeded out of its concern for the spiritual care that believers practice with other believers. It aimed to make God's Word happen in people's lives as it kills sinners and makes them alive anew in Christ. This way of practicing theology focused on how God acts in the lives of believers, individually and as the called, gathered, enlightened people of God, the church.

This way of doing the tasks that constitute the application of God's Word to people's lives presumed that God made his human creatures in two dimensions. In the first they are human (or righteous) passively, simply receiving the gift of life from their Creator and their Recreator, and in the second they are human (or righteous) actively, practicing and performing the life God made them to live with him in trust and with other creatures in loving care and concern. On the basis of this presupposition, in the face of the mystery of the continuation of sin and evil in the lives of the baptized, the Wittenberg way distinguishes law and gospel in order to bring the proper and appropriate message to the defiant sinner or to the broken sinner. The Wittenberg way sees law and gospel as Words of God that are accomplishing his will as they are delivered in human speech by his people to one another.

What Wengert has given us in this volume is a catechism for the practice of the Wittenberg way of using God's Word in the twenty-first century. The text of the Epitome is helpfully supplied within each chapter; discussion questions will facilitate further thinking especially in small groups; and the glossary will answer many queries. This is a book that sparks the imagination for better reading of the texts of the Lutheran tradition, and other Christian traditions as well. It is a book that impels readers into a better reading of the lives of fellow believers and of those outside the faith for the more effective delivery of God's Word into their lives. It is a book for preachers and counselors and all who proclaim God's Word and thus convey his saving action. It is a book for all those involved in the witness and conversation that delivers the Word of life to others, a conversation to which all believers are called — every last baptized one of us!

ROBERT KOLB

Abbreviations

Ap	Apology of the Augsburg Confession, translated by Charles Arand, in *BC 2000*
BC 2000	*The Book of Concord*. Edited by Robert Kolb and Timothy J. Wengert. Minneapolis: Fortress, 2000.
CA	The Augsburg Confession, translated by Eric Gritsch, in *BC 2000*
Ep	Epitome of the Formula of Concord, translated by Robert Kolb, in *BC 2000*
FC	Formula of Concord
LC	Luther's Large Catechism, translated by James Schaaf, in *BC 2000*
LW	Luther, Martin. *Luther's Works*. American Edition. Edited by Jaroslav Pelikan and Helmut Lehmann. 55 vols. St. Louis: Concordia; Philadelphia: Fortress, 1955-1986.
SA	The Smalcald Articles, translated by William Russell, in *BC 2000*
SC	Luther's Small Catechism, translated by Timothy J. Wengert, in *BC 2000*
SD	The Solid Declaration of the Formula of Concord, translated by Robert Kolb, in *BC 2000*
Sources and Contexts	*Sources and Contexts of the Book of Concord*. Edited by Robert Kolb and James A. Nestingen. Minneapolis: Fortress, 2001.
TR	*Tischreden* (Table Talk)
WA	Luther, Martin. *Dr. Martin Luthers Werke*. Weimar: Böhlau, 1883-1993.

Introduction

This book arose out of the conviction, confirmed by fifteen years of teaching in a Lutheran seminary, that Lutherans have underused and sometimes even misused their definitive collection of Lutheran confessions of faith first published in 1580, *The Book of Concord*. For the most part, like its counterpart for laity, the Small Catechism, *The Book of Concord* is taught in the Lutheran seminaries of North America either as important, albeit "ancient," history (the Lutheran equivalent of Alex Haley's famous *Roots*) or as dogmatic theology (believe it, or else!). As important as it is to know one's history and to take the doctrinal claims of the Lutheran confessional documents seriously, these approaches can leave readers with the narrow, mistaken impression that *The Book of Concord* is merely preparation for the *actual* task of being a pastor. Then, clergy and laity alike miss the very practical origins of these documents and the down-to-earth ways the teachings they contain may shape life in today's congregations.

Already in my 1989 interview for a professorship in Lutheran Confessions at the Lutheran Theological Seminary at Philadelphia, this question arose. When asked how I would teach the Confessions, I responded (somewhat recklessly), "On internship!" At the time, having been pastor of a rural Wisconsin parish for six years, the answer seemed obvious, although my interlocutors were not amused. Despite my apparent glibness, they offered me the position. I then wrote lectures for the basic course in the Confessions while still living in Wisconsin, and many of the stories and anecdotes with which I regaled my students at the time reflected the freshness of my parish work.

I am by no means the only scholar to make this connection. I still remember the reaction of the late Lou Smith, then a parish pastor in New Jersey, who was sitting in on the course in Lutheran Confessions as a tutor for a foreign student. He came into the seminar room for a discussion group, plopped *The Book of Concord* on the table, and exclaimed in his thick New York accent, "I am amazed by how practical this all is!" The students, worried about papers, exams, and deadlines, looked at him like cows staring at a new gate. Despite weeks of stories from the trenches in my lectures, they still could not imagine what he was talking about.

The Formula of Concord as Practical Theology

In the 1960s George Forrell produced a widely read study of the Augsburg Confession along practical lines: *The Augsburg Confession: A Contemporary Commentary* (Minneapolis: Augsburg, 1968). He took the articles of the Augsburg Confession and showed how modern issues related to them. This present book will attempt much the same thing, except using a much less well-known portion of *The Book of Concord:* the Formula of Concord. The Formula, published in 1580, was written years after the deaths of the reformers Martin Luther (1483-1546) and his colleague Philip Melanchthon (1497-1560), both of whom authored the other sixteenth-century documents in *The Book of Concord.*

The Formula consists of twelve articles and deals with issues that threatened to break the Lutheran church apart in the period after Luther's death. In this way the authors of the Formula were much like us. They, like us, were heirs of the churchly explosion we call the Reformation. They, like us, struggled to appropriate the basic insights of the Reformation and make them relevant for a new generation of believers. They were also pastors and teachers of the church, committed to the very practical, experiential spirit of the Reformation. Although their style of arguing and language may leave the casual reader with the impression that they were interested only in the "right answer" to the theological problems they faced, in fact they understood profoundly how their answers impacted the parishes they and their students served.

One of the reasons American Lutherans are not as familiar with the Formula of Concord as one might expect is because most Scandinavian churches never accepted it as a doctrinal standard. (The exception was the Swedish church, which adopted it in the late seventeenth century.) One king is said to have exclaimed that he did not want to import that "German plague" into his lands. He did not, it seems, understand that the topics in the Formula were "Lutheran questions" (see below) that will come up one way or another wherever Lutherans gather to profess their faith. Perhaps, rightly used as a source of Lutheran conversations over the critical questions of the faith in the context of parish life, the Formula presents more an inoculation against disease than a German Lutheran theological illness.

History of the Formula

The history of the Formula of Concord properly begins on 18 February 1546, when Luther died. Up until then, serious disagreements among Luther's followers had been settled by appeal to the theological faculty of the University of Wittenberg, and thus indirectly to Luther himself. His death, however, was shortly followed by the outbreak of war between Lutheran princes of the Smalcald League (including Luther's prince, Elector John Frederick of Saxony) on the one side and the emperor and his allies (including all the Roman Catholic princes and a smattering of evangelical ones, especially Duke Moritz of Saxony) on the other. This Smalcald War was short and ended with the imprisonment of John Frederick, the confiscation of much of his Saxon territory (including Wittenberg), and the transfer of the electoral title to his cousin, Moritz. (The seven imperial electors [four secular princes and three archbishops] were the highest-ranking princes in the Holy Roman Empire, whose duty it was to elect the emperor.)

When Emperor Charles V called for an imperial parliament, or diet, to meet in Augsburg from 1547 to 1548, he was sure he had finally defeated the evangelical party (Lutherans) and could impose his own religious settlement on the empire, in the interim before a church council could meet and discuss the theological issues. The result, nicknamed the Augsburg Interim, allowed the evangelicals little more than married priests and communion using both bread and wine. Other-

3

wise it was a return to Roman rites and theology. Moritz, now in control of the University of Wittenberg, tried to lessen the effect of this decree in his newly won, evangelical lands by enlisting the help of Wittenberg's theologians in coming up with a compromise. At first Melanchthon, Luther's colleague for twenty-eight years and now Wittenberg's star theologian, steadfastly refused. Indeed, when his written attack on the Augsburg Interim was published in the summer of 1548, he found himself in trouble with the imperial court itself. A later proposed compromise, upon which he and other theologians worked in the summer and fall, allowed for changes in neutral practices (called by the Greek term *adiaphora*) to match Roman demands, but no changes in doctrine. It was presented to but never accepted by the Saxon estates (princes and city representatives) meeting in Leipzig in December 1548. The document's willingness to compromise with the Roman party on nonessentials *(adiaphora)* even in the face of persecution sparked fierce opposition. The antagonists (later nicknamed Gnesio-Lutherans [genuine Lutherans]) called it the Leipzig Interim.

From this initial fight over nonessentials (addressed in article 10 of the Formula) sprang a host of others (articles 1-6) regarding sin, free will, justification by faith, good works, law and gospel, and the "third use" of the law. In the meantime, however, the political situation had changed dramatically. Moritz, realizing that the emperor intended to strip the imperial princes and cities of all meaningful authority, changed sides and orchestrated the Princes' Revolt in the early 1550s, which led first to the Truce of Passau in 1552 and then the Peace of Augsburg of 1555, where evangelicals (Lutherans) were finally given legal standing in the empire. (This peace, incidentally, was the longest enjoyed in central Europe to the present day, lasting until the outbreak of the Thirty Years' War in 1618.) Political peace may have reigned in the empire, but theological, internecine warfare between Gnesio-Lutherans and Philippists (followers of Melanchthon) raged throughout the 1550s and 1560s.

Along with these debates surrounding the Interim, another set of conflicts arose over the Lord's Supper, first in Hamburg and Bremen in northern Germany and then in 1559 at the University of Heidelberg in the Rhenish Palatinate. Shortly before his death in 1560 Melanchthon wrote a memorandum regarding this latter controversy for the Palatine elector, criticizing one of his own student's defense of the real presence of Christ in the Lord's Supper. Then, in the late 1560s and 1570s, theologians at the University of Wittenberg, who believed themselves to be drawing the logical consequences of Melanchthon's teaching, began promulgating ideas that other Lutherans strongly denounced as reducing Christ's presence in the Supper to a spiritualized one. These Wittenbergers did this fairly subtly without the clear knowledge or approval of their prince, the pious Lutheran Duke August, Saxony's elector since Moritz's death in 1553. Thus, later scholars nicknamed them crypto-Calvinists (secret followers of John Calvin, the Reformed theologian in Geneva who held similar views), although they are more accurately termed crypto-Philippists. When August discovered this secret movement among his theologians, some of whom were also his closest advisers, he arrested some, sent many into exile, and left a gaping hole in German Lutheranism.

As a result of these struggles, several theologians from the second generation of Lutherans began to explore ways for Lutherans to come to agreement. But how could they accomplish this? Convening a major gathering of Lutheran theologians had been tried and found wanting in the 1550s and 1560s. It seemed, too, that producing a common confession was out of the question, since each major Lutheran territory seemed bent on producing its own standards for teaching or "body of doctrine" (called in Latin a *corpus doctrinae*). Thus, in Saxony, Lutheran pastors were trained using a collection of Melanchthon's works, called the *corpus Philippicum*. In other places various collections were used containing some of Luther's works and the Augsburg Confession, the key confessional document by which the Peace of Augsburg itself defined Lutheran princes.

A first, tentative step toward concord came from Jakob Andreae, a theologian from Württemberg in southern Germany who was generally Gnesio-Lutheran in persuasion but moderate in tone. In 1573, at the behest of his prince Duke Christopher, he wrote *Six Sermons on the Disputes Dividing the Theologians of the Augsburg Confession*. They were actually essays addressing a variety of contested Lutheran questions. He sent this statement to several theologians. These included Martin Chemnitz, a Gnesio-Lutheran church leader in central Germany (specifically the Lower Saxon principality of Braunschweig-Wolfenbüttel), and David Chytraeus, one of Melanchthon's favorite students, who taught at the northern German University of Rostock in Mecklenburg and who was also more Gnesio-Lutheran in his outlook. They requested a more formal statement from Andreae's theological faculty in Tübingen, which Andreae fulfilled by writing the Swabian Concord in 1574. Chemnitz and Chytraeus then revised this document in 1575 to form the Saxon-Swabian Concord. At the same time, Duke Ludwig succeeded his father Christopher in Württemberg and requested another statement of faith for his land and neighboring Lutheran lands in Baden. Andreae and others met in the onetime Cistercian cloister in Maulbronn, and in January 1576 produced what became known as the Maulbronn Formula.

Of course, all was not well in electoral Saxony following the discovery and ouster of the elector August of Saxony's chief theological advisers for crypto-Philippism. However, Nicholas Selnecker, a fairly consistent Philippist until 1569 when he began working with Chemnitz and Andreae, remained on the Wittenberg faculty. He and Andreae were called in to help restore Lutheran teaching to that school. At this point August decided to join with other princes in working toward Lutheran concord in the empire. A committee of theologians was formed, now including Selnecker, Chytraeus, Andreae, and Chemnitz. When the elector of Brandenburg (whose capital was Berlin) also wanted a part in the negotiations, he sent Andreas Musculus and Christopher Körner to join in.

In 1576 these theologians took the Swabian-Saxon Concord and the Maulbronn Formula and formed them into a single document, the Torgau Book, which was sent to Lutheran territories throughout the empire for comment and resulted in the revised Bergen Book of 1577, later called the Solid Declaration. Because some princes objected to the length and complexity of the arguments, Andreae was given the task of producing a "Reader's Digest Condensed Version," called appropriately enough an epitome. Thus, the Formula of Concord consists of two parts: the longer Solid Declaration and its condensation, the Epitome. Andreae and others worked tirelessly to gain the support of other Lutheran theologians for this Formula of Concord, and they succeeded through a series of discussions and colloquies to convince theologians from about two-thirds of the evangelical territories to sign it. The Formula was then combined with earlier Lutheran confessional statements. Besides the ecumenical creeds (Apostles', Nicene, and Athanasian), these included the Augsburg Confession and its Apology

6

(defense) by Melanchthon, and Luther's Small Catechism and Large
Catechism, as well as his Smalcald Articles and Melanchthon's Treatise
on the Power and Primacy of the Pope. Along with the Formula, these
writings make up *The Book of Concord,* published on the fiftieth anniver-
sary of the public presentation of the Augsburg Confession to Emperor
Charles V (25 June 1530) and signed by the territorial rulers. Its preface,
a model of ecclesiastical compromise, dealt with many of the outstand-
ing issues and helped obtain the signature of yet another Lutheran
elector, Count Ludwig of the Palatinate.

Lutheran Questions and an Outline of This Work

Dogmaticians and historians have often defined the Christian denomi-
nations that inhabit North America by the *answers* they traditionally
gave and still give to the burning theological debates over such topics
as justification by faith, the Lord's Supper, sacraments, or the structure
of the church. However, these obvious differences among denomina-
tions (even if the beliefs of individual members or pastors deviate
markedly from the "party line") beg the question of the origins of such
answers and focus attention instead on the divisions themselves.

    Another way to characterize Christian variations is to focus on
the questions that arise within a tradition and are debated continu-
ously there. Put in its simplest form, every constellation of Christians
may be defined by the questions they most typically ask of themselves
and others, questions that stand at the heart of their witness to the
gospel. To be sure, all Christians hold certain questions in common,
concerning the two natures of Christ, the Trinity, and Jesus' death and
resurrection. However, Roman Catholics still debate the question of
the relation between pope and bishops or pope and council. The Greek
Orthodox may debate matters related to *theosis,* the divinization of the
individual. Congregationalists, Presbyterians, and Episcopalians may
debate, among other things, questions of church polity, as their names
imply. Millennially minded churches debate such things as whether the
rapture comes before or after the tribulation. Churches in the Wesleyan
tradition are more likely to debate matters of holiness, perfection, and
the work of the Holy Spirit.

    For Lutherans, most questions revolve around justification by faith alone. How deep does the human sickness we call sin run? When we say we are justified by God's grace alone, does this exclude all human activity in coming to faith? What is the relation between faith and works? What role does God's Word play in justification? If we are saved by grace alone, what should we say about predestination? What is the nature of Christian freedom? A second but related set of questions concerns the Lord's Supper. Lutherans are convinced that God's justifying activity in Christ is not restricted to the past, but that God continues to work in the present in the same way, by assuming the weakness and limitations of human flesh. "The finite is able to hold the infinite." What, then, may we say about the nature of Christ and the nature of Christ's presence in the Lord's Supper?

Because of these "Lutheran questions," the Formula of Concord should be of continuing interest to Lutherans in parish life. The authors, whom we will call here concordists, managed in twelve articles to summarize the heart of our Lutheran "questions." Because we hold so dearly to the gospel that God justifies (forgives) sinners by grace through faith on account of Christ, these questions about sin, grace, law, gospel, freedom, and Christ's presence in the Supper will not go away. They are our questions, and the more we know about them and their connection to the gospel, the more they will strengthen and enrich our faith and life. In fact, as I often discovered to my amazement while working on this book, many of the practices peculiar to Lutheran churches have their origins in these very questions and our continuing debates over them.

Before the articles of the Formula begin in earnest, there is a brief introduction to the sources and authorities used by the formulators: Scripture, the ecumenical creeds (the Apostles', Nicene, and Athanasian), and the other documents in *The Book of Concord*. This section, called the "Rule and Norm," functions more as a list of sources and authorities than as an introduction to the topic of authority in theology. It reminds us ever so briefly that all theology is done drinking from the "pure, clear fountain of Israel," the Scriptures, and listening to the witnesses of Christians who have gone before us. As the Epitome reminds us, quoting Psalm 119, God's Word is "a lamp to my feet and a light to my path." It is in this light that the specific Lutheran questions of the Formula emerge.

In the Formula the first six articles deal with questions most directly related to justification by faith alone without works. First, in relation to original sin, Lutherans debated just how deep our "inherited sin" goes. This has direct consequences for our understanding and practice of Holy Baptism. Second, the concordists asked the related question of human choice in salvation and soundly rejected the notion that our hope for salvation rests in any way on ourselves. Instead, the gospel itself brings us to faith. In a society where "deciding for Jesus" has become a major preoccupation among Christians, the admission that we are "in bondage to sin and cannot free ourselves" comes as a great relief. Third, the concordists devoted an entire article to the heart of the Lutheran gospel: justification by grace through faith on account of Christ. In a church where this is often taken for granted (rather than shouted from the rooftops), perhaps this article ought to receive the most attention. Fourth, the question of good works arises, and the concordists succeed in putting works in their (rightful) place, as fruit from good trees and not as causes of salvation. This is a point often missing from Lutheran sermons and instruction, where too often the faithful get their ears boxed by well-intentioned but legalistic preachers. Fifth and sixth, the question of good works led to two related questions about the relation of "law and gospel" and the definition of a "third use" of the law. Here, too, these Lutheran questions help us think more clearly about the nature of preaching and teaching in our congregations. What stands at the heart of our proclamation, good news or bad?

The next three articles (7-9) deal with the Lord's Supper and the related questions of Christology. I still remember a Christmas sermon by Roy Harrisville, a professor at my seminary in the 1970s. It consisted of a conversation in heaven among the angels who were about to frighten some of Bethlehem's shepherds. Discussing the incarnation, Gabriel said: "It will be the death of him [God], I just know it." It is in the incarnation, the angel went on to say, that God does the impossible: creates a stone too heavy to lift. That impossibility marks the incarnation (God becoming a human being), the crucifixion (God dying), our salvation (God dying for and saving sinners), and the Lord's Supper (God present in earthly means for the forgiveness of sins). The seventh article of the Formula is so important that I divided it into two parts. In the first part we hear Lutherans amazed by Christ's presence in the bread, under the bread, and with the bread. The second part examines questions of actual practice addressed by the concordists: how long is Christ present and who is worthy to receive the Supper. The eighth article connects our understanding of the Lord's Supper to the birth, death, and resurrection of Christ. Here, surprisingly, is one of the most neglected parts of Christian preaching and teaching today: that "we live on a visited planet" (J. B. Phillips) where God died for us. The ninth article, on the unlikely question of Christ's descent into hell, arose out of the eighth, but also allowed the concordists, in the way they discussed it, to examine the very limits of our theological questions. Sometimes, when faced with the mystery of God becoming flesh, dying, and rising for us, it is best to adore rather than investigate (as Melanchthon had written already in 1521).

The last three articles turn out to be among the most practical of all. The tenth article, on *adiaphora,* touches on issues raised in the first six, although historically speaking it was questions over *adiaphora* that gave rise to the debates in articles 1-6. The concordists provide also for today's congregations the parameters for discussing disagreements over important but "neutral" matters. If the rediscovery of this article resolves even one congregational fight over some incidental practice, the Formula will have again proven its worth. The eleventh article deals with the reverse side of the second article: our bondage to sin as seen from God's perspective of unconditional grace and mercy. Here the question is God's electing us to faith. As in the second article, the concordists move quickly away from needless speculation about what is going on in God's mind to God's revelation in Christ, who is "the Book of Life," on whose heart our names are engraved. Here, almost more than anywhere else in the Formula, the concordists reflect on the amazing comfort and grace of the gospel that bears our election. The final article, a rejection of certain teachings of the Anabaptists and antitrinitarians of the age, served in the first instance simply to distance Lutherans from some of the sects active in western Europe. "Our questions are not these sectarian questions," the article seems to say. However, under this expressed intention lurks one of the most practical Lutheran questions of all: How do Christians relate to the real world? What comes to expression here is a question that is one of the most important (for its time) and often neglected (in our time): that daily life *is* the Christian life.

The Structure of This Work

This book is intended as an introduction to the Formula of Concord for pastors, teachers, and other interested laypersons. Each chapter begins with a vignette from my experience as a pastor and a Christian, and ends by making connections to modern Lutheran parish life. These stories and associations are meant to function not prescriptively but suggestively, allowing the reader to make even better links to his or her situation and experience. There follow in each chapter a section on the history of the dispute that gave rise to the article and an analysis of the text of the Epitome. If my thesis concerning the relevance of the Formula for today's parishes is correct, then the history and the analysis should not only lead us to want to study further this history and to read the Solid Declaration itself, but also to relate these issues to congregational life.

In the center of each chapter is a section labeled "The Heart of the Matter." Here I delve into the deeper theological issues within each article. These were never minor issues that the concordists addressed. They all went to the very core of their appropriation of the gospel. When we recover that core, then the distance between us and them shrinks to where we can look through the personalities and problems, the language and method, and hear again the witness of believers in Christ. Without gainsaying the extraordinary differences between our time and theirs, we can allow the concordists to do what indeed they set out to do in each article, namely (using their own words), "believe, teach, and confess."

To help the reader with the many unfamiliar terms and persons, I have added a small glossary at the very end of the book. In it are short definitions of the most important theological terms used here and brief descriptions of the important persons and events referred to in the historical section of each chapter.

Sources

Mostly I write books with lots of footnotes. But here is one with none. I have done this purposely, so that the reader is not distracted from the text. However, this does not mean that I am not beholden to many others who know far more about these topics than I and on whose shoulders I am pleased to stand. First, I am indebted to Prof. Charles Anderson of Luther Seminary, who taught me the Lutheran Confessions and whose final exam consisted of a case study of modern congregational life — an approach to final examinations that I have adapted to my own teaching. At the same time, I must thank Prof. Gerhard Forde, who inadvertently taught the Lutheran Confessions by confessing them daily in class in his own winsomely dour way. His little book *Where God Meets Man: Luther's Down-to-Earth Approach to the Gospel* (Minneapolis: Augsburg, 1972) made my late wife Barbara and me into fairly good Lutherans. I have already mentioned George Forrell, who in my early days in Philadelphia taught systematic theology beside me and whose book showed me that such a project could indeed succeed in print.

By far the most important source for this book's historical sections comes from the one English-speaking scholar who knows more about the Formula of Concord and the disputes leading up to it than anyone else since his teacher, Arthur Carl Piepkorn, died, namely, my collaborator on the English edition of *The Book of Concord,* Robert Kolb. He not only wrote the introduction to and translated the Formula of Concord in that book, but he also gave me a preliminary copy of his own contributions to the historical commentary on *The Book of Concord,* which he is writing with James Nestingen and which should appear shortly from Fortress Press. Although on some topics I have included my own research and knowledge of the Reformation, in large measure the historical insights and particularities are his. As we were editing *The Book of Concord* together, I was constantly amazed by his youthful sense of discovery. Footnotes were being rewritten down to almost the last day, based on his continuous research of the documents. I wish I had even an inkling of his erudition. I recommend his work heartily to all readers who want to know more about the history of these debates.

There are two other scholars whose research deserves mention, even though most English-speaking readers will not have access to their work. Every scholar of the Lutheran Confessions has had a veritably encyclopedic resource at his or her fingertips ever since Gunther Wenz published his two-volume *Theologie der Bekenntnisschriften der evangelisch-lutherischen Kirche* (Berlin: De Gruyter, 1996-97). Now a professor of systematic theology at the University of Munich, Wenz has produced an exhaustive study of the documents and theology of *The Book of Concord.* No one can do research on any topic in the Lutheran Confessions without discovering that Wenz has already covered both the primary and secondary literature in detail. The other scholar, Irene Dingel, professor of church history at the University of Mainz, has written the definitive study of how *The Book of Concord* was received after its publication in 1580, *Concordia controversa: Die öffentlichen Diskussionen um das lutherische Konkordienwerk am Ende des 16. Jahrhunderts* (Gütersloh: Gütersloher Verlagshaus, 1996). Her work shows that these "Lutheran questions" continued to enjoy a healthy life into the seventeenth century. The Formula was far from the last word in debates sparked by Luther's death and the Smalcald War of 1547, and Dingel demonstrates just how deeply these debates ran among Lutherans and how the Formula represented one more stage in that discussion. Her thorough, convincing investigation proves just how real these Lutheran questions were.

In addition to the books just mentioned, here are some important books on topics dealt with in this work.

Arand, Charles. *Testing the Boundaries: Windows to Lutheran Identity.* St. Louis: Concordia, 1995.

Elert, Werner. *The Structure of Lutheranism.* Translated by Walter A. Hansen. St. Louis: Concordia, 1962.

Forde, Gerhard. *Justification: A Matter of Death and Life.* Philadelphia: Fortress, 1982.

Gassmann, Gunther, and Scott Hendrix. *Fortress Introduction to "The Book of Concord."* Minneapolis: Fortress, 1999.

Grane, Leif. *The Augsburg Confession: A Commentary.* Translated by John H. Rasmussen. Minneapolis: Augsburg, 1987.

Gritsch, Eric. *Fortress Introduction to Lutheranism.* Minneapolis: Fortress, 1994.

Gritsch, Eric, and Robert Jenson. *Lutheranism: The Theological Movement and Its Confessional Writings.* Philadelphia: Fortress, 1976.

Kolb, Robert. *Confessing the Faith: Reformers Define the Church, 1530-1580.* St. Louis: Concordia, 1991.

————. *Andreae and the Formula of Concord: Six Sermons on the Way to Lutheran Unity.* St. Louis: Concordia, 1977.

Kolb, Robert, and James Nestingen, eds. *Sources and Contexts of "The Book of Concord."* Minneapolis: Fortress, 2001.

Nestingen, James A. "Preaching Repentance." *Lutheran Quarterly* 3 (1989): 249-65.

Wengert, Timothy. "Luther and Melanchthon on the Consecrated Communion Wine (Eisleben 1542-43)." *Lutheran Quarterly* 15 (2001): 24-42. (This article forms the basis of comments in article 7, part 2. Prof. Thomas Manteufel of Concordia Seminary, St. Louis, first pointed us to this dispute and to the incorrect foot-notes in earlier translations and editions of *The Book of Concord*.)

—————. "Reflections on Confessing the Faith in the New English Translation of *The Book of Concord*." *Lutheran Quarterly* 14 (2000): 1-20.

—————. "Georg Major (1502-1574): Defender of Wittenberg's Faith and Melanchthonian Exegete." In *Melanchthon in seinen Schülern,* edited by Heinz Scheible. Wiesbaden: Harrassowitz, 1997.

—————. *Law and Gospel: Philip Melanchthon's Debate with John Agricola of Eisleben over Poenitentia.* Grand Rapids: Baker, 1997.

Acknowledgments

Finally, I would be remiss if I did not mention other important sources for this work. First, much of this was written during a sabbatical leave from the Lutheran Theological Seminary at Philadelphia in the fall of 2003, for which leave I am most grateful to the faculty, administration, and board of the seminary. Most helpful have been the comments of students in my graduate seminar, "Lutheran Confessions for Parish Practice," held in January 2005. They each took a section of this book and not only made helpful suggestions for improvement (one of which led to the construction of the glossary), but also proposed discussion questions that became the basis for those that grace the conclusion to each chapter. Thus, I owe a special thanks to William Flammann, Gary Steeves, Joel Pancoast, Mark Huffman, Pat Harris, Kimberly van Driel, Paul Collinson-Streng, Kenneth Ruppar, Anne Deneen, Katherine Braun, Lois Martin, Kimberly Cottingham, Eric Childers, and Cynthia Krommes.

Second, during that sabbatical I was the Eric W. Gritsch Resident Theologian at the Melanchthon Institute of Christ the King Lutheran Church in Houston, Texas. Several of these chapters first saw the light of day in adult studies prepared for that congregation. I am deeply indebted to that congregation's members and to its pastors, especially Dr. Robert Moore, for their encouragement. Most moving for me was the effect one chapter (on our worthiness at the Lord's Supper) had on a member who, until that time, had been plagued with feelings of unworthiness and often stayed away from the Supper. Not only did this person, as a result of class discussions, start coming to Holy Communion, but after my departure she also became a communion assistant. Imagine my surprise and joy, upon returning to Houston the next year, when I received the cup at her hands. I am also grateful to three pastors who read and commented on this manuscript: the Reverend Amandus Derr, the Reverend Irving Sandberg, and the Reverend James Tallman, as well as to Prof. Paul Rorem and Prof. Robert Kolb for their suggestions.

Third, inspiration for this work came from the people to whom I dedicate this book. The members of Cross Lutheran Church, Roberts, Wisconsin, supported me as their pastor from 1983 to 1989 and provided many of the stories in the following pages. Long after I became a teacher at the seminary in Philadelphia, their faith has continued to support mine. Thanks go to them, to my children, David and Emily, and, as a delightful latecomer to this creative process, the woman who on 16 April 2005 became my wife, the Reverend Ingrid Fath.

TIMOTHY J. WENGERT

QUESTIONS FOR DISCUSSION

- ▶ Why is it important for the church to read and understand historical documents related to its existence?
- ▶ What might we learn from the concordists about strife and reconciliation?
- ▶ Are there any questions that come up repeatedly in the life of the church today? What might be some of the controverted questions among Lutherans now? Are they "Lutheran questions"?
- ▶ In preparation to work through this book, what is the role of "compromises" or "accommodations" in the church's life? What is the role of "confession"?

"But Babies Are So Cute!"
The Original Problem with Human Beings

Somehow, when I began work as my congregation's new pastor, I did not expect theological questions on my first day at the office. However, there she was, waiting for me as I pulled into the parking lot of the rural Wisconsin parish that would be my home for the next six years. That morning we talked about many things of a pastoral nature. However, the one question that stuck in my mind was strictly theological.

The conversation began something like this. "In baptism our sins are washed away, right?" I learned after several years as a seminary professor never to walk into a question like that. In fact, I duck such questions so regularly by asking in turn, "Why do you ask that question?" that students often preface their questions with "The reason I'm asking you this is . . ." That day, however, I unwittingly said yes; baptism washes our sins away.

"Then why do we baptize babies? They're too young to commit sins. In fact, they're just too cute."

My first, unspoken reaction was to ponder why such cute babies grew up to ask their pastors trick questions. Common sense bridled my tongue, and instead I gave some long since forgotten (and forgettable) answer. After all, baptism is much more than simply forgiving some mistakes we have made. It goes rather to fixing the heart of the human problem: our enslavement to bad choices and actions, our delight in bad company, the prevalence of evil, and the universality of "the last enemy," death itself. That is why the Bible and the early Christian church preferred to associate baptism with new birth (John 3: birth "from above"; Titus 3: regeneration) or with the death of the old and the birth of the new (Rom. 6 and Col. 2-3), or even with salvation through the flood (1 Pet. 5).

The woman's real problem, however, lay somewhere else: with her view of humanity. Despite all the wrongs others had recently committed against her — the subject of our pastoral conversation — she preferred not to acknowledge that human nature was flawed from the outset. After all, that truth might reflect on her as well. Surely, if babies were okay, then some of us might be fine, too.

There are actually two extremes operating here. On the one hand, some people view humanity (or at least portions of it) as worms, dirt, garbage, or worse. There is not anything good in human nature or about human beings. We encounter a psychological version of this belief in people who hate others or themselves completely. Moreover, some deterministic psychological theories, which argue that human nature (whether from nature or nurture!) possesses no freedom, can lead people to assume that they are trapped in their behavior forever and may blame their genes or their upbringing for it. In past generations people who may otherwise have defended their own personal freedom, nevertheless argued that certain races or nationalities were genetically inferior to their own, that their very essence had some fatal flaw. Some people still think that way. In Christian circles some found support in Bible verses where God pronounced a curse on one group (the descendants of Ham) or another (the offspring of Esau).

On the other hand, people like my early-morning visitor insist on the basic innocence of human beings. Whatever their flaws, human beings have a spark of goodness that shines through no matter what. Very often Christians who want to argue this way refer to the creation story in Genesis 1, which describes human beings as made in God's image. Surely we cannot be all that bad!

The authors of the Formula of Concord witness to a very different view of human beings, a position that contrasts with both those who find humanity (or at least some human beings) totally evil and those who insist on humanity's fundamental goodness. The concordists do this by reframing the question entirely. When we consider human nature and "original sin," as this doctrine is called, we generally make a mistake before even opening our mouths: we think we know human nature, or we think it is up to us to determine what our nature is. The concordists consider the question not from our perspective at all, but rather from God's perspective: what *God* has created and what *God* says about that creation and the subsequent disaster that befell it. From that perspective Christians can affirm both the goodness of God's creation and humanity's blindness to its dire predicament, that is, to its own rebellion against God.

The Historical Context

History is the process of discovering from the record of humans of the past just how different our world is from theirs. Yet, in confessional documents such as the Formula of Concord, the more seriously we take the vast differences between these sixteenth-century confessors of the faith and us, the greater the possibility that the echoes of their confessing may speak to us today. Sometimes people have used Christian confessions in such a way as to gloss over or ignore these differences. Then such testimonies of faith become little more than laws, under which the recipients must bend or else. Or they become fonts of proof texts used to uphold the readers' most cherished theological opinions. Either way the vibrancy of confessing the faith under adversity lies undetected under the debris of history, and we greatly impair the documents' ability to function as testimonies to our Lord and his gospel.

The controversy behind article 1 of the Formula of Concord arose as a result of fights over the concept of *adiaphora* and the so-called Leipzig Interim, a document drafted by Wittenberg's foremost theologian after Luther's death, Philip Melanchthon, but never officially recognized. We will get to this dispute in our discussion of article 10. One of the disturbing aspects of that document for the "Genuine Lutheran Party" (Gnesio-Lutherans, as they were called) was its weak view of sin and (as we will see in article 2) its high regard for the human will. In fact, these characteristics were to some extent implied in the third edition of Melanchthon's famous and widely used textbook on theology, the *Loci communes theologici*, first published in 1543. Earlier discomfit with that text and its author broke into the open when the compromise language of the Leipzig Interim came to light.

One particularly fervent opponent of Melanchthon's theology

was Matthias Flacius of Croatia. He had been a student and later teacher of Hebrew at the University of Wittenberg. His uncle had died as a Protestant at the hands of the Roman inquisition in what is now northern Italy. At the time of the reconstitution of the University of Wittenberg after the debacle of the Smalcald War, Flacius was in Magdeburg, the one major northern German city that had not capitulated to the imperial troops and remained under siege until several years after the war had concluded elsewhere. The headstrong Flacius, who made major scholarly contributions to biblical interpretation and the study of history, attacked the Leipzig Interim without mercy, not only on the basis of its stand on *adiaphora* but also because of its less-than-adequate description of original sin.

However, an incident several years into these disputes in 1560 illuminates the nature of the debate. By that time Flacius had been a professor of theology at the newly founded University of Jena for three years. His colleague in the arts faculty was Viktorin Strigel, a confirmed student of Melanchthon. Like his teacher and true to his calling as an instructor of philosophy, Strigel attempted to use proper philosophical categories in the service of the gospel. To protect the human being's dignity and God's creation, he insisted (using Aristotelian categories) that original sin was not part of the "substance" (essence or quiddity) of the human being but only an "accident" (a technical term in philosophy denoting a changeable quality). His concern? To make sure God was not seen as the cause of evil. Flacius was much more prone to use biblical language and, based on his wide reading in Luther (he was involved in the University of Jena's publication of Luther's works), to employ the most radical expressions of the reformer.

What happened next is right out of the movies. The pious duke of Saxony, John Frederick the Middler (his father had been Luther's elector), insisted that all the professors at his University of Jena subscribe to a Gnesio-Lutheran statement of faith. When Strigel refused, soldiers were sent out to prevent him from leaving the territory and to arrest him. They broke down the door to his house and dragged him off to jail. Lengthy negotiations led to the duke calling for a formal disputation on this topic in 1560. Flacius tried to counter Strigel's low view of sin by employing philosophical language. He claimed that the "fall" into sin had so damaged the "formal substance" of human beings that they were in the image of Satan (although what he called the "material substance" of human beings retained its created, God-given image). The duke and some of his advisers were shocked at Flacius's language.

With this the battle was joined. Strigel and his supporters, nicknamed Philippists because of their association with Philip Melanchthon, claimed Flacius had revived the ancient Manichaean heresy, which taught that God created evil and which denied the good of creation. Flacius and his followers, the Gnesio-Lutherans, returned the compliment by accusing Strigel of "Pelagianizing tendencies." This referred back to the English monk and opponent of Augustine. In the fifth century Pelagius reduced God's grace to God's law and creation and argued that human beings possessed the power to become righteous before God on their own steam. The ensuing paper war between the two sides raged for decades. Even after Flacius's death in 1575, several of his most ardent supporters continued the fight, even attacking the Formula of Concord itself.

The Heart of the Matter

Manichaean? Pelagian? Substance? Accidents? What was the fuss all about? It may be easy for us, as "enlightened" Christians, to dismiss the name-calling and polemics. However, perhaps we simply do not appreciate the importance of this topic for our Christian faith. Sometimes when we read in history about Christians fighting over what may look like an esoteric matter, we behave like supposed friends of a person whose spouse habitually arrives home late and drunk. "What are you so upset about?" we ask in our superior tone. "You need to learn to manage your anger." Flacius and his supporters often lost their jobs over this dispute and lived in exile, and the Philippists were perennially charged with abandoning the central teaching of the Reformation. Strigel had briefly been imprisoned before the 1560 debate. The question of human sin is deadly serious, even if today we would hardly arrest someone for holding one view or another.

In fact, as the Formula of Concord points out, every major Christian doctrine we confess in the creed depends on our approach to this topic; creation, sin, redemption, the work of the Holy Spirit, and even the resurrection of the dead all hinge on how we look at this doctrine! None of us behaves quite as cavalierly as did the queen from *Alice in*

Wonderland, who on occasion could believe as many as six impossible things before breakfast. We generally (and automatically) connect what we believe about one thing to what we then will say about another. If we magnify human sin to the extent that we obscure God's handiwork, we denigrate God's creation and call the resurrection of the body into question. If we diminish sin and the human predicament, we are at the same time reducing the importance of Jesus' saving death and resurrection and the work of the Holy Spirit in declaring us righteous and making us holy in God's sight. There is plenty to shout (and fight) about when it comes to this topic, and plenty for us to learn.

What is the heart of the matter of sin? There is something wrong with our heart. Sin, finally, is not just a matter of crimes of omission and commission or transgressions of "thought, word, and deed." On that basis babies are more or less innocent — on the surface. Sin, especially the "original" sin, goes to the core of who we think we are (free persons) and who we really are (bound persons). When the liturgy has Lutherans in the United States and Canada saying, "We are in *bondage* to sin and cannot free ourselves," it has us confessing the heart of the matter. Human nature is good — insofar as it is God's creation. However, because of sin it is bent, "curved in upon itself," to use Luther's famous saying, and worse yet, it thinks it is straight as an arrow.

The Text of the Epitome

Concerning Original Sin

Status controversiae

The Chief Question in This Dispute

[1] Whether original sin is really, without any distinction, the corrupted nature, substance, and essence of the human creature, or indeed the most important and best part of its essence, as the rational soul itself at the height of its development and powers? Or whether, even after the fall, there is a distinction between the human substance, nature, essence, body and soul, and original sin, in such a way that human nature is one thing and original sin, which is imbedded in the corrupted nature and which corrupts this nature, is another?

Article One

Affirmative Theses

The Pure Teaching, Faith, and Confession on the Basis of the Guiding Principle and Summary Explanation Set Forth Above

[2] 1. We believe, teach, and confess that there is a difference between original sin and human nature — not only as God originally created it pure, holy, and without sin, but also as we have it now after the fall. Even after the fall this nature still is and remains a creature of God. This difference is as great as the difference between the work of God and the work of the devil.

[3] 2. We also believe, teach, and confess that we must preserve this difference very carefully because the teaching that there is supposedly no difference between our corrupted human nature and original sin is contrary to the chief articles of our Christian faith on creation, redemption, sanctification, and the resurrection of our flesh, and it cannot coexist with them.

[4] For God created not only the body and soul of Adam and Eve before the fall but also our body and soul after the fall, even though they are corrupted. God also still recognizes them as his own work, as it is written, Job 10[:8], "Your hands fashioned and made me, together all around."

[5] Furthermore, the Son of God assumed this human nature into the unity of his person — of course, without sin — and what he assumed was not another kind of flesh but our flesh. In this way he became our true brother. Hebrews 2[:14], "Since the children share flesh and blood, he himself likewise shared the same things." And [2:16, 17], "He did not [assume the nature of] the angels but of the descendants of Abraham; thus, he had to become like his brothers and sisters in every respect," apart from sin.

[6] Therefore, Christ also redeemed human nature as his creation, sanctifies it as his creation, awakens it from the dead, and adorns it in glorious fashion as his creation. But he did not create, assume, redeem, or sanctify original sin. He will also not bring it to life in his elect. He will neither adorn it with glory nor save it. Instead, it will be utterly destroyed in the resurrection.

[7] From all this, it is easy to distinguish between the corrupted nature and the corruption which is embedded in this nature — through which this nature is corrupted.

[8] 3. On the other hand, we believe, teach, and confess that original sin is not a slight corruption of human nature, but rather a corruption so deep that there is nothing sound or uncorrupted left in the human body or soul, in its internal or external powers. Instead, as the church sings, "Through Adam's fall human nature and our essence are completely corrupted." [9] The damage is so indescribable that it cannot be recognized by our reason but only from God's Word. [10] The damage is such that only God alone can separate human nature and the corruption of this nature from each other. This separation will take place completely through death, at the resurrection, when the nature which we now have will rise and live eternally, without original sin — separated and severed from it — as it is written in Job 19[:26, 27], "I will be covered in my own skin, and in my flesh I shall see God, whom I shall see for myself, and my eyes shall behold."

Negative Theses

Rejection of the False Contrary Teaching

[11] 1. Therefore, we reject and condemn the teaching that original sin is only a *reatus,* that is, guilt, which results from someone else's fault, without being any kind of corruption of our own nature.

[12] 2. Likewise, that evil desires are not sin but are essential characteristics of our nature as it was created, as though the defect or damage discussed above were not truly sin for which the human creature apart from Christ is to be regarded as a child of wrath.

[13] 3. Likewise, we also reject the Pelagian error, which asserts that even after the fall human nature has remained uncorrupted and especially in spiritual matters remains completely good and pure in its *naturalia,* that is, in its natural powers.

[14] 4. Likewise, that original sin is only a slight, insignificant smudge that has been smeared on top of the human nature, a superficial stain, underneath which human nature retains its good powers, even in spiritual matters.

[15] 5. Likewise, that original sin is only an external obstacle for these good spiritual powers, and not a loss or lack of them, comparable to smearing a magnet with garlic juice. The juice does not take away the magnet's natural

powers but merely interferes with them. Or, it is said that this spot can easily be washed away, like a smudge from the face or paint from the wall.

[16] 6. Likewise, that in the human being, human nature and its essence are not completely corrupted but that people still have something good about them, even in spiritual matters, such as the capability, aptitude, ability, or capacity to initiate or effect something in spiritual matters or to cooperate in such actions.

[17] 7. On the other hand, we also reject the false teaching of the Manichaeans, when it is taught that original sin is something essential and autonomous that Satan infused into human nature and mixed together with it, as when poison and wine are mixed.

[18] 8. Likewise, that not the natural human being, but something extraneous and alien within the person commits sin, and thus not human nature but only original sin itself, which is in this nature, stands accused.

[19] 9. We also reject and condemn as a Manichaean error when it is taught that original sin is really, without any distinction, the very substance, nature, and essence of the corrupted human being, and thus that there should be no suggestion of a difference between human nature after the fall in and of itself and original sin, nor should they be differentiated from each other in our thinking.

[20] [10.] Luther calls this original sin 'nature-sin', 'person-sin', 'essential sin', but not in the sense that the nature, person, or essence of the human being in and of itself is original sin, without any distinction between the two. Rather with these expressions he made clear the difference between original sin, which is embedded in human nature, and other sins, which are called actual sins.

[21] [11.] For original sin is not a sin that a person commits; rather it is embedded in the human being's nature, substance, and essence. That means that even if no evil thought ever arose in the heart of the corrupted human being, no idle word were uttered, no evil deed done, nonetheless our nature is corrupted by original sin, which is implanted in us at birth in the sinful seed and which is a source of all other, actual sins, such as evil thoughts, words, and deeds, as it is written, "Out of the heart come evil intentions . . ." [Matt. 15:19], and, "The inclination of the human heart is evil from youth" [Gen. 8:21].

[22] [12.] It is therefore good to note the different definitions of the word "nature," through which the Manichaeans conceal their error and lead many simple people astray. For sometimes it means the essence of the human being, as when we say, "God created human nature." Sometimes, however, it means the good or bad quality embedded in a thing's nature or essence, as when it is said, "It is the nature of the snake to bite," and, "It is the nature or quality of the human being to sin; thus human nature is sin." Here the word "nature" does not mean the substance of the human being but rather something which is embedded in that nature or substance.

[23] [13.] Concerning the Latin words *substantia* and *accidens,* since they are not biblical terms and are words unfamiliar to common people, they should not be used in sermons delivered to the common people, who do not understand them; the simple folk should be spared such words.

[24] But in the schools and among the learned these terms are familiar and can be used without any misunderstanding to differentiate the essence of a thing from that which in an "accidental" way adheres to the thing. Therefore, these words are properly retained in scholarly discussion of original sin.

[25] For the difference between God's work and the devil's work can be made most clear through these words because the devil cannot create a substance but can only corrupt the substance, which God has created, in an "accidental" way, with God's permission.

Commentary

Affirmative Theses (pp. 487-89)

Paragraph 1. Here Jakob Andreae, author of the Epitome, gives a short description of the debate. (For more detail, see SD I.1-2, in *BC 2000,* 530-31.) True to their attempt at bringing concord among Lutherans, the concordists state positions never held by the major disputants. No one said there was no distinction between sin and the human being; everyone claimed some distinction existed there. The real issue first comes to light in the following paragraphs, where the concordists rehearse what is at stake in raising this question in the first place.

Paragraph 2. *There is a difference between God's creation and human sin.* I am reminded of that poster of the late sixties. A defiant little boy stands in a vacant lot in front of a dilapidated tenement. The caption: "God made me, and God don't make no junk." However we describe the depth of our sin (and it is deep), we cannot confuse God's creative work with our destructive mess of things. Think of what this means to-day! Here we should not so much worry about those who believe we are products of fate or a star-crossed upbringing or a rotten environment. We should rather consider how often *we* act as if this were true — if not about ourselves, then at least about others. Whatever we may say about sin, *God* don't make no junk!

Paragraphs 3-7. Without the difference between human nature and human sin, the entire Christian message falls apart. We are totally God's creatures. As Luther put it, "God has given me and still preserves my body and soul." Jesus is "a true human being, born of the Virgin Mary" (SC, Apostles' Creed, 2 and 4, in *BC 2000,* 354-55). He assumed not another kind of flesh but our flesh, and thereby redeems and sanctifies human nature. At the last day he will not raise sin from the dead but the redeemed and sanctified sinner.

Paragraphs 8-10. Lest the reader think there is basically nothing wrong with the human being — that sin is just a slight blemish — the concordists make clear just how devastating our predicament is. It is "a corruption so deep that there is nothing sound or uncorrupted left in the human body or soul." Babies are not cute, they are dying, and they are caught in the same web of sin that we are. When Jesus hugged the children in Mark 10, it was not because they were so blessed but because they so desperately needed blessing. When 1 Peter announces that "bap-tism now saves us," it is because we all need saving — from the youngest to the oldest.

Paragraph 9 adds a comment that could easily be overlooked. The reason we fight over the extent of human sin is because we are human sinners. Our reason immediately searches for ways to mitigate our cir-cumstances. We do not wake up one fine morning and announce to the world, "Boy, am I ever a sinner!" Only God's Word (especially the law, as we'll see in article 5) illumines our darkness; only God will finally sepa-rate our good human nature from our sin. This leads to a final point: the separation between sin and the creature will take place only at the end. Christian faith, and especially the Lutheran witness to the gospel, always looks forward to what the spiritual called "that great gettin' up day." Then "I will know fully even as I am fully known" (1 Cor. 13:12). Until that day we live as sinners in desperate need of God's grace. No wonder we baptize babies, forgive sinners, commend our dying, and bury our dead! It is in the sure and certain hope of forgiveness, life, and salvation.

Negative Theses (pp. 489-90)

The negative theses reverse the process of the positive by first rejecting those who hold that our rebellion against God is a minor matter. Here the concordists peer over the fence and reject what they believed their Roman Catholic neighbors were saying about original sin at the Council of Trent, that Roman Catholic gathering of bishops that met from 1545 to 1563 and rejected many Lutheran teachings. Thus, the concordists reject the notion that original sin is just guilt for someone else's sin (**par. 11**) and that evil desires are not really sin (**par. 12**). The Pelagians come in for an attack in **paragraph 13**, when the concordists reject the notion that human nature (a.k.a. cute babies) is "completely good and pure." (One always wonders how people who raise their own children could come to this conclusion.)

Next, the Philippist party itself comes under scrutiny (**par. 14-16**). Original sin is not just a smudge on the face or garlic juice on a magnet (a more accurate modern example might be interference on a cell phone — easily fixed if we just move to a window — "Can you hear me now?"). In spiritual matters we cannot simply appeal to some better part of human beings in the hope that they will improve. This puts the lie to many modern views of human beings: from the spirituality of New Age religion to the naive belief that "every day, in every way, we're getting better and better." Babies, cute or not, are in trouble, and so are we! Ask any pastor who has imposed ashes on his or her own children and said, "Remember that you are dust and to dust you shall return!"

In **paragraphs 17-19** the concordists attack the other side of the equation: their understanding of where the Flacian position might lead: not to Pelagianism but to Manichaeanism. The latter believed that the world was locked in a battle between evil and good substances. Thus sin corrupts human nature itself, is an uncontrollable force, and constitutes the very nature of the nonelect human being. This, too, undercuts contemporary views of humankind. We are not robots, forced to do things against our better judgment because of bad upbringing or genes.

Definitions (pp. 490-91)

One thing that may seem odd to us is the importance the concordists regularly placed on definitions of terms. Given the fact that Luther and Melanchthon, and in the 1560s their own disputants, had used various terms in different ways, the concordists attempted partially to solve the dispute by eliminating fights over words. So when Luther called original sin "nature sin" (**par. 20**), he did not mean there was no difference between original sin and human nature. Our "original" sin (**par. 21**) is not some action we did (or failed to do) but a condition — a sickness embedded in us. From the very beginning of our lives we are estranged and alienated from God. The word "nature" itself is subject to different meanings (**par. 22**). Finally, although those versed in philosophy may in scholarly debate use terms like "substance" (i.e., the essence of something) and "accidents" (i.e., the changeable qualities in something), when proclaiming the gospel to simple folks, theologians should keep it simple (still good advice today) (**par. 23-25**).

A Formula for Parish Practice

So, what to do with cute babies and bad gene pools or upbringing? Celebrate and nurture their lives, **and then baptize them**! The waters of baptism are just where each and every one of us needs to begin new life with God. The introduction to the liturgy of Holy Baptism in the *Lutheran Book of Worship (LBW)* hits the nail on the head. "In Holy Baptism our gracious heavenly Father liberates us *from sin and death* by joining us to the death and resurrection of our Lord Jesus Christ. *We are born children of a fallen humanity;* in the waters of Baptism we are reborn children of God and inheritors of eternal life" (p. 121). Here the pastor says what seems so hard for us to believe: the child — all of us, really — is in desperate need of God's grace and mercy in Jesus Christ. That need does not disappear when the baptismal service is over. In fact, to use Luther's language in the Large Catechism, "baptism remains forever" (Baptism, 77, in *BC 2000*, 466). It puts us on the ship of the church.

Luther goes on to say that, unfortunately, sometimes we fall off the boat. "However, those who do fall out should immediately see to it that they swim to the ship and hold fast to it, until they can climb aboard again and sail on in it as before" (Baptism, 82). Again, our practical, down-to-earth liturgy (cited above) comes to our rescue each week, throwing us a life preserver: **confession and forgiveness** (*LBW*, p. 56). First, we begin with our baptism into the name of the triune God, sealed by the cross of Christ forever. Then "We confess that *we are in bondage to sin and cannot free ourselves.*" That is, we've fallen off the ship and can't get back in on our own. The old creature may have drowned in baptism, but (as one of my students, quoting Karl Barth, once told me) it is a good underwater swimmer. So, back under the water we go to hear the baptismal promise all over again: "Almighty God, in his mercy, has given his Son to die for us and, for his sake, forgives us all our sins. . . . I therefore declare to you the entire forgiveness of all your sins," in the name in which you were baptized.

If that does not help, there are other gracious life rafts: counseling, private confession and forgiveness, and the mutual support from friends and fellow members of the congregation. This means that the Formula of Concord and its statements about original sin really do matter in the daily life of the congregation. They remind us about the goodness of creation, the depth of sin, and the marvel of our restoration in Christ. Not a bad way to get practical about our confession of faith!

DISCUSSION QUESTIONS

- ▶ In light of Genesis 1:1-25 and the discussion above, what is it about creation that is good, and why? Is this the same kind of good as when we say something, or someone, is good?
- ▶ What does it mean to be created in the image of God (cf. Gen. 1:26-27)?
- ▶ In what ways has sin broken human life? (You may wish to refer to Genesis 3 for this discussion.)

▶ John 3:16 states, in a nutshell, God's response to human rebellion. How do baptism into Christ and confession and forgiveness overcome the ills brought on by sin? What other helps does God provide you?

Article Two

"I'll Do It My Way":
What Happens When Human Beings
Demand to Be in Charge of Everything

My mother grew up in Milwaukee in a mixed religious household. Her father had been brought up Roman Catholic and her mother Lutheran. However, as the youngest of eleven children, she had never become a member of any congregation. So, in her early twenties, she finally began instruction to join a Lutheran church. When her schedule as a nurse and her pastor's schedule fit together, she would take the streetcar from her house to Bethany Lutheran Church to receive personal instruction from Pastor Beiderwieden, whose daughter was one of her best friends. She went for weeks. Then one Saturday as she made her way back to the streetcar stop, it suddenly struck her: "Jesus Christ died for me!" The insight was so overwhelming that she kept repeating it. In tears, she turned around and walked all the way back to the church. Bursting in on the unsuspecting pastor, she blurted out, "Pastor Beiderwieden, Jesus died for me!" He looked up from his desk. "Yes, Janet," he replied with a broad smile. "That's what I've been trying to tell you."

He could also have said, "What a Lutheran way to come to faith!" For complicated historical reasons, American Christianity insists almost without exception that our faith depends on us. We make decisions to follow Jesus. We accept Jesus as our personal Lord and Savior. Every evangelistic tract that has been handed to me in an airport, placed on my windshield in a parking lot, or e-mailed to me on my computer has had that bent: "It's up to you! You must decide!" Television and radio evangelists are perhaps the most insistent about this.

No matter how grace-filled the message may appear, at some point the speakers insist that it is up to us to make a commitment — and incidentally, to write and tell them about it. But my mother's story has a different ring to it. There was no "decision" at all. If anything, an "anti-decision" was involved. She was walking toward a streetcar stop in Milwaukee in the 1930s, and it (the gospel spoken by her pastor) hit her. One might be tempted to say that her story has much more in common with Saint Paul's account of his conversion than most of the tales that fill the airwaves and the Christian bookstores. Paul was not deciding anything, but Christ came and knocked him off his high horse, confronting him with his sin and his savior. Nor was it much different from Jesus' encounters with Peter in the boat in Luke 5 or with Zacchaeus in Luke 19. It is God who takes the initiative, sweeps into our lives, catches us off guard, and announces, just plain *announces,* to us the good news: "I will make you fish for people"; "Come down, for I am going to your house today"; "I am Jesus, whom you are persecuting"; "Jesus died for you, Janet!"

History

The fight over the human will's participation in salvation began with a famous exchange between Martin Luther and Erasmus of Rotterdam between 1524 and 1528. When Erasmus wrote *On the Freedom of the Will* in 1524, Luther responded in 1525 with *On the Bondage of the Will.* Erasmus's answer, *Hyperaspistes,* the title of which could be translated "Treading on Snakes," was dismissed in comments contained in Philip Melanchthon's 1528 commentary on Colossians. By the 1530s, however, Melanchthon had become much more sensitive to the charge that holding too strictly to the will's bondage made God the cause of evil and made human beings less than human. He, with Luther, also rejected the suggestion that God's election undercut the efficacy of God's promise to the sinner in Word and sacraments. As a result, in 1535 Melanchthon revised his textbook on theology, the *Loci communes theologici,* to say that there were three causes for salvation: the Holy Spirit (the effective cause), the Word of God (the instrument used), and the human will (which he seemed to label a "material" cause — the material on which the Spirit and Word worked).

The dispute that triggered the debate prior to the Formula of Concord started in 1555, when a student of Melanchthon and professor at the University of Leipzig, Johann Pfeffinger, defended in a debate at the university a role for the human will in conversion. The venerable Nicholas von Amsdorf, one of Luther's closest friends and onetime bishop of Naumburg, took exception and attacked Pfeffinger in print for reintroducing the medieval notion of merit into salvation. Pfeffinger, never one to shy away from a fight, responded and continued to defend the notion that in some small way and very weakly, the human will could cooperate (Greek: *synergos*) with the Holy Spirit and God's Word. Thus was born the "synergistic controversy." Pfeffinger argued that although the sun alone provides heat, human beings can run for the shade or, alternatively, let themselves be drawn to the light.

This high regard for human activity in salvation concerned many Gnesio-Lutherans. It seemed that in his eagerness to protect God's honor and to respect the integrity of the human mental capacities, Pfeffinger had simply returned to the very theology Luther had opposed. Gabriel Biel, the author of the medieval theology textbooks Luther owned, had written, "To those who do what is in them, God will not deny grace," and Luther attacked this notion mercilessly. Suddenly, Pfeffinger, too, made grace depend on human cooperation. In addition to von Amsdorf's initial attack, Matthias Flacius joined the fray, using Luther's assertion that human beings are completely passive and are worse than blocks of wood, since they willfully resist God. In less inflammatory language, von Amsdorf replied that the human will is captive to Satan and therefore cannot cooperate with God. Later in the controversy Nicholas Gallus, a preacher in Regensburg, turned the attack toward Melanchthon himself and his statements in the *Loci*.

In 1560 this debate became entangled in the controversy over original sin between Viktorin Strigel and Flacius, described under the first article above. Strigel, ever the philosopher, insisted that God had endowed human beings with a certain *modus agendi* (an ability to act [freely]). When this kind of language made it into a Lutheran confession of the 1560s, von Amsdorf and others opposed it, even when it was explained that this ability was purely passive. Despite or perhaps because of the careful blending of Luther's and Melanchthon's concerns in the Formula of Concord, some of Flacius's supporters continued to object to the language there.

33

Article Two

The Heart of the Matter

The human will is bound! If the concordists are right, think about how this changes our understanding of evangelism and, even more, our view of our relation to God. No one has to wake up in the morning wondering how well he or she is doing with God. Did I really decide? Couldn't I backslide? What if I didn't really mean it? Am I really living up to my decisions? Have I done enough?

The point is not how well we are doing for God but what God has promised us. This means that in the face of our doubts or unbelief the question to ask is not "How could I be doing better?" but rather, "What is God's promise to me today?" We need to develop the theological skill of "turning the verbs," as one Lutheran theologian put it, that is, making God the subject of the theological sentence and not the object of our works and resolutions. Faith, our trusting relation to God, is not a product of our efforts but a miracle of hearing. In fact, perhaps the best story in the Bible for showing both the human predicament and God's action comes in Mark 7, where Jesus speaks to a deaf man to make him hear. The paradox of this action — speaking words to someone incapable of hearing them — is precisely what happens to us every time we wander into a worship service. This paradoxical speaking to the deaf (or, in the case of the young man at Nain in Luke 7, to the dead!) begins in baptism and continues every day thereafter. No wonder the crowd in Mark 7 exclaimed, "He has done everything well!" They did not exclaim, "We (or at least the deaf man) listen well or have decided everything well."

This is not to say that human beings are robots, incapable of any decisions at all. We decide things all the time, but we cannot decide about things outside of ourselves. We cannot wake up one morning and decide to be someone else. Or, rather, we can decide all we want, but it will never happen. In the same way, we cannot decide to become new persons. We are stuck with ourselves and on ourselves. Any decision we make regarding God will always end up making ourselves God and making God our slave, bound to do what we say, now that we have imperiously decided. No wonder Luther could exclaim in the Large Catechism, "What is this but to have made God into an idol . . . and to have set ourselves up as God?" (Ten Commandments, 23, in *BC 2000*, 389).

34

The Text of the Epitome

Concerning the Free Will

Status controversiae

The Chief Question in This Dispute

[1] Because the human will is found in four dissimilar situations (1. before the fall; 2. after the fall; 3. after new birth; 4. after the resurrection of the flesh), the primary question concerns only the human will and capacity in the second situation: what kind of powers do human beings have after the fall of our first parents, before rebirth, on their own, in spiritual matters? Are they able, with their own powers, before they receive new birth through God's Spirit, to dispose themselves favorably toward God's grace and to prepare themselves to accept the grace offered by the Holy Spirit in the Word and the holy sacraments, or not?

Affirmative Theses

The Pure Teaching concerning This Article on the Basis of God's Word

[2] 1. On this article it is our teaching, faith, and confession that human reason and understanding are blind in spiritual matters and understand nothing on the basis of their own powers, as it is written, "Those who are natural do not receive the gifts of God's Spirit, for they are foolishness to them and they are unable to understand them" [1 Cor. 2:14] when they are asked about spiritual matters.

[3] 2. Likewise, we believe, teach, and confess that the unregenerated human will is not only turned away from God but has also become God's enemy, that it has only the desire and will to do evil and whatever is opposed to God, as it is written, "The inclination of the human heart is evil from youth" [Gen. 8:21]. Likewise, "The mind that is set on the flesh is hostile to God; it does not submit to God's law — indeed, it cannot" [Rom. 8:7]. As little as a corpse can make itself alive for bodily, earthly life, so little can people who through sin are spiritually dead raise themselves up to a spiritual life, as it is written, "When we were dead through our trespasses, God made us alive together with Christ" [Eph. 2:5]. Therefore, we are not "com-

petent of ourselves to claim anything [good] as coming from us; our competence is from God" (2 Cor. 3[:5]).

[4] 3. However, God the Holy Spirit does not effect conversion without means, but he uses the preaching and the hearing of God's Word to accomplish it, as it is written (Rom. 1[:16]), the gospel is a "power of God" to save. [5] Likewise, faith comes from hearing God's Word (Rom. 10[:17]). And it is God's will that people hear his Word and not plug their ears. In this Word the Holy Spirit is present and opens hearts that they may, like Lydia in Acts 16[:14], listen to it and thus be converted, solely through the grace and power of the Holy Spirit, who alone accomplishes the conversion of the human being. [6] For apart from his grace our "willing and exerting," our planting, sowing, and watering, amount to nothing "if he does not give the growth" [Rom. 9:16; 1 Cor. 3:7]. As Christ says, "Apart from me, you can do nothing" [John 15:5]. With these brief words he denies the free will its powers and ascribes everything to God's grace, so that no one has grounds for boasting before God (1 Cor. [9:16]).

Negative Theses

Contrary False Teaching

[7] Therefore, we reject and condemn all the following errors as contrary to the guiding principle of God's Word:

[8] 1. The mad invention of the philosophers who are called Stoics, as well as the Manichaeans, who taught that everything that happens has to happen just so and could not happen in any other way, and that people do everything that they do, even in external things, under coercion and that they are coerced to do evil works and deeds, such as fornication, robbery, murder, thievery, and the like.

[9] 2. We also reject the error of the crass Pelagians, who taught that human beings could convert themselves to God, believe the gospel, be obedient to God's law with their whole hearts, and thus merit forgiveness of sins and eternal life out of their own powers apart from the grace of the Holy Spirit.

[10] 3. We also reject the error of the Semi-Pelagians, who teach that human beings can initiate their conversion by means of their own powers, but cannot complete it without the grace of the Holy Spirit.

[11] 4. Likewise, the teaching that, although human beings are too weak to initiate conversion with their free will before rebirth, and thus convert themselves to God on the basis of their own natural powers and be obedient to God's law with their whole hearts, nonetheless, once the Holy Spirit has made a beginning through the preaching of the Word and in it has offered his grace, the human will is able out of its own natural powers to a certain degree, even though small and feeble, to do something, to help and cooperate, to dispose and prepare itself for grace, to grasp this grace, to accept it, and to believe the gospel.

[12] 5. Likewise, that the human being, after rebirth, can keep God's law perfectly and fulfill it completely, and that this fulfilling of the law constitutes our righteousness before God, with which we merit eternal life.

[13] 6. Likewise, we also reject and condemn the error of the Enthusiasts, who contrive the idea that God draws people to himself, enlightens them, makes them righteous, and saves them without means, without the hearing of God's Word, even without the use of the holy sacraments.

[14] 7. Likewise, that in conversion and new birth God completely destroys the substance and essence of the old creature, especially the rational soul, and creates a new essence of the soul out of nothing.

[15] 8. Likewise, when this wording is used without explanation: that the human will resists the Holy Spirit before, in, and after conversion, and that the Holy Spirit is given to those who intentionally and stubbornly resist him. For, as Augustine says, in conversion God makes willing people out of the unwilling and dwells in the willing.

[16] Some ancient and modern teachers of the church have used expressions such as, "Deus trahit, sed volentem trahit," that is, "God draws, but he draws those who are willing"; and "Hominis voluntas in conversione non est otiosa, sed agit aliquid," that is, "The human will is not idle in conversion but also is doing something." Because such expressions have been introduced as confirmation of the natural free will in conversion contrary to the teaching of God's grace, we hold that these expressions do not correspond to the form of sound teaching, and therefore it is proper to avoid them when speaking of conversion to God.

[17] On the other hand, it is correct to say that in conversion God changes recalcitrant, unwilling people into willing people through the drawing

power of the Holy Spirit, and that after this conversion the reborn human will is not idle in the daily exercise of repentance, but cooperates in all the works of the Holy Spirit which he performs through us.

[18] 9. Likewise, when Dr. Luther wrote that the human will conducts itself *pure passive* (that is, that it does absolutely nothing at all), that must be understood *respectu divinae gratiae in accendendis novis motibus,* that is, insofar as God's Spirit takes hold of the human will through the Word that is heard or through the use of the holy sacraments and effects new birth and conversion. For when the Holy Spirit has effected and accomplished new birth and conversion and has altered and renewed the human will solely through his divine power and activity, then the new human will is an instrument and tool of God the Holy Spirit, in that the will not only accepts grace but also cooperates with the Holy Spirit in the works that proceed from it.

[19] Therefore, before the conversion of the human being there are only two efficient causes, the Holy Spirit and God's Word as the instrument of the Holy Spirit, through which he effects conversion; the human creature must hear this Word, but cannot believe and accept it on the basis of its own powers but only through the grace and action of God the Holy Spirit.

Commentary

The Chief Question (p. 491)

Paragraph 1. The concordists begin with some standard Augustinian distinctions. The church has been arguing this point for a long time. In the fifth century the North African bishop Augustine of Hippo came under intense attack from the moral rigorist and monk Pelagius for having prayed in his *Confessions,* "Give what you command, and command what you will." Augustine left people with the impression, Pelagius argued, that salvation did not depend on them and their freedom to choose. In response, Augustine, too, carefully divided the human story. Before their rebellion the first human beings trusted God and at least had the ability not to trust God. Afterward, like an addict after the first hit, they and their descendants were hooked on themselves and would do anything to get another fix of power and choice.

Once God makes these deaf and dead people hearing and alive, they once again can live as people trusting God and fighting sin. Finally, they will truly be free in the end, when they will be completely bound to God. The question up for debate is simple. In this second state, do people have the power, without the Holy Spirit, "to dispose themselves favorably toward God's grace and to prepare themselves to accept the grace offered by the Holy Spirit in the Word and the holy sacraments"?

Affirmative Theses (pp. 491-92)

Paragraph 2. We are talking about the dead here, about the blind, about the deaf! We "understand nothing." But what do the concordists mean? They are not talking about cognitive powers. Anyone can *know* that Jesus died for the sins of the world or rose again. But, like my mother sitting in the streetcar, it is all theoretical, all a matter of something done for everyone else or for no one, but certainly not for me. And no matter how many times a person says "Janet, Jesus died for you," it will be water off a duck's back until, finally, by the mercy of God it strikes you. Otherwise we are clueless — deaf, blind, dead.

Paragraph 3. Now here comes a description of the human being that Hollywood, that great spokesperson for a humanity "turned in upon itself" (to use Luther's phrase), just hates. A recent television series, *Joan of Arcadia,* has the protagonist subject to visions of a God who assures her right off the bat that human beings have complete freedom of choice. Such a view is right where it should be, in the world of make-believe. Our will is not just turned away from God, but is an enemy of God. We are at war for control over our heart, and as long as we claim to decide, we stay in control. Things are so serious that the concordists have to shift metaphors from the blind to corpses, a picture of the human condition also used by the author of Ephesians. Either God stops the funeral procession and raises us "with Christ," or we are done for.

Paragraph 4-6. The Holy Spirit uses real, concrete, down-to-earth means to effect this resurrection in our lives. Consider the Word as Jesus' *Ephphatha* to our deaf ears, and consider the sacraments as the spittle, mud, and touch of God. This part of the paradox Lutherans refuse to give up on. God uses means — the actual preaching of the Word; the water and Word of baptism; the bread, wine, and Word of the Supper; and even the kind word of Pastor Beiderwieden: "That's what I've been trying to tell you, Janet."

The reason for this caveat has to do with insights the reformers gained in the 1530s, as they began to encounter people who, realizing they could not choose God, had come to the (false) conclusion that God had not chosen them, that is, that God's Word and sacraments were not *really* for them. They were beset by doubts and plagued by sin, so they followed what Luther often called the devil's logic. "God is angry at sinners; you are a sinner; therefore God is angry with you." (Or, to use our metaphor, deaf people cannot hear God's word; I am deaf; therefore I cannot hear.) Not so, replied Luther. God's Word is bigger than our doubts and deafness, bigger than our sin. But it is a real word, spoken to real people with real ears. And God uses that very Word to make you alive, and hearing, and new. Anything that undermines the "for me" of the gospel leads to dangerous speculation and turns the good news into the worst news yet. Both here and in article 11, as we shall see, the concordists reject any attempts to undermine God's word of promise with dangerous speculation about some sort of secret will of God.

They use the example of Lydia (they did not know my mother). She heard the Word of the apostle Paul and was converted, "solely through the grace and power of the Holy Spirit." Ah, the Holy Spirit! What few Lutherans realize is that among all the Christian churches in North America, Lutherans, when judged from their theology, are most likely to be the Holy Spirit church. For without the Holy Spirit we are deader than doornails, insistent on resisting God at every turn. No wonder Luther says in the Small Catechism, "I believe that by my own understanding or strength I cannot believe in Jesus Christ my LORD or come to him, but instead the Holy Spirit has called me through the gospel, enlightened me with his gifts, made me holy and kept me in the true faith" (Apostles' Creed, 6, in *BC 2000*, 355).

One time a woman came to Luther claiming not to have faith. He approached her dilemma much as his own confessors had counseled him. He requested that she recite the Apostles' Creed and then asked her whether she believed it. When she answered in the affirmative, he said that was enough. Faith is not some complicated affair involving penetrating mental powers, deep commitments, and a steadfast will. It is also not some magic trick that God performs on us while we are outside the room. No! It is the real Jesus placing fingers in our ears, spitting, sighing, and speaking a word that we hear, truly hear. It is our mouth proclaiming "I believe in Jesus Christ . . . our Lord" or "I believe, help my unbelief." Thus, Luther could paraphrase the creed in the Small Catechism: "God created me . . . Jesus . . . is my LORD . . . the Holy Spirit calls me."

Negative Theses (pp. 492-94)

Paragraph 7. As we will also see in other parts of the Epitome, the negative theses express more clearly the contours of the historical debate. It is also worth noting that they talk here about the "guiding principle of God's Word." The Scripture is not some sort of celestial answer book for these believers. It is a plumb line (German: *Richtschnurr*) for determining whether a wall is going to stand up or fall over. This means that the concordists are not so much interested in finding one verse or another to prove their point, but they are looking at what happens when, instead of celebrating God's mercy, we insist on our choice.

  If one hears those familiar "proof texts" for free will ("Choose this day!" or "I stand at the door and knock" or "Ask, and you shall receive"), one could answer them point for point (Joshua gives them a choice between the gods of the Amorites and the gods of the Egyptians; the door is open for the sixth church in Revelation; the "ask" is an invitation to uncertain believers, not a command to the godless). However, that would be to miss the central point of the Scripture, which is *always* and *only* the mercy of God, not the strength of human powers. As Paul says in Romans 9:16, "So it depends not on human will or exertion, but on God who shows mercy."

  Paragraph 8. Lutherans are not determinists. God is not forcing you to wear a certain pair of socks, to read a fascinating book on the Formula of Concord, to marry a certain person, to try firing your pastor, or to do anything else of the kind. Not only that, we do not have to exhaust ourselves, as some folks do, trying to figure out what "God is trying to tell us," as if, like the Wizard of Oz, God were in a back room behind a screen scaring us with random acts. God is telling us that for the things of this world, we may use the words of my mother when she sent me off to school each day: "Think! Use your head!" Now it is true that sin and the devil make doing the right thing difficult, but we still have relative freedom in this life. Our mistake is imagining that we control God.

Paragraphs 9-10. Here the opposite group comes in for criticism. The "crass Pelagians" are those who think they can convert themselves to God. The concordists would be amazed at how many such folk are gallivanting around North America claiming to be spreading true Christianity. Better we should consider the confession of C. S. Lewis, who claimed, I believe, to have been dragged kicking and screaming into the kingdom of God. The "half-Pelagians," to use Luther's term for them, turn the Pelagians' difficult climb up God's Mount Everest into a jump onto an escalator. We make the first step; God does the rest. Luther thought this by far more insidious, because it hid how fully we attempt to control God through our choices. This was the theology that Luther encountered in the monastery and the university before the Reformation and strenuously objected to his entire life.

Paragraph 11. Here the concordists attempt to summarize the synergists' position, around which the fights of the 1550s centered. It is also the first objection I often hear from my students when they encounter talk about the unconditional mercy of God. "Well, can't we do something? Surely, we can object, can't we?" To which one must ask pointedly, "Why do you ask that question?" The problem here resides in the metaphors we use for thinking about this issue. Stuck inside such questions is already the assumption that our will has some freedom vis-à-vis God. It would be like a blind person saying, "Do I have to open my eyes?" or a deaf person saying, "Do I have to hear?" or the dead saying . . . but certainly there the metaphor breaks down completely. When our true Love says, "I love you," what sense does it make if we say, "Well, of course I can reject you, can't I?" To this, God replies, "What do you think you have been doing (and are bound to do) all along?" When we receive a gift from God, we never have to say, "What did I do to deserve this?" "Surely, I can turn it down, can't I?" To such questions the believer finally has to say, "Who would want to do that?" As the liturgy in *The Lutheran Book of Worship* has us sing (from Peter in John 6), "Lord, to whom shall we go?"

Paragraphs 12-13. Here the concordists cast their nets a bit more broadly and attack two groups: those who practiced rebaptism with the belief that one could not sin afterward, and a Roman Catholic piety that assumed that certain strict monastic orders not only were in a "state of perfection" but could actually reach perfection in this life. More importantly, the concordists reject the notion that our relation to God can occur without means. The group named here, the *Enthusiasten,* literally those who worship the God within (Greek: *en-theou*), were also related to an ancient heresy of monks who rejected Scripture and sacraments in favor of unmediated inspiration from the Holy Spirit. As a marginal note in the original *Book of Concord* said, they "wait for heavenly enlightenment of the Spirit without the preaching of God's Word."

This summarizes so much of modern religiosity in the United States that it is hard to know where to begin. It is present in the self-anointed spiritual guru for an individual or a congregation, who claims to have a direct pipeline to God. It fills the shelves of the "spirituality" section of bookstores. It is underneath many a pious justification: "Well, God told me to . . ." It is also behind much of the denigration of and contempt toward the public office of ministry. It is also the myth we hide behind when we refuse to share the good news of God with our neighbor, claiming that faith is a private affair. Paul wrote, "How shall they believe without a preacher?" Someone must play the part of Pastor Beiderwieden or there will be no tears at Milwaukee streetcar stops! On one occasion Luther equates this "en-thusiasm" with the original sin of our first parents (see SA III.8.3-13 in *BC 2000,* 322-23). Contrary to all the "en-thusiasm" of the old creature, God enjoys using means: words ringing in our deaf ears, water over our heads, and bread and wine in our mouths. (Article 8 will make the same point regarding the incarnation.)

Paragraphs 14-15. In an attempt to be evenhanded, the concordists also issue some minor corrections to the Gnesio-Lutheran (Flacian) side of the debate. Although Flacius never held the view, the concordists reject the notion that God has to destroy our minds to make us believers. In fact, God uses deaf ears, blind eyes, and corpses to do his work, or as Augustine put it, makes "willing people out of the unwilling." Seems foolish, perhaps, but look at how he used the crucified One to bring life to the world. And think how he continues to use means of grace: a pastor's broken words, water in a bowl, bread and wine. The other objection, in paragraph 15, is what happens when someone loses focus in a debate and, to make a point, exaggerates. The concordists do not reject this shocking language ("the human will resists the Holy Spirit before, in, and after conversion") completely, just when it is used for its shock value, without explanation. The fact is, drowned though it is in our baptism, the old creature *is* a good swimmer. No wonder one of Luther and Melanchthon's favorite verses in the Gospel was that of the poor father whose son has a demon. When Jesus says faith is necessary, the father responds for all of us: "Lord, I believe; help my unbelief!" We are, at the same time, saint and sinner, believer and unbeliever. But it is important to offer explanation when we say such radical things.

Paragraphs 16-18. The concordists also must do something they hate doing: correcting one of their own teachers, Melanchthon. In his standard textbook for theology, the 1543 *Loci communes theologici* [General Theological Topics], Melanchthon had used these quotes from the Greek Fathers John Chrysostom and Basil of Caesarea (or so Melanchthon thought; it was actually Eusebius of Emesa). The concordists try to be gentle, arguing that the citations have been wrongly applied to the question of free will, but in the end they have to say "it is proper to avoid them." In the next paragraph Andreae summarizes another way to construe these passages: as descriptions of the human being in whom the "drawing power of the Holy Spirit" is at work. Believers, as we will discover in article 6, do good (insofar as they are truly believers) out of sheer joy and willingness.

As in other articles, the concordists have to explain Luther's own comments, over which there had been plenty of fighting. One can almost hear Luther and Melanchthon's theological descendants throwing quotes from these two dead giants back and forth. "God draws those who are willing," says one. "The human will is *pure passive* [Latin for purely passive]." Then we are off to the races. Our pure passivity has to do with our bound will apart from faith, not with our freed will in faith. One way to say it is that God does not work faith on us while we are out of the room. That is, in the end, it is our deaf ears that hear, our blind eyes that see, our dead bodies that are made alive. Then, from the perspective of faith alone, one could talk about cooperating, but (note well) as a musical instrument in the hands of a virtuoso, the Holy Spirit. Then, paraphrasing Shakespeare, we (instruments with healed ears and wills) respond, "If music be the food of faith, play on!"

Paragraph 19. There was one more problem with Melanchthon's textbook. In the second edition he had written that three causes combine in our salvation: the Holy Spirit, the Word, and the human will. Scholars have since shown that he understood this third "cause" as a "material cause" (in Aristotelian terms), that is, the material the Holy Spirit works on to bring about faith. Melanchthon, ever worried about fatalism, meant that our conversion does not take place apart from us. However, in later debates this phrase came to mean that the human will could cooperate in bringing about salvation. There are, thus, only two actual causes for our faith: the Word and the Holy Spirit. Luther says as much in his explanation to the first two petitions of the Lord's Prayer in the Small Catechism (Lord's Prayer, 3-8, in *BC 2000,* 356-57).

A Formula for Parish Practice

What would evangelism look like in our congregations if we believed human beings are in bondage to sin and cannot free themselves? One thing is clear. We can set aside all calls to decision. Christians never have to play the part of religious hucksters, trying to convince people to buy into this particular brand of religious conveyance. David T. Niles was close to the mark when he said, "Evangelism is one beggar telling another where to get some bread." It is not decision but invitation. But more than that! Our evangelism can really be the good news of God's unleashed, unconditional promise. "Jesus Christ died and rose again for you!" This is the Word that the Holy Spirit loves to use. Of course, we must realize that the old creature, hearing such a message, will resist with all its might and main. Either it will assume that it is actually a trick and there is something left to do, or it will get mad at or make fun of such a foolish message.

When the Word does not seem to work, there are two things to do. First, it could be that what we intend to say (good news of God in Christ) may not always be what people hear (especially given all the false gospels out there). That is why true evangelism involves actually knowing the people with whom we are speaking. Listening is twice as important as speaking, as Dietrich Bonhoeffer noted when he reminded us that the Christian pastor has two ears but only one mouth. Second, we can pray the first two petitions of the Lord's Prayer, which mean, according to Luther, "Father, bring in the Word and through the Holy

Spirit make us believers." God must hear such a prayer and promises to answer our deepest pleas. There may also be a third point to remember, namely, that the Word we speak may first sprout in a person's life years later (this may especially console parents and loved ones). Jesus' parable in Mark 4 of the secretly growing seed is a special comfort. Think what our congregations' evangelism would look like in light of the Formula! There might be many more people crying at trolley stops and bursting unannounced into pastors' studies.

DISCUSSION QUESTIONS

- ▶ What is God's promise for you today, and what in your life interferes with or undermines your hearing the gospel message for you?
- ▶ What does it mean to rely on God in sharing the gospel promise with others?
- ▶ Metaphorically speaking, what are points in your life when you have felt deaf or even dead to the Word (cf. Mark 7:31-37 and Luke 7:11-17)? What is your experience of hearing words that you were incapable of hearing? How did those words come to you?
- ▶ How would the concordists' approach to "free will" change your approach to evangelism?
- ▶ People "will truly be free in the end, when they will be completely bound to God." How do you make sense of this paradox? How might we experience this freedom provisionally now?

Article Three

Getting Right(eous) with God:
Christians Are Declared, Not Made

He leaned over and whispered in my ear. Everything about that action was uncharacteristic for our culture and our relationship. He was my young next-door neighbor Larry, a devout Presbyterian with a wife and two young children. And I was grieving, standing in the receiving line at the funeral of my wife of twenty-seven years, a widower at fifty. When Larry shook my hand, he leaned over and whispered, "Just remember, Tim, Jesus said, 'I am the resurrection and the life.'" He could not have known that my dear Barbara had chosen that very selection from the Gospel of John to be read at her funeral, which was to start in twenty minutes. Nor could he have fathomed that of all the wonderful things said to me that day (and contrary to rumor and perhaps our own feelings of inadequacy, people really do by and large say the right thing at funerals), his would be the only comment I really and truly remembered. Hearing those words was for me like hearing the very voice of Jesus as he spoke to the grieving Martha in John 11.

The first two articles in the Formula of Concord were building toward article 3, "Concerning the Righteousness of Faith before God," and the next three build upon it. It is, to use an old designation, the article upon which the church stands or falls: justification by faith alone without the works of the law. Yet, to use words like "article" and "doctrine" to describe justification misses the point entirely and misconstrues what the concordists were trying to confess. Justification by grace through faith alone is not a theory but an event, something that happens to us. Moreover, it is an event centered in a word, the Word, of God's promise. It requires dramatic stories, like the one above, in order to begin to make sense of it. More importantly, it requires the spoken, unconditional declaration of God's grace from one person's mouth to another person's ears. Although we may not often hear that Word in such a dramatic fashion or with such lasting results, it is nevertheless that Word that, in Luther's pithy language, does what it says: forgives sinners, comforts mourners, encourages the hopeless and the helpless.

History

The authors of the Formula had two purposes in mind as they composed this article. On the one hand, as they expressly state in the first two paragraphs, there was a fight among Lutherans about which nature of Christ actually bestowed righteousness on us. In some ways, 425 years later, this dispute seems rather lame and the solution (why, both natures, of course!) rather obvious. But, as we shall see, there is plenty at stake underneath this dispute. On the other hand, and less obviously, the concordists were also reacting to some of the teachings of their Roman opponents, especially as expressed at the Council of Trent, and they used this venue to explain once more the entire doctrine. Perhaps underneath both purposes lies a third: these Christians simply love to talk about justification! Like the bride and groom who just have to talk about the wedding weeks and months after it has happened — to the consternation of all their friends — the concordists cannot say enough about this teaching.

The instigator of the debate over justification by faith was Andreas Osiander. Already as an evangelical (Lutheran) pastor in Nuremberg, he had been involved in a small skirmish over the meaning of this doctrine. In the 1530s he objected to the general absolution often announced from the pulpit after the sermon in evangelical parishes. Both Luther and Melanchthon responded by defending the practice, but neither seemed to notice that Osiander's position on the absolution was related to his Platonic philosophy. In 1548, with the imposition of the Augsburg Interim (see below, article 10), Osiander fled Nuremberg for the safety of the Prussian court in Königsberg, where he became professor of the fledgling university there. Almost immediately he attacked Melanchthon's perspective on *adiaphora* (see article 10). At the same time, however, he began to express more fully his peculiar view of justification.

In a 1550 tract arguing that Christ would have become incarnate even if human beings had not sinned — an old and, frankly, dangerous debate — Osiander spoke of God in ways that began to cause concern among other Lutherans (both Philippists and Gnesio-Lutherans). God was a single, inseparable, pure essence whose (essential) presence always carried with it God's attributes. Thus, to become righteous in Christ meant that a human being had to be touched by God's essence and thereby receive God's perfect righteousness. Osiander viewed justification as a process whereby human creatures came into direct contact with the essential righteousness of God, not simply with verbal signs of that righteousness. He failed to grasp Luther's more biblical, Hebraic understanding of God in terms of relationship and promise, and preferred instead to view theology in terms of essence and spirit.

Soon Osiander was arguing that Christians were justified precisely when they received the divine essence of Christ's righteousness. Thus, Christ's divinity, not his humanity, is the source of the believer's righteousness. Faith is the channel for receiving this divine essence into the human being. In justification the soul of the believer participates in the divine righteousness of Christ. In his opponents' eyes this undercut both the Word of God (a mere sign for Osiander and not the bearer of God's creative work) and Christ's redemption on the cross (an event in the past for him). Christ's human nature was not the source of our righteousness, Osiander insisted, only his divinity was.

In the debate that followed, Osiander was attacked from all sides. The young ducal librarian in Königsberg, Martin Chemnitz (later one of the chief authors of the Formula of Concord), combed the church fathers for refutations of the view. As a result, he became very familiar with the theology of the ancient church, and he became friends with Osiander's chief opponent among the Gnesio-Lutherans, Joachim Mörlin. At the same time, Melanchthon joined the fray, realizing that the chief article of the faith was under attack. Not only did Osiander's position seem to undercut the centrality of Christ's incarnation and his death on the cross, it also rejected outright the center of Melanchthon's understanding of justification: that God pronounces us righteous through his promise, to which faith clings, trusting that promise to be our righteousness in Christ before God. A third opponent, Francesco Stancaro (who later returned to the Roman Church), simply fell off the horse on the other side by arguing that Christ's human nature alone was mediator between God and humanity and thus alone provided righteousness to believers. Stancaro was also roundly attacked by everyone. Only Johann Brenz, the reformer from Württemberg who was from Luther's generation but had never studied with Luther, gave faint credence to Osiander's position, in part because of earlier personal contact between the two when both were reformers in south Germany.

Osiander died in 1552, before any final action could be taken on his challenge, in 1552. Stancaro soon returned to the Roman fold, and, with few exceptions, everyone else agreed with Luther that justification by grace through faith alone meant that God pronounces us righteous and that faith, receiving that promise, has what it says, namely, God's full righteousness given in Christ (human and divine). Of course, when the old creature hears this full and free Word of forgiveness, it dies with all of its self-righteous works. At the same time, the new creature, which trusts in Christ's righteousness alone, comes to life in faith. Everything depends on God's Word alone. This, in essence, was also the approach of Melanchthon, who was very worried about the uncertainty Osiander's position implied. If justification meant an infusion or union with Christ's divine righteousness, the believer could easily despair in the face of continuing sins, doubts, and anxieties, and could imagine that God's righteousness was completely absent. The only certain thing is the promise of God's forgiveness, which comes from outside the sinner and to which faith clings.

The Heart of the Matter

Justification before God is about *grace alone.* "God forgives us our sins by sheer grace" (Ep III.4). Justification is about *faith alone.* "Faith alone is the means and instrument through which we lay hold of Christ" (Ep III.5). This faith, by the way, "is not a mere knowledge . . . [but] a gift of God . . . in the Word" (Ep III.6). Thus justification is not about feelings or some essential qualities poured into our souls, but is about *the Word alone.* "'To justify' in this article means 'to absolve,' that is, 'to pronounce free from sin'" (Ep III.7). To sum it all up, despite our weakness and frailty, we need not doubt this righteousness, reckoned to us through faith, but "should regard it as certain that [we] have a gracious God for Christ's sake, on the basis of the promise and the Word of the holy gospel" (Ep III.9).

The heart of justification is precisely this certainty. Certainty, despite the way we may construe it popularly, is not a feeling. Imagine how easily one's feelings change. Here our children are the best mirrors we have. A young child in a toy store wants everything he or she lays eyes on. Based on this principle, grocery stores long ago learned to put a display of candy in the checkout line. Yet, adults fare scarcely better — if they did, Madison Avenue would collapse.

Certainty can also not be found in theories. For example, some Christians insist, somewhat in the spirit of Andreas Osiander, that in justification they are infused with some sort of divine force, disposition, or power — so that when God justifies us we become intrinsically holy, participants in God's divinity. But if this were true, how could one be certain that this was truly happening? It sounds good in theory, but — I ask myself — do I show such holiness and righteousness in my life? Do you in yours? Does anyone? Suddenly the one, chief comfort in a Christian's life becomes a threat. "Be holy! Be righteous! Or else!" What always haunts approaches similar to Osiander's is the specter of uncertainty and our addiction to discovering how well we are faring in our relation to God. We are always curved in upon ourselves.

Much earlier in the Reformation Melanchthon and Luther had a conversation with their fellow reformer Johann Brenz of Schwäbisch Hall (and later of Württemberg) over this very issue. Brenz thought, in line with Saint Augustine, that when Christ declares us righteous, he is simply anticipating the work of the Holy Spirit in making us righteous. In an uncharacteristic joint letter, written by Melanchthon with a lengthy appendix in Luther's hand, both reject this approach, because it, too, leaves sinners uncertain, dependent on how well they do righteous deeds and not on God's promise alone. Here is a portion of what they wrote to Brenz. Melanchthon urged him to "cast your eyes back to the promise and Christ and away from this renewal. . . . Thus we are righteous by faith alone, not because (as you write) it is the root [of human righteousness] but because it apprehends Christ, on account of whom we are accepted whatever kind of renewal is there." Luther's approach gives these same arguments his own unique twist. "And I am accustomed . . . to think of it in these terms: as if there is no quality in my heart that might be called 'faith' or 'love,' but in that place I put Jesus Christ and say, 'This is my righteousness; he is the quality and (as they say) formal righteousness. . . . I want him to be gift and teaching in himself, so that I may have all things in him.' Thus Christ says, 'I am the way, the truth, and the life'; he does not say I give you the way, truth, and life, as if Christ stood outside of me and worked such things in me."

But can we say that any word of comfort justifies? Aren't we only talking here about the forgiveness of sins? After all, whispering comfort into the ear of the newly widowed is not the same as forgiving sins. Or is it? Our habit of separating forgiveness, comfort, freedom, and the like from one another may say more about our theology than the truth of the gospel. But perhaps the problem can be put more narrowly. Perhaps we do not understand that consoling a widower with the gospel *is* the forgiveness of sin, because we do not understand sin.

Like Erasmus, Luther's famous humanist opponent, we always tend toward moralism, that is, the belief that sin is essentially comprised of "sins," that is, discrete acts. What "sin" could a grieving person possibly commit? But if sin is a condition — marked always by a lack of fear, love, and trust in God — then the exchange between my neighbor and me makes more sense. Nowhere does a person experience being out of line with God more poignantly than when faced with death. Being "put right" with God means precisely hearing that God has put things right for us. In the face of death this means precisely the promise that Jesus Christ is resurrection and life. Yet, this cannot be a general statement; it must be whispered in my ear with my name attached — like Jesus' encounter with another grieving person in chapter 20 of John's Gospel, Mary Magdalene. What brought her from sin and death to faith and life was precisely Jesus calling her name. Whether that whispered name comes in a graveyard, from a pulpit, washed over us at a font, or poured out for us from a chalice, the effect is the same: we are declared right with God for the sake of Christ alone. Now, that is something to believe!

The Text of the Epitome

Concerning the Righteousness of Faith before God

Status controversiae

The Chief Question in This Dispute

[1] Our churches unanimously confess on the basis of God's Word and in accord with the content of the Augsburg Confession that we poor sinners become righteous before God and are saved only through faith in Christ, and that therefore Christ alone is our righteousness. He is truly God and human because in him the divine and human natures are personally united with each other (Jer. 23[:6]; 1 Cor. 1[:30]; 2 Cor. 5[:21]). Because of this confession, the question arose: According to which nature is Christ our righteousness? Thus, two mutually contradictory errors emerged in some churches.

[2] The one party held that Christ is our righteousness only according to his divinity, when he dwells in us through faith. In comparison to this divinity which dwells in us through faith, the sins of all human creatures are to be regarded as a drop of water compared to a huge sea. On the other side, some have held that Christ is our righteousness before God only according to his human nature.

Affirmative Theses

The Pure Teaching of the Christian Church against Both These Errors

[3] 1. Against both of these errors we believe, teach, and confess unanimously that Christ is our righteousness neither according to his divine nature alone nor according to his human nature alone. On the contrary, the whole Christ, according to both natures, is our righteousness, solely in his obedience that he rendered his Father as both God and a human being, an obedience unto death. Through this obedience he earned the forgiveness of sins and eternal life for us, as it is written, "Just as by the one man's disobedience the many were made sinners, so by the one man's obedience the many will be made righteous" (Rom. 5[:19]).

[4] 2. Accordingly, we believe, teach, and confess that our righteousness before God consists in this, that God forgives us our sins by sheer grace, with-

out any works, merit, or worthiness of our own, in the past, at present, or in the future, that he gives us and reckons to us the righteousness of Christ's obedience and that, because of this righteousness, we are accepted by God into grace and regarded as righteous.

[5] 3. We believe, teach, and confess that faith alone is the means and instrument through which we lay hold of Christ and, thus, in Christ lay hold of this "righteousness which avails before God." Because of him "faith is reckoned to us as righteousness" (Rom. 4[:5]).

[6] 4. We believe, teach, and confess that this faith is not a mere knowledge of the stories about Christ. It is instead a gift of God, through which in the Word of the gospel we recognize Christ truly as our redeemer and trust in him, so that solely because of his obedience, by grace, we have the forgiveness of sins, are regarded as godly and righteous by God the Father, and have eternal life.

[7] 5. We believe, teach, and confess that according to the usage of Holy Scripture the word "to justify" in this article means "to absolve," that is, "to pronounce free from sin": "One who justifies the wicked and one who condemns the righteous are both alike an abomination to the Lord" (Prov. 17[:15]); "Who will bring any charge against God's elect? It is God who justifies" (Rom. 8[:33]). [8] When in place of this the words *regeneratio* and *vivificatio,* that is "new birth" and "making alive," are used as synonyms of justification, as happens in the Apology, then they are to be understood in this same sense. Otherwise, they should be understood as the renewal of the human being and should be differentiated from "justification by faith."

[9] 6. We believe, teach, and confess that in spite of the fact that until death a great deal of weakness and frailty still cling to those who believe in Christ and are truly reborn, they should not doubt their righteousness, which is reckoned to them through faith, nor the salvation of their souls, but they should regard it as certain that they have a gracious God for Christ's sake, on the basis of the promise and the Word of the holy gospel.

[10] 7. We believe, teach, and confess that for the retention of pure teaching concerning the righteousness of faith before God, it is particularly important to hold steadfastly to the *particulae exclusivae,* that is, the following expressions of the holy apostle Paul that completely separate the merit of Christ from our works and give honor to Christ alone. The holy apostle Paul

writes, "by grace," "without merit," "apart from the law," "apart from works," "not through works," etc. These expressions all mean nothing other than that we become righteous and receive salvation "alone through faith" in Christ.

[11] 8. We believe, teach, and confess that although the contrition that precedes justification and the good works that follow it do not belong in the article on justification before God, nevertheless, a person should not concoct a kind of faith that can exist and remain with and alongside an evil intention to sin and to act against the conscience. Instead, after a person has been justified by faith, there then exists a true, living "faith working through love" (Gal. 5[:6]). That means that good works always follow justifying faith and are certainly found with it, when it is a true and living faith. For faith is never alone but is always accompanied by love and hope.

Antithesis or Negative Theses

Rejection of Contrary Teaching

[12] Therefore we reject and condemn all the following errors:

[13] 1. That Christ is our righteousness only according to the divine nature, etc.

[14] 2. That Christ is our righteousness only according to the human nature, etc.

[15] 3. That in texts from the prophets and apostles, when they speak of the righteousness of faith, the words "to justify" and "to be justified" are not supposed to mean "to pronounce free from sin" or "to be pronounced free from sin" and "to receive the forgiveness of sins." Instead they mean to be made righteous before God in fact on account of the love and virtues which are infused by the Holy Spirit and through the works which result from this infusion.

[16] 4. That faith should look not only to the obedience of Christ but also to his divine nature, as it dwells in us and produces results, and that through this indwelling our sins are covered.

[17] 5. That faith is the kind of trust in Christ's obedience that can exist and

remain in a person who does not truly repent, demonstrates no love resulting from this faith, and perseveres in sin against the conscience.

[18] 6. That not God himself but only the gifts of God dwell in believers.

[19] 7. That faith saves because renewal, which consists in love toward God
and the neighbor, has begun in us through this faith.

[20] 8. That faith has the primary role in justification, but at the same time
renewal and love also constitute a part of our righteousness before God in
this way, that although they are not the most important cause of our righteousness, nevertheless, our righteousness before God cannot be complete
or perfect without such love and renewal.

[21] 9. That believers are both justified before God and receive salvation
through the righteousness of Christ reckoned to them and through the new
obedience which has begun in them, or partly through the reckoning of
Christ's righteousness to them and partly through this new obedience
which has begun in them.

[22] 10. That the promise of grace is made our own through faith in the
heart and through the confession of the mouth and through other virtues.

[23] 11. That faith does not justify without good works, that is, that good
works are necessarily required for righteousness, and without their presence
a person cannot be justified.

Commentary

The Controversial Issue (pp. 494-95)

Paragraph 1. In a single sentence Jakob Andreae summarizes the heart
of justification by faith alone from Scripture and the Augsburg Confession. We are, first of all, "poor sinners." Our righteousness, holiness,
goodness, purity, salvation, and anything else you can think of do not
come from us and our works but "through faith in Christ." Therefore,
"Christ alone is our righteousness." Not a bad way to start!

Paragraph 2. Here the concordists state the surface problem.
Which nature of Christ provides our righteousness: the human nature
or the divine nature? Is our sin just a drop of water in the vast sea of

God's divine righteousness? Or is Christ's righteousness open to us only through his human suffering and death? As we shall see, this is only the tip of a much more serious issue: the nature of our salvation.

Affirmative Theses (pp. 495-96)

Paragraph 3. "The whole Christ, according to both natures, is our righteousness." This obvious solution to the positions of Osiander and Stancaro holds within it a far more profound insight: that we are saved by Christ alone. Although most Lutherans can rattle off other *solas* (*sola gratia* [grace alone], *sola fide* [by faith alone], *sola Scriptura* [the Scripture alone]), the one most near and dear to Luther's heart and theology was actually *Christus solus*, Christ alone. (For example, see SA II.1.1-5, in *BC 2000*, 301.) If the whole Christ *(totus Christus)* and Christ alone *(Christus solus)* are not the heart of every aspect of our congregation's life, it is not clear why we should call ourselves Christian at all. Thus, Paul asked his squabbling Corinthians, "Was Paul crucified for you?" (1 Cor. 1:13), and said to the Galatians, "May I never boast of anything except the cross of our Lord Jesus Christ" (Gal. 6:14).

Paragraph 4. Now the concordists tell us that our right relation with God is a matter of "sheer grace." What a relief! How often do sermons, Sunday school curricula, and well-meaning friends try to turn things upside down and make everything depend on us and on our works! Moreover, our righteousness is "reckoned" to us. It is not a matter of something we possess or even, as Luther warned Brenz, something Christ works in us. It is a reckoning of Christ's obedience to us, who are disobedient. As we sing in the Lenten hymn: "What punishment so strange is suffered yonder! / The shepherd dies for sheep who love to wander. / The master pays the debt the servants owe him, / who would not know him" (*Lutheran Book of Worship*, no. 123).

Paragraphs 5-6. Now comes "faith alone." Here the concordists consider both the order (par. 5: grace precedes faith) and the meaning of the word "faith" (par. 6). It is God's grace, not human effort, that is the heart of our relation to God. Faith is "means and instrument." For this reason Melanchthon had it right in the Augsburg Confession IV, when he wrote that we are justified *by* grace *through* faith. But please understand what faith is. It is not just knowledge of the facts. (How often do we not unintentionally convey to children in confirmation instruction that we are justified by right answer alone!) "It is instead a gift of God." If faith is not understood as a gift, then we will end up trusting ourselves, not Christ. In the Solid Declaration, III.13 (in *BC 2000*, 564), the concordists write: "For faith does not make people righteous because it is such a good work or such a fine virtue." Too often Christians have reduced faith to a decision, some virtuous work that we pull off. It is not. It is precisely what happens to us (that is, what the Holy Spirit works in us) through the Word of forgiveness. This relationship of faith "comes to us," so that suddenly God's promise comes alive for us and we discover that God is *for us,* not against us. No wonder faith follows God's grace!

Paragraph 7-8. As is their habit, the concordists also define disputed terms. The easiest way to define "justify" is to use a metaphor from the law courts: "to pronounce [the criminal on death row] free from sin [and death]." Of course, if a judge were to act that way, he or she would soon be fired (that is the gist of Prov. 17:15); but for us sinners, "it is God who justifies" (Rom. 8:33). While it is true that sometimes words like "new birth" and "making alive" can refer to the life of the now justified Christian, there are also places in Scripture where these terms are just metaphors, or pictures, of justification itself. One can well imagine a freed prisoner speaking in just those terms: "I feel as if I have gotten a whole new lease on life!" Indeed we have.

Paragraph 9. Let's be honest. As true as forgiveness may be, it does not make us any less a sinner. In fact, this paragraph admits as much and, at the same time, provides such "sinner-saints" great comfort. When we discover our sins, frailties, fears, and anxieties (usually daily), we need not despair. We have "a gracious God for Christ's sake, on the basis of the promise and the Word of the holy gospel." Thank heavens!

Paragraph 10. Here is a Latin phrase worth learning: *particulae exclusivae,* "exclusive terms." One of the criticisms of the so-called Leipzig Interim (see below, article 10) was that it lacked such terms, especially "faith *alone.*" If Saint Paul himself saw fit to exclude our works from the equation of our relation with God, we can, too. And think of how comforting these exclusive "particles" are: our relation to God is right where it should be, in God's hands, not ours.

Paragraph 11. Here the concordists anticipate the arguments of the next three articles. On the one hand, do not mix works and faith together. Of course we may feel sorry for our sins, but that does not earn us grace (no matter how many crocodile tears we shed). Of course our lives are filled to overflowing with good works, but we are not saved by depending on them. On the other hand, do not dream up a faith that has no life in it. Faith just abounds in goodness and love, as we will see in article 6.

Negative Theses (pp. 496-97)

Paragraphs 12-14. The reader can sense how easily the concordists can put aside the stated argument over Christ's divinity and humanity in our salvation. However, the other theses show that there were much more important debates than whether Christ saves us by his humanity or his divinity.

Paragraph 15. Here they attack not simply Osiander (who may not actually have held this position) but also certain statements by the Roman Catholic Council of Trent. When God wants to make someone right, God just says the Word. This is no different from creation itself, where God said, "Let there be," and there it was. Justification is not a matter of anything inside us ("love and virtues . . . infused by the Holy Spirit") or anything that comes from us ("works which result"); it results from an external Word that, by its very alien nature, kills the old and brings the new to life.

Paragraph 16. Here Osiander's peculiar view of Christ's divinity comes in for attack. However, this view of Christ is by no means dead. How often are people so transfixed by Christ's divinity and spirit that they forget the good news: "To you this day is *born* a savior" (Luke 2)? We never have to encounter God outside his flesh.

Paragraphs 17-23. The rejected positions in this list all have to do with faith. One of the most helpful pictures of faith comes from one of my teachers, Gerhard Forde, who said that "faith is falling in love." This view helps clarify what concerns the concordists here. First, faith coexisting with sheer contempt of God (par. 17) is as foolish as a person who gets married *so that* he or she can commit adultery. Imagine the lover saying to the beloved, "Ask me anything!" and the beloved responding, "Mind if I cheat on you?" Second, referring to a dispute between two medieval theologians (Peter Lombard and Thomas Aquinas), the concordists take Lombard's side and argue that God himself dwells in believers (par. 18). The difficult philosophical problem (how can the perfect touch the imperfect?) is simply God's to figure out, not ours. God in Christ is not distant.

Third, the concordists again struggle against false definitions of faith (par. 19-23). Paragraph 19: do not imagine that faith depends on our renewal! It depends on God's grace and merciful promise alone. Paragraphs 20-21: do not think faith is not strong enough to get the job done. There are not two sources for our standing before God (faith and works of love). If there were, we would be robbed of the certainty of God's mercy. The problem of our imperfection is not ours to solve but God's to absolve. It is not that God's righteousness goes part of the way and our righteousness makes up the difference. As Paul reports God saying to him in 2 Corinthians 12:9, "My grace is sufficient for you, for power is made perfect in weakness." Paragraph 22, though small, packs a punch. Here the concordists reject redefining faith as a virtue, something good we do or decide for God. In paragraph 23 they are again anticipating the fight in article 4. We dare not mix our good works with God's overwhelming mercy! In the face of such good news, who would want to do a thing like that anyway?

A Formula for Parish Practice

Above all else, justification by grace through faith on account of Christ alone occurs through God's direct address to us. The "I baptize you" at the font, joining my name to God's; the eating and drinking around the table with its "body of Christ" and "blood of Christ *for you*"; and all words of forgiveness and comfort that put people right with God qualify, whether heard in Sunday morning worship or in a receiving line at a funeral.

In the Smalcald Articles III.4 (in *BC 2000*, 319), Luther includes in his definition of the gospel "mutual conversation and consolation of the brothers and sisters." That was precisely what my neighbor Larry provided for me. When one looks around, however, one can find this same personal sharing of the gospel all over the place. The parents teaching their children to pray, the friend inviting someone to worship, a child reminding a relative of God's love — all these and more give God the opportunity to make people right(eous). In most congregations God is doing more justifying than we can even imagine.

Nowhere is this word of absolution and forgiveness more crucial than in the sermon — that often neglected part of Christian worship. Some think of the sermon as a time to tell funny jokes and poignant stories. Others turn the sermon into a dialogue or a morality play, simply underscoring our need to lead good Christian lives. However, the sermon is where God gets the job done, speaks the actual word of forgiveness, reconciliation, and resurrection to the weak and broken and dying. The sermon, in the words of one of my teachers, *does* God to us. That is, it delivers a word that pronounces us righteous in God's sight because of Christ alone. And that very Word in the hands of the Holy Spirit destroys the old creature and its works-righteous ways and brings a new, "faith-righteous" creature to life. To be sure, the sermon has to be a more general word, applicable to a roomful of people. Thus, as Luther himself admitted, sometimes the sermon may miss you and leave you cold. For that reason, he said, God instituted the Lord's Supper — God's visible word of justification in which those distributing (to my knowledge) never miss the mouth or ears of the person receiving the good news: "The body of Christ for you; the blood of Christ for you for the forgiveness of sins." In whatever form it comes, what a Word! What a formula for the life of any parish!

DISCUSSION QUESTIONS

▸ What was the issue raised by Andreas Osiander? How did Melanchthon and other followers of Luther respond to this?

▸ What is sin? How is sin described as something other than separate and "discrete acts"?

▸ How are we "justified" or forgiven for our sin? How does this happen to us, and how can we be certain that we are justified?

▸ Faith is described and defined in a number of ways. What is faith? How would you describe faith to avoid turning it into a work or decision?

▸ Along with the opening story, what are some other concrete examples of justification by grace through faith at work?

▸ How is the sermon a place where God gets the job of justifying sinners done? Have you heard a sermon recently that "did God" to you?

God Does Not Need Your Good Works
(But They Won't Hurt You Either)

Ed and Mary Jo had four feisty kids; that much was certain. When they moved to town, she, a lifelong Lutheran, and her children joined the congregation immediately. Within a few months Ed, who had grown up in the Roman Catholic Church, decided to join as well by taking adult instruction. The class always started with justification by grace through faith, and Ed, a big man who worked for the railroad, caught on immediately. "So, it's all a matter of God's grace," he began. "Yes, Ed," I replied, thinking to myself what a great teacher I was. "And there's nothing you have to do." "You've got it, Ed!" I beamed. Then he paused. "Well, just don't tell the kids!"

When we finally "get it," that is, when we finally realize that the gospel has to do with the unconditional grace of God, one of the first things we wonder about is our works. Specifically, what happens to our motivation to do good works if they are not what establishes or cements our relation to God. Along with the question of predestination (see article 11), the question of works is one of the questions people most often raise when they hear of God's mercy with no strings attached. I often call the question about works question 6 and the question about election question 9, because Paul in Romans 6 asks, "Should we continue in sin in order that grace may abound?" and in Romans 9 inquires, "Is there injustice on God's part?" In fact, unless God's grace and mercy are unconditional, we will never ask those (Pauline) questions. When they arise, it is a sign that we are on the right track. So, too, with the concordists. As soon as they nail down justification by grace through faith (article 3), they must deal with the question of good works.

History

The dispute over the relation between faith and works can be traced back to an attack on the Lutherans by John Eck just prior to the Diet of Augsburg in 1530. Eck, a professor at Ingolstadt and an archenemy of Luther, claimed that the evangelicals forbade good works in their preaching and teaching — a sure sign of treasonous behavior to the emperor's ears. As a result, Melanchthon added article 20 to the Augsburg Confession and entitled it "Faith and Good Works." (See CA XX in *BC 2000*, 52-57.) He concluded with Jesus' words in John 15:5, "Apart from me you can do nothing."

In the mid-1530s an intra-Lutheran fight broke out over Melanchthon's comment that good works were a necessary condition for the Christian life. The strife ended quickly, but not long afterward Luther himself became embroiled in a related dispute over the role of the law in the Christian life with John Agricola, an "antinomian" (someone against the law) who denied that the law applied to believers. (See articles 5 and 6 for details.)

The struggle over good works that most concerned the concordists began in the wake of the fights over the so-called Leipzig Interim (see article 10). In June 1548 the emperor promulgated a decree from the diet (parliament) meeting in Augsburg that was to regulate Germany's religious life "in the interim," until a churchwide council could be called. Nicknamed the Augsburg Interim, it allowed Protestants little more than married priests and communion in both kinds (bread *and* wine). In December of that year a memorandum from the theological faculties of the electoral Saxon church (Wittenberg and Leipzig) became public. Its opponents called it the Leipzig Interim because it was presented in Leipzig to the Saxon lesser nobility and cities for approval, which they never gave. Written in large part by Melanchthon and signed by other theologians, including the Wittenberg theology professor George Major, this document used a form of compromise in attempting to protect Saxony's churches from the Augsburg Interim.

Practices that were neither commanded nor forbidden *(adiaphora)* could be reinstated as long as the theology remained evangelical. However, the memorandum also restated evangelical theology in a way that raised questions for other Lutherans, especially for the venerable Nicholas von Amsdorf, one of Luther's closest friends from the early days of the Reformation.

When von Amsdorf, a former professor at Wittenberg and bishop of Naumburg, published a tract against the Leipzig Interim in 1551, he attacked among other things its failure to use the phrase "faith alone." Moreover, a sermon by Major from this period had implied that works were necessary for salvation. When Major, who had worked as a teacher under von Amsdorf when the latter was rector of a Latin school in Magdeburg, took it upon himself to respond, he thought he had caught the older man in a basic antinomian error — denying good works were necessary in the Christian life. Thus, he wrote in his response of 1552, "This I confess, that I have always taught, still teach, and will continue to teach all my life that good works are necessary for salvation [or: blessedness]. . . . Just as no one will be saved [or blessed] through evil works, so no one will be saved [or blessed] without good works." One can just imagine the furor that these comments provoked. Major probably meant simply that good works necessarily flow from Christian faith. What he wrote sounded like a betrayal of the entire Reformation. Thus, the so-called Majoristic Controversy began.

In many ways George Major spent the rest of his career trying to distance himself from his (in)famous dictum. Time and again he tried to refute the notion that we earn salvation through our works (at one point even denying that he had written such a thing). He even promised to write the word "alone" (in the phrase "faith alone") in capital letters wherever it occurred in his works. In a life marked by professional disappointment and personal tragedy (his four sons predeceased him, one succumbing to rabies), even a work from 1570, published at his retirement from public life at the age of sixty-eight, tried to defend his view of good works. At his death in 1574, Wittenberg's rector wrote on the official death notice for the community that Major had throughout his career fought off the *"rabies theologorum,"* the rabies of theologians.

Throughout this period until his own death in 1565, von Amsdorf and other Gnesio-Lutherans kept up the attacks. At one point von Amsdorf, in an attempt to make clear that our works did not constitute even the smallest part of our standing before God and in an obvious rhetorical flourish found also in the young Luther, claimed that good works were harmful for salvation. Most understood the nature of this exaggeration and its source, but the comment simply added more fuel to the fire. Major and von Amsdorf did not agree on terms, especially on the meaning of the phrase "Good works are necessary for salvation [blessedness]." What von Amsdorf understood as salvation, Major construed as the blessed fruit of saving faith. What Major understood as a necessary consequence, von Amsdorf treated as an actual cause. What von Amsdorf viewed as external deeds, Major took as the outpourings of a believing heart. Melanchthon, who quite early distanced himself from Major's position, nevertheless continued to construe Major's opponents as simple "antinomians," in league with Agricola, who was also a chief defender of the hated Augsburg Interim. Melanchthon claimed that Major's enemies simply wanted to eliminate the law from the Christian life, which was never the case.

Other controversies followed from this initial one. As the result of some struggles in ducal Saxony, Justus Menius, a faithful student of Melanchthon, and von Amsdorf clashed over whether one could even say that works were necessary under the law "in the abstract." Other echoes from this dispute reverberated in a fight over the meaning of the words "free" and "necessary" that arose at the University of Frankfurt an der Oder in eastern Germany. Finally, and throughout these disputes, the specter of antinomianism lingered: whether Christians perform good works on the basis of the law or only on the basis of the gospel.

With the deaths of the chief instigators of the dispute, the concordists could resolve this issue quite straightforwardly through properly defining terms (a technique learned from their teacher, Melanchthon) and rejecting extremes. However, because this topic, like the one in article 3, touched on matters central to the Lutheran confession of faith, they were glad to try their hand at proclaiming a law-free, unconditional gospel of grace, which a person could still "tell the kids."

The Heart of the Matter

The necessity of works and unconditional grace do not mix. That is, any attempt to smuggle works into one's grace-filled relation to God always ends up missing the point and destroying that very relationship. I suppose it is as bad as a lover imagining that the relationship to the beloved is less than unconditional. The result is either doubt ("Does she really love me?") or desperation ("Perhaps if I try harder, he will *really* love me"), but in the midst of such frenzy the bond of love itself simply dissolves. The trust and love that make up the heart of the relationship cannot by definition allow any works to define it, simply because works always force us to turn inward, wondering how well we are doing, if we measure up, or whether we are acceptable.

Many of us, adept at playing the part of the elder brother in the parable of the waiting father (Luke 15), do not realize the damage we do when we insist directly or indirectly that, at some level, works must play a role in our salvation. I still remember visiting in the hospital the dying mother of a woman who was a member of our congregation. She must have been subjected to moralistic sermons throughout her many years in Lutheran parishes. She knew she was dying, and she knew that I knew, too, so she blurted out as she sat on the side of her bed, "I've tried to live a good life. But have I done enough?" The problem with George Major and with all the pietistic preachers who follow in his train rests not in their intentions (to combat lawlessness) but in the effect of their words. Proclaiming the necessity of works in our relation with God will always leave the weak dangling their feet over the bed wondering, especially at the end of life, whether they have done enough.

Yet, on the other side, there are Paul's rhetorical question ("Should we continue in sin?") and Ed's family concern ("Don't tell the kids!"). However, Paul's response gives no space to the moralist. "By no means! How can we who died to sin go on living in it?" (Rom. 6:2). He does not say, "Oh, I was just kidding about all that grace and faith stuff." Instead, he talks of death and resurrection. The new life of faith itself changes who we are because it changes whose we are. We do not avoid sin to earn salvation. Instead, faith does not live in the old way, because we have died and were raised in baptism, and we die and rise daily with Christ by faith alone. Works come into a Christian life not as a cause for earning salvation but rather as a result of good trees bearing good fruit.

The Text of the Epitome

Concerning Good Works

Status controversiae

The Chief Question in the Controversy over Good Works

[1] Regarding the teaching on good works two controversies arose in some churches:

[2] First some theologians split over the following expressions. The first party wrote: good works are necessary for salvation; it is impossible to be saved without good works; and no one has ever been saved without good works. Against this position the other party wrote: good works are harmful to salvation.

[3] Later a split occurred among some theologians over the two words "necessary" and "free." One party argued that the word "necessary" should not be used in regard to new obedience, which does not flow from necessity and compulsion but rather from a spontaneous spirit. The other party retained the word "necessary" because such obedience is not subject to our discretion, but rather reborn human beings are bound to render such obedience.

[4] From this semantic argument a further controversy developed over the substance of the matter, when one party argued that the law should not be preached at all among Christians but people should be admonished to do good works only on the basis of the holy gospel. The other party contradicted this position.

Affirmative Theses

> The Pure Teaching of the Christian Churches
> concerning This Controversy

[5] As a thoroughgoing explanation and disposition of this dispute, it is our teaching, faith, and confession:

[6] 1. That good works follow from true faith (when it is not a dead faith but a living faith), as certainly and without doubt as fruit from a good tree.

[7] 2. We also believe, teach, and confess that at the same time, good works must be completely excluded from any questions of salvation as well as from the article on our justification before God, as the apostle testifies in clear terms, "So also David declares that salvation pertains to that person alone to whom God reckons righteousness apart from works, saying, 'Blessed are those whose iniquities are forgiven, and whose sins are covered'" (Rom. 4[:6-8]), and also, "For by grace you have been saved through faith, and this is not your own doing; it is the gift of God — not the result of works, so that no one may boast" (Eph. 2[:8-9]).

[8] 3. We also believe, teach, and confess that all people, particularly those who have been reborn and renewed through the Holy Spirit, are obligated to do good works.

[9] 4. In this sense the words "necessary," "should," and "must" are used correctly, in Christian fashion, also in regard to the reborn; in no way is such use contrary to the pattern of sound words and speech.

[10] 5. Of course, the words *necessitas, necessarium* ("necessity" and "necessary") are not to be understood as a compulsion when they are applied to the reborn, but only as the required obedience, which they perform out of a spontaneous spirit — not because of the compulsion or coercion of the law — because they are "no longer under the law, but under grace" [Rom. 6:14].

[11] 6. Accordingly, we also believe, teach, and confess that when it is said that "the reborn do good works from a free spirit," that is not to be understood as if it were up to the discretion of the reborn human beings to do good or not to do good as they wish, and that they would nevertheless retain their faith even as they deliberately persist in sin.

[12] 7. This is, of course, not to be understood in any other way than as the Lord Christ and his apostles themselves explain it, that is, regarding the liberated spirit, which acts not out of fear of punishment, like a slave, but out of the love of righteousness, as children (Rom. 8[:15]).

[13] 8. However, in the elect children of God this spontaneity is not perfect but is encumbered with great weakness, as St. Paul complains about himself in Romans 7[:14-25] and Galatians 5[:17].

[14] 9. Of course, because of Christ, the Lord does not reckon this weakness

against his elect, as it is written, "There is therefore now no condemnation for those who are in Christ Jesus" (Romans 8[:1]).

[15] 10. We also believe, teach, and confess that not our works, but only God's Spirit, working through faith, preserves faith and salvation in us. Good works are a testimony of his presence and indwelling.

Negative Theses

False and Contrary Teaching

[16] 1. Accordingly, we reject and condemn the following manner of speaking: when it is taught and written that good works are necessary for salvation; or that no one has ever been saved without good works; or that it is impossible to be saved without good works.

[17] 2. We also reject and condemn the bald expression that "good works are harmful to salvation" as offensive and harmful to Christian discipline.

[18] For particularly in these last times it is no less necessary to admonish the people to Christian discipline and good works and to remind them how necessary it is that they practice good works as a demonstration of their faith and their gratitude to God than it is to admonish them that works not be mingled with the article on justification. For people can be damned by an Epicurean delusion about faith just as much as by the papistic, Pharisaic trust in their own works and merit.

[19] 3. We also reject and condemn the teaching that faith and the indwelling of the Holy Spirit are not lost through intentional sin, but that the saints and elect retain the Holy Spirit even when they fall into adultery and other sins and persist in them.

Commentary

The Chief Question in the Controversy (pp. 497-98)

Paragraphs 1-2. Andreae begins with a simple sketch of the initial controversy. It is interesting that the concordists describe these positions by emphasizing that these things were written (not necessarily confessed). The paraphrase of George Major's famous dictum then follows. As the antithesis, the concordists mention the overblown rhetorical response of von Amsdorf, which claimed that good works were actually harmful to salvation. Their condemnation of the old man's saying in paragraph 18 will be quite mild.

Paragraph 3. Because Andreas Musculus, one of the parties to the dispute at the University of Frankfurt an der Oder, was also involved in drafting the Formula of Concord, the concordists include a reference to the fight over the terms "freedom" and "necessity." However, they quickly reduce it to a war of words. One party emphasized the spontaneity of works; the other the necessity of Christian obedience.

Paragraph 4. Here the concordists show that, like Melanchthon, they are sensitive to the antinomian ramifications of this dispute and its role in preaching. Do we admonish Christians with the law or only with the gospel? This problem will play itself out more fully in articles 5 and 6.

Affirmative Theses (pp. 498-99)

Paragraph 5. This might be a good place to consider the way in which the concordists describe what they are doing. They speak about "pure teaching" and state repeatedly that "it is our teaching, faith, and confession." These two concepts work together. On the one hand, like the Renaissance thinkers they were, they believed that the closer they came to the original sources, the purer the teaching. In this case they claimed that they based their teaching on Scripture and other pure sources of the church (the church fathers and the original Augsburg Confession). The result of this encounter with such sources was not law ("You must believe what I say") but witness in the form of teaching, faith, and confession.

Paragraph 6. We always mess up our view of good works when we use the wrong picture. The picture we most frequently use might be described as "condition — response"; that is, we set the condition with our works so that God must respond. Then the question will always come down to how much must we do; how much must God do. In paragraph 6 the concordists use a very different metaphor — that of a good tree bearing fruit — found in Jesus' comments (Matt. 7:15-20), in

Paul's writings (Gal. 5:22-23), and in the Augsburg Confession (VI.1, in *BC 2000*, 40-41). By "dead faith" they mean precisely a faith defined as knowledge of the facts rather than trust in the midst of relationship.

Paragraph 7. "Good works must be completely excluded from any questions of salvation as well as from the article on our justification before God." Nothing could be more clearly stated, and yet it is rather sad how quickly Christians, perhaps especially Lutherans, fall back into some works-righteous trap or another. Andreae is so adamant about this that he does something very unusual for the Epitome. He quotes the Scripture! Whereas the Solid Declaration is filled with discussions of Scripture passages and citations of Lutheran sources, the Epitome, true to its name, gives a *Reader's Digest* version with few frills. Yet here Andreae brings in two sources also used in the Augsburg Confession, Romans 4 (cited in CA IV.4) and Ephesians 2 (CA XX.10). In the first we hear "apart from works," and in the second "by grace . . . through faith . . . not the result of works." Perhaps if we tattooed them on the inside of preachers' eyelids. . . . No, that would just make body decorations a new law for saving seminarians! The facts are that our self-justifying ways are hardwired into us from Adam and Eve, and so the church must always struggle with its inability to believe the best news we know: God's grace in Christ is unconditional.

Paragraphs 8-10. The concordists take aim at the more recent controversy over freedom and necessity, trying to find a way to use both expressions. First, the reborn are obligated to do good works (par. 8). Thus, it is not wrong to use terms that express such obligation (par. 9). However, these words do not signify compulsion because those reborn (notice the language of new relationship!) do things spontaneously, not because they *have to* but because of grace itself (par. 10). Too bad the concordists did not consider the language of love. Imagine the beloved whose response to the true love is, "Do I *have* to kiss you?" or "I suppose I'll kiss you because it's the right thing to do." To be sure, an obligation remains, but it is, so to speak, an obligation of the relationship itself, not an obligation to follow the rules for a good relationship. Now, it may happen that the Christian, reborn by grace through faith alone, is bone ignorant. Then, the law reveals what God really likes, much to the delight of the hearer, not unlike what happens when the beloved learns that his lover has a thing for chocolate. "Buy her chocolate," we whisper to him. And the command to buy melts into invitation under the power of the relationship itself. "Love God; love your neighbor," we hear, and faith cannot imagine doing anything else.

Paragraphs 11-14. Here the language of freedom comes under scrutiny. Freedom is not "license" to follow the old creature's every whim (par. 11). It is not the kind of relationship-destroying attitude that insists on doing whatever we want. "How can we who have died to sin still live in it?" What being declared righteous (justification by grace through faith alone) does to us is clear: we die (daily) to sin and rise (daily) to new life. At the same time, this is not the grudging love of a slave or the forced humility of Charles Dickens's ever 'umble Uriah Heep, but instead is the spontaneous love of children. This metaphor conjures up many of the tenderest stories in Scripture: Jesus blessing the little children in Mark 10; Paul crying "Abba, Father" in Romans 8; and especially Jesus calling his disciples friends, not slaves (John 15:12-17). Every parent who knows the amazing, spontaneous affection of children, who themselves are surrounded and bathed in that parent's unconditional love, recognizes the power of this picture. As with all pictures, this one, too, has its limits. "Say thank you to Aunt Linda for your wool socks, David." To this command comes the sorry reply, "Thank you, Aunt Linda. I guess." But when the relation is one of love, then in Luther's explanation of "Our Father" (added to the Small Catechism when his oldest child was five), "we may ask [God] boldly and with complete confidence, just as loving children ask their loving father." (See SC, Lord's Prayer, 2, in *BC 2000*, 356.) The facts are that such spontaneity is never perfect (par. 13-14). If Paul complains about weakness (Rom. 7:14-25; Gal. 5:17), then we certainly will experience it as well. But underneath all our good works rests the unconditional love of Christ, who never, ever reckons this weakness against us. "There is therefore now no condemnation for those who are in Christ Jesus." How is that for unconditional?

Paragraph 15. This little paragraph might be easy to skip over, and yet the danger it averts is enormous. We need never sit on the side of our deathbed and wonder, "Have I done enough?" It is, finally, not about us at all. God is not nearly as stingy and mean as Christian preachers may be tempted to portray him. Instead, it is his Holy Spirit who not only gives us faith through the Word but keeps us in that faith. And if by some miracle we should happen to see one of our own good works, we need never imagine that such a work is a testimony to how good we are, how far we have advanced, or how close to perfection we have come. Instead, even such good works simply point us away from ourselves to the Holy Spirit, who is doing more in our lives for good than we can ever ask or imagine.

Negative Theses (pp. 499-500)

Paragraph 16. Here the unfortunate dictum of poor George Major is roundly condemned. It should not be taught or written. I always wonder why, if the concordists could say something so clearly, their successors could manage to ignore them so completely. Many sermons would be much shorter were this advice followed. Unfortunately, many preachers *think* they are speaking salvation despite the fact that what comes out of their mouths is judgment and law — as if there is something so dangerous about God's unconditional promises that we try to avoid telling not only the kids but the adults as well!

Paragraph 17. The concordists are much gentler with dear old von Amsdorf's saying. The problem is not the expression ("Good works are harmful to salvation") but the *bald* expression (that is, one without explanation). It does not harm salvation but only "Christian discipline." The kids will simply get the wrong idea.

Paragraph 18. There is a twist in this paragraph that helps explain the urgency of the entire Formula. The writers understand, perhaps much more profoundly than we do, the brevity and fragility of life, so they write, "in these last times." It is just as important to encourage free people to exercise their freedom as it is to keep good works and justification separate. The reason we preach good works is not to save our listeners but rather to help our listeners' families, fellow workers, community, society, and the human family. We can as easily wreck our lives by imagining that we can do "whatever we damn well please" as by imagining that what we do "damn well ought to please God." That is, in our relation to God, trusting in bad works (Epicurean delusion) or counting on good works (Pharisaic boasting) means there is no relation at all.

Paragraph 19. Of all the words in the Formula, this paragraph gives students fits. If God's grace is unconditional, they cry, how can the Holy Spirit be lost without finally crediting the keeping of the Holy

Spirit to human works? Does this not finally make our salvation dependent on us? Before wading in and answering such a question, it is good to pause and realize that the only form of Christianity that worries about such things is one that places God's unconditional grace at its center. It is crucial to understand what the concordists are worried about: people who imagine that God's grace is more like an inoculation than a relationship! The use of adultery as the only example here had to do with some particularly contemptuous ways in which people had justified abandoning spouse and children in the name of faith. The old creature is always sniffing out opportunities to turn God's grace into something we can control, so that we can boss God around and destroy our neighbors. Do not imagine that that kind of contempt arises from and is blessed by the Holy Spirit! However, as in the story of King David's adultery, do not imagine that God leaves the sinner forever. Instead, Nathan's word of law and gospel simply clobbers David and drives him running into the arms of God's merciful forgiveness. Similarly, the concordists' strictures here are meant to convey law and judgment to hardened sinners, so that they may hear the gospel and believe (the subject of the next chapter). For the weak (whose weakness forever tries to separate them from God's mercy), there are these comforting words of Martin Chemnitz in the Solid Declaration: "Likewise these [propositions] regarding the necessity of good works for salvation deprive troubled, distressed consciences of the comfort of the gospel, give them reason to doubt, and are in many ways dangerous" (IV.23, in *BC 2000*, 578). Let us stick with the good news of God in Christ and leave the judging where it belongs: in God's hands (through the law).

A Formula for Parish Practice

Many congregations (unfortunately) are built upon good works. We are so busy putting programs in place, seeing that they run properly, and getting (coercing) enough volunteers that we sometimes miss the point. It is not about our works at all. Some of the most grace-filled moments in the life of a congregation may come when everything is swept away. I recall some news program in the aftermath of a tornado in Alabama providing snatches of a pastor's sermon in the ruins of a Baptist church. Suddenly what mattered were God's gifts of life and salvation *alone*. Works had no place. The same happens on a smaller scale at many funerals, where — whatever we may say about the deeds of the deceased — what matters finally is that God raises the dead and promises eternal life. Our works cannot pull that off. That is why African American spirituals are so filled with hope and with God's grace, despite what the slaves were experiencing outwardly. "Didn't my Lord deliver Daniel?" "There is a balm in Gilead."

Our works have a place where they belong: witnessing to the power of the Holy Spirit in establishing our relation to God and helping our neighbor in need. They are never things we do, insofar as we are reborn, "under the gun," but instead they come as free and spontaneous fruit from a tree. Arnold Lobel, the author of children's books about Frog and Toad, tells a story called "The Garden," where Toad plants seeds and yells at them to sprout. Frog warns Toad that he has frightened the seeds, and now they will never grow, so Toad tries a variety of tricks to sweet-talk his seeds out of the ground. Finally, as in Mark 4:26-29, Toad falls asleep and the seeds come up all on their own, although he still wants to take the credit. So much of our well-intentioned talk in church about good works is no more than yelling at or cajoling either the good seed of the Word to sprout (Mark 4:1-20) or good trees to bear good fruit. The gospel works in our very hearing and accomplishes its goal of creating new creatures in Christ, moving us in faith toward God and fervent love toward one another. Perhaps it is best if, when we begin our harangues, our congregations fall asleep in the gospel and get up Monday morning refreshed to help the neighbor in need without our having yelled at them. Go ahead and tell the kids!

DISCUSSION QUESTIONS

▶ Understanding good works as not "necessary for salvation" but rather as fruits of the good tree of faith may change how we look at many parts of parish life. For example, how might this perspective change our approaches to stewardship? Do you know of some ways this has been done legalistically?
▶ In daily life many Christians are forced to make decisions that may seem to hurt other people. How might the Lutheran understanding of good works help in such ethical dilemmas?

► Good works can easily become bad news when we put our trust in them rather than in God, whose Holy Spirit brings all good things to fruition in us. Can you think of examples where people trusted in or boasted about their good works? What happens to others when this occurs?

► In the mid–sixteenth century Nicholas von Amsdorf and George Major, among others, were embroiled in a controversy over the role that good works play in life, death, and salvation. Article 4 of the Epitome summarized a proposal for resolution to this conflict. Can you describe a situation in your own church where the Epitome can help you to understand how God acts to give life and salvation?

Article Five

What God's Word Does to You:
Death (Law) and Resurrection (Gospel)

It is certainly not unusual that parents are proud of a child who is ordained to the public office of ministry. Mine certainly were. It is perhaps less frequent that parents give the ordinand free advice. Yet, the advice my mother gave me that day in 1977 was perhaps the best preaching course I ever had. She hugged me and then, looking me square in the eye (as only a mother can), she said, "Now, Tim, when you preach, comfort the people." I suppose I could have responded, "You've been reading article 5 of the Formula of Concord again," but all I did was hug her back, and I've never forgotten what she said.

"When you preach, comfort the people." One of the things for which Lutherans are (rightly) best known is their emphasis on the distinction between law and gospel. However, this concept is often reduced to a formal distinction between commands and promises in the Bible. In the sixteenth century the reformers and concordists alike were far more interested in the functional distinction. Through the Word of God (spoken, read, or visible), God works on us. First, in creation God speaks a word of law that initially ordered the universe and our lives in it but that now, subsequent to sin, restrains evil and rewards good as well. This is often called the first or civil use of the law. Then, for the sake of our salvation, God speaks a word of law and gospel, that is, a word of law that reveals our sin, terrifies and kills the old creature, and thereupon a word of gospel that forgives our sin, comforts and makes us alive in and by faith alone. This second, or theological, use of the law is matched by the good news and comfort of the gospel. Especially in this context, Luther often realized that whether the word was a command or promise, *how* it functioned was the most important thing. Any word, even a description of Christ on the cross, functions as "law" when the result is a revelation of sin, terror, and death for the old creature. Similarly, any word that witnesses to the Savior, comforts, and creates faith is gospel.

History

The development of the categories of law and gospel and their uses emerged in Christian theology over centuries. In fact, the notion that God's word does not just sit there (for us to observe and figure out) but *does* something to us goes back to the Hebrew understanding of the word for "word," *dabar* (דבר). Thus, God said through the prophet, "Is not my word like fire, says the LORD, and like a hammer that breaks a rock in pieces?" (Jer. 23:29). In the New Testament, too, God's Word works on its hearers. No wonder Jesus often ends his parables with the words "Let anyone with ears to hear listen!" In Romans Paul talks about the gospel as the "power of God" (1:16) and the law as showing us our sins (3:20). The word of our justification results in our having "peace with God" (5:1). Saint Augustine, bishop of Hippo in North Africa, also picked up on this distinction between commands and promises and used it in several of his writings.

However, Martin Luther and Philip Melanchthon were the first to make this distinction the centerpiece of their theology. Already in his famous tract of 1520, *The Freedom of a Christian,* Luther distinguished law and gospel and linked them inextricably to his argument that we are justified by faith alone. The next year Melanchthon followed suit in his theological textbook, the *Loci communes theologici.* In that same year Luther prepared sermon helps on Galatians 3:23-29, the Epistle for New Year's Day. He may well have used a medieval commentator on the text, Nicholas of Lyra, who had identified several uses of the law for the Jews. However, Luther applied Lyra's comments to all human beings. God uses the law, first, to keep order in society and restrain evil, and second, to reveal our sin and drive us to the gospel. Thus, explicit talk of a "first" use of the law to order civil affairs did not come to full expression in Luther's theology until after the "second" use had already been developed. After all, the "chief use" of the law was its theological use to reveal our sin and drive us to the gospel, to forgiveness in Christ.

Even though earlier controversies over the law during Luther's lifetime probably did not figure directly in the issues discussed in the Formula of Concord, they do provide an important backdrop. In 1527 a small dispute broke out between two students of Luther, Melanchthon and John Agricola, over repentance. Does sorrow for sin arise from the law and, hence, from fear of punishment (so Melanchthon), or from the gospel and love of God (so Agricola)? Although Luther settled this dispute with compromise language that allowed both, stating that the penitent can hardly distinguish his or her motives, it was a victory for Melanchthon, who had championed Luther's understanding of law and gospel. Melanchthon best expressed his position in the Augsburg Confession (XII.1-6, in *BC 2000*, 44-45) and its Apology (IV.5-6, in *BC 2000*, 121, and XII.28-58, in *BC 2000*, 191-96). The movement of the Christian life in God's Word is not from gospel to law but from law to gospel, that is, from terror to comfort, from death to resurrection.

By the late 1530s Agricola had become Luther's colleague at the University of Wittenberg. Agricola was quickly labeled an "antinomian" (one opposed to the law) because he and some of his followers seemed to restrict the law to civic affairs. (One slogan attributed to this party was "Das Gesetz bleibt auf dem Rathaus" [The law remains in city hall].) In a series of disputes Luther argued that such an approach missed the central function of the law to expose our sin and put to death the old creature — a function that pertained as much to believers (who always remain sinners) as to unbelievers. One cannot simply declare the law and its accusation of our sin ended by a theological sleight of hand. Outside the gospel of God's mercy, the law will always accuse us. Finally, what matters are not the labels "law" and "gospel" but their effects, condemning and comforting, putting to death and making alive. The former always works as law; the latter always as gospel, truly good news.

After Luther's death, debates over the law broke out in connection with the dispute over the necessity of good works (article 4). Many of these disputes involved the third use of the law, which will be dealt with under article 6. However, the one that directly triggered the formulation of this article came from a debate over the nature of the gospel that arose during the 1550s between Melanchthon and Matthias

Flacius, the Gnesio-Lutheran. By the 1540s Melanchthon taught that, as important as it was to distinguish law and gospel, sometimes the Scripture used the word "gospel" to designate both the condemnation of the law (repentance) and the proclamation of God's mercy in Christ (faith). Flacius, always suspicious of Melanchthon's motives and eager to maintain the comfort of the gospel, argued that such a broad definition of gospel would only confuse people and lead them to think that human effort (in repenting) was a requirement of the gospel. In the 1570s followers of Melanchthon at Wittenberg continued to clash with another Gnesio-Lutheran, Johannes Wigand, over the same issue, but the dispute never amounted to very much.

The Heart of the Matter

God's Word, the author of Hebrews writes, "is living and active, sharper than any two-edged sword, piercing until it divides soul from spirit, joints from marrow" (4:12). This relatively minor dispute over the meaning of the word "gospel" gave the concordists an opportunity to highlight this central aspect of evangelical theology. The whole point of forensic justification (God proclaiming us righteous gratis, for the sake of Christ alone by faith) is that *God* proclaims. That proclamation is not simply information, nor does it point to some sort of hidden agenda that we must perform in order truly to be saved or to become righteous. Instead, the proclamation of God's Word cuts to the heart, smashes our hard hearts like a hammer, and puts to death and makes alive, so that we can truly live as believers.

The law and its accusation sound throughout our lives (and not merely in church). Indeed, we are surrounded daily by the reality of sin, death, and evil. Outside the proclamation of the gospel (God's free forgiveness, life and salvation in Christ), human beings can only try to master the law or, failing that, be crushed by it. All our ruses to deny our rebellion against God, the pervasiveness of sin, the reality of death, or our complicity in this world's evil are simply symptoms of both our inability to fulfill the law and our addiction to sin. Preaching the law in the Christian community is not so much making people feel guilty as it is telling the truth about our human condition. Because of our deep denial of sin and death, such preaching could be characterized as "mentioning the unmentionable," that is, borrowing the terminology of some twelve-step programs, naming the elephant in the room, the existence of which everyone is covering up. In this case the elephant is our addiction to sin. The gospel, on the other hand, tells the truth about God, that Jesus Christ — "the mirror of the Father's heart," as Luther calls him — saves and redeems us. Just as the law reveals sin and crushes the old creature, so the gospel forgives sin and brings us to the new life of faith.

The Text of the Epitome

Concerning Law and Gospel

Status controversiae

The Chief Question in This Dispute

[1] Whether the preaching of the holy gospel is really not only a preaching of grace, which proclaims the forgiveness of sins, but also a preaching of repentance and rebuke, which condemns unbelief (something condemned not in the law but only by the gospel).

Affirmative Theses

The Pure Teaching of God's Word

[2] 1. We believe, teach, and confess that the distinction between law and gospel is to be preserved with great diligence in the church as an especially glorious light, through which the Word of God, in accord with Paul's admonition, is properly divided.

[3] 2. We believe, teach, and confess that the law is, strictly speaking, a divine teaching which gives instruction regarding what is right and God-pleasing and condemns everything that is sin and contrary to God's will.

[4] 3. Therefore, everything that condemns sin is and belongs to the proclamation of the law.

[5] 4. However, the gospel is, strictly speaking, the kind of teaching that reveals what the human being, who has not kept the law and has been con-

demned by it, should believe: that Christ has atoned and paid for all sins and apart from any human merit has obtained and won for people the forgiveness of sins, "the righteousness which avails before God," and eternal life.

[6] 5. However, because the word "gospel" is not used in just one sense in the Holy Scripture — the reason this dispute arose in the first place — we believe, teach, and confess that when the word "gospel" is used for the entire teaching of Christ, which he presented in his teaching ministry, as did his apostles in theirs (it is used in this sense in Mark 1[:15], Acts 20[:24]), then it is correct to say or to write that the gospel is a proclamation of both repentance and the forgiveness of sins.

[7] 6. When, however, law and gospel are placed in contrast to each other — as when Moses himself is spoken of as a teacher of the law and Christ as a preacher of the gospel — we believe, teach, and confess that the gospel is not a proclamation of repentance or retribution, but is, strictly speaking, nothing else than a proclamation of comfort and a joyous message which does not rebuke nor terrify but comforts consciences against the terror of the law, directs them solely to Christ's merit, and lifts them up again through the delightful proclamation of the grace and favor of God, won through Christ's merit.

[8] 7. In regard to the disclosure of sin: the veil of Moses [2 Cor. 3:13-16] hangs in front of the eyes of all people as long as they only hear the preaching of the law and nothing of Christ, and thus they never learn to recognize the true nature of their sin from the law. Instead, they either become presumptuous hypocrites, like the Pharisees, or they despair, like Judas. Therefore Christ takes the law in his hands and interprets it spiritually (Matt. 5[:21-48]; Rom. 7[:14]). Thus, God's wrath, in all its enormity [Rom. 1:18], is revealed from heaven upon all sinners; through this revelation they are directed to the law, and only then do they learn properly to recognize their sin through the law. Moses would never have been able to wring this acknowledgment out of them.

[9] Therefore, it is true that the proclamation of the suffering and death of Christ, God's Son, is a sobering and terrifying proclamation and testimony of God's wrath. Through it people now are really led into the law, after the veil of Moses is taken away from them, so that they now really recognize what great things God demands from us in the law (none of which we can keep), and that we therefore should seek all our righteousness in Christ.

[10] 8. Nonetheless, as long as all of this (that is, Christ's suffering and death) proclaims God's wrath and terrifies people, it is still not, strictly speaking, the preaching of the gospel, but the preaching of Moses and the law and is thus an alien work of Christ, through which he comes to his proper function, which is the preaching of grace, comforting, and making alive. This, strictly speaking, is the preaching of the gospel.

Negative Thesis

Contrary Teaching, to Be Rejected

[11] 1. Accordingly, we reject and regard it as incorrect and harmful when it is taught that the gospel is, strictly speaking, a proclamation of repentance or retribution and not exclusively a proclamation of grace. For in this way the gospel is again made into a teaching of the law, the merit of Christ and the Holy Scriptures are obscured, Christians are robbed of true comfort, and the door is opened again to the papacy.

Commentary

The Chief Question in This Dispute (p. 500)

Paragraph 1. This rather cryptic paragraph points out that this dispute was terminological at heart. How does one define the words "law" and "gospel" on the basis of Scripture? Does the law condemn all sins save unbelief, which is then condemned only in the gospel? Like so many things in life and in theology, everything depends on how one defines the terms. The affirmative theses outline these definitions.

Affirmative Theses (pp. 500-501)

Paragraph 2. The notion of "properly dividing" Scripture comes from a uniquely Lutheran interpretation of 2 Timothy 2:15. ("Do your best to present yourself to God as one approved by him, a worker who has no need to be ashamed, rightly explaining [ὀρθοτομοῦντα] the word of truth.") The NRSV translates the Greek to refer to interpretation in general, but Luther and Melanchthon invariably used it to refer specifically to distinguishing the two chief words of God (law and gospel) and their functions. What was at stake? Although only stated explicitly in the negative thesis, the concordists feared a "returning to the papacy," that is, a turning of the Bible's witness to the good news of God's love in Christ into the bad news of a law we must fulfill to earn or keep God's favor.

Paragraphs 3-4. Here and in paragraph 5 the concordists define law and gospel in terms more of what they *are* than of how they *function.* The law (par. 3) is simply any instruction about what pleases God, and it condemns everything not done according to God's will. Even in this simple definition, note that the emphasis is not on a particular kind of word (command), but on *any* word that instructs and condemns. Paragraph 4 makes clear that the concordists are describing the law "strictly speaking" as any word that condemns. This is particularly important for preachers, teachers, and evangelists. Often, what the preacher takes to be "friendly advice" actually hits the ears of the weak as sheer condemnation. Thus, the focus of the one delivering God's Word cannot be on what he or she intends ("I was *only* trying to help"), but on what actually happens when a person hears what we are saying.

Paragraph 5. The gospel, in contrast, is a word not about works (what pleases or angers God) but about faith. It is not just any word of human comfort ("Everything will be all right"), but a word with specific, theological content ("In Christ you are all right with God"). In the final analysis, that is why showing a person our works of love is not the same as sharing the good news of Jesus Christ. Not only can most anyone do good things to and for others — regardless of religious persuasion — but also there is no way for a work or a kind gesture unequivocally to convey God's mercy in Christ unless we say something. Of course, we dare not restrict ourselves to the particular expression of the gospel given here ("Christ has atoned and paid for all sins and apart from any human merit has obtained and won for people the forgiveness of sins, 'the righteousness which avails before God' [cf. Rom. 1:17], and eternal life"). One look at Luther's sermons or Melanchthon's theology, or at Scripture itself, proves that there are endless possibilities for how we may share the gospel. What *is* clear is that the gospel is not, strictly speaking, law. It provides a way out from under the condemnation of the law, namely, salvation for the sake of Christ alone. One can almost hear strains of Luther's explanation to the second article in the

Small Catechism: "I believe that Jesus Christ . . . is my Lord. He has redeemed me, a lost and condemned human being. He has purchased and freed me from all sins, from death, and from the power of the devil" (Apostles' Creed, 4, in *BC 2000,* 355).

Paragraph 6. As with justification in article 3, the concordists simply enjoy talking about these things. The dispute, at least as they define it, comes down to the definition of the gospel. Scripture itself uses the term in several ways. Sometimes it denotes the whole kit and caboodle. Then the gospel means both repentance (what happens when we are cut down to size by the law) and faith (the result of the good news of God's grace and mercy in Christ). After all, when Mark (who invented an entire genre of literature we call Gospels) says in 1:15 that Jesus preached the gospel, he goes on to define it as repentance *and* faith (forgiveness of sins). In this sense Melanchthon was correct.

Paragraph 7. At this point the concordists move closer to functional definitions of law and gospel, which indeed stand at the center of the distinction for Luther and Melanchthon. How God uses the Word in our lives matters more than anything else. In these uses we discover that God's Word, Christ's incarnation, and our life of faith converge. As Jesus died and rose again, so God's Word kills and makes alive. This is nowhere clearer than in baptism itself, the waters of which signify the daily drowning and rising of the Christian and in which we are linked to the death and resurrection of Christ. (See SC, Baptism, 12-14, in *BC 2000,* 360.) Here the concordists contrast the terror of the law with the "delightful proclamation" of God's grace and favor in Christ. This is a "proclamation of comfort and a joyous message." As the Christmas carol echoes, "O tidings of comfort and joy."

Paragraphs 8-10. What happens (as often occurs) if one hears only the law? The concordists use the grim image of the "veil of Moses" (2 Cor. 3:13-16). The law is there and it does something to us, but it never reaches its goal of revealing the true nature of our sin and driving us to the Redeemer. Instead, we are stuck in either presumption or despair. The law in the hands of Christ makes matters worse for the old creature. Then the true depth of sin becomes clear and both pride and despair are eliminated as responses to the law. In this sense (par. 9), even the death of Christ is terrifying, here described as God's wrath.

God's wrath is often a foreign concept to many Christians today. To these writers, as paragraph 10 makes clear, "God's wrath" is not central to God's true nature or true attitude toward humanity. Instead, they call it "an alien work of Christ." This label, "alien," comes from Isaiah 28:21, a text often alluded to in Reformation discussions of law and gospel. In the Solid Declaration the writers explain that God "must perform an alien work — which is to convict — until he comes to his proper work — which is to comfort and to proclaim grace" (V.11, in *BC 2000,* 583). Perhaps a useful analogy is the phrase "tough love" used by some twelve-step groups. To confront an addict with his or her destructive behavior in an intervention can seem mean-spirited and unkind. In fact, it is loving only when connected with its proper goal: to bring a person to sobriety. In a much more basic sense, any word or work of God (law, wrath, punishment, etc.) that terrifies and kills the old creature is alien to God's true nature, contradicts who God is. That alien word works to drive us into the arms of the Savior, where, according to God's true and proper nature, we hear "the preaching of grace, comforting, and making alive." This is the goal of God's Word and, by extension, of good preaching and teaching. The veil is lifted; the truth is ours.

Negative Thesis (p. 501)

Paragraph 11. "The papacy" in this context is not simply some institution connected to the bishop of Rome. It is instead a designation for a way of thinking that confuses law and gospel in the worst possible way, by reducing the word "gospel" to a proclamation of repentance or retribution. How often does this not occur in our pulpits and classrooms? In a recent poll of Lutherans, over half thought they were saved by doing good works and not by God's grace alone. This fundamental belief of the old creature can come to an end only in the unconditional word of God's grace in Christ. We can never preach it too often, too loudly, or too joyously.

A Formula for Parish Practice

This article addresses the two single most important functions in a Christian congregation: preaching and teaching. How many pastors and parishioners imagine that the goal of preaching is to get the congregation to do something, to concoct some virtuous act or another that is pleasing to God? How many, when hugging their favorite ordinands after ordination, would know enough to remind them that the bottom line, the "proper work" of preaching, is to comfort, not to heap upon their hapless hearers more works and rules? The law has its functions, to be sure, but we dare not confuse it with the gospel or, intentionally or unintentionally, put it over the gospel. Legalistic preaching may whine, "Yes, Jesus saves you, but only if you get serious, only if you commit." "Of course God is loving and gracious, but that is just an example for you to follow — or else!" However, preaching that does not make the gospel the last word (that is, the end or goal of the law) leaves its hearers with no comfort, no life, and no hope. In short, it leaves them to their own devices, stuck in either pride or despair. We would not hesitate to give water to a thirsty man or food to a hungry woman or clothing to a naked child. Yet, why do we not give the comfort of the gospel to those burdened with the law, the truth of grace to those misled by the falsehood of works, and the life of Christ to those who are dying? Perhaps, like the slavish elder brother in the parable (Luke 15), we would just as soon our younger brothers and sisters never hear the waiting father's amazing words, "This, my child, who was lost and dead, is now made alive and found."

Of course, the cutting edge of the gospel, by its very gracious nature, means death to the old creature. As a pastor once wrote to me, "Would the old self really want to spend eternity with a god who is this generous?" At the same time, deeply hidden within the law is God's heart for grace and protection. Police presence in a dangerous neighborhood may restrain the evildoer and at the same time bring some level of comfort to the defenseless. Or, as Luther implies in the Large Catechism (Lord's Prayer, 10-11), the command not to misuse God's name but instead use it to call upon God reveals that God is eager to hear from us. When Johann Schlagenhaufen, one of Luther's table companions, groaned, "Dr. Luther, I cannot pray because I am a sinner," Luther snapped back, "Schlagenhaufen, I pray because I am a sinner."

Preaching involves both law and gospel, not as stale categories to distinguish commands from promises but as a stripping bare of the truth about the human condition and a revealing of the truth about God's gracious heart. Luther, reflecting on the dilemma of preaching, once complained that when he preached the unconditional grace of

God in the gospel, the lazy and licentious always took it as an opportunity to remain in their sin. When he preached the law, the weak despaired. Either way, preaching seemed to miss its goal. However, Luther added, for the sake of the weak he would proclaim the gospel, since those who use its forgiveness as an excuse to sin would manipulate everything to their advantage anyway. "When you preach, comfort the people."

What about programs of Christian education? How many Sunday school programs are not centered on human works and morality? This may be fine instruction as law, but it cannot finally replace the good news of God in Christ. Or, rather, when it does replace that message, then there is no comfort, no new life, no hope, no faith, no Christ. Then, the Holy Scripture — this amazing love story of God's continuing, enduring affection for the whole human race, culminating in Christ's death and resurrection — is lost, and there is only hell to pay. Why do we find it so hard to speak the comforting truth that makes Christians Christians? That is, the truth that God was in Christ reconciling the world, that God so loved the world and that we are saved by grace through faith on account of Christ alone.

The Formula of Concord may seem to be a distant, obsolete book, until we use it to illumine our own situation with the authors' witnesses to the faith. They would have us preach Christ crucified and risen, so that we, too, may die and rise again each day. Is there any sweeter word to a sinner than forgiveness? Is there any more consoling sound to the mourner than resurrection? Is there any more encouraging voice to the lonely than "Look! I am with you always"? Tell the truth about the human condition, to be sure. But then look around in your congregation, for "Everything that provides comfort — everything that offers the favor and grace of God to those who have transgressed the law — is and is called the gospel in the strict sense. It is good news, joyous news, that God does not want to punish sin but to forgive it for Christ's sake" (SD V.21, in *BC 2000*, 585). Let the preaching and teaching of God's Word, the right dividing of law and gospel, begin. As Paul reminds us, "Since we are justified by faith, we have peace with God" (Rom. 5:1). This is true comfort indeed!

DISCUSSION QUESTIONS

- Lutherans divide the Word of God into law and gospel. What does this mean? How do "law" and "gospel" function in the lives of believers?
- What does it mean to say that the Word of God kills and makes alive? What makes Lutherans talk about God's wrath in this situation?
- Where are some places you have encountered the law in the world?
- Have you ever been comforted by the gospel? How? What was going on? Who spoke that word to you?
- Consider a recent sermon you have heard. Can you identify the preaching of the law? Of the gospel?
- To what extent must programs in a congregation be based on the law? To what extent on the gospel?

A Free and Merry Spirit:
When Is the Law Not the Law?

Every other year in my parish in rural Wisconsin the stewardship program did not emphasize giving. Instead, we focused on other aspects of the congregation's life. So one year the entire congregation was invited to come to church to fill out an inventory of their spiritual gifts. By answering a 100-item questionnaire, members could get some sense of which gifts (out of twenty) they might have to share with the congregation, including such things as music, administration, teaching, and even faith. I sat with one group that dutifully filled out the form and tallied up their scores. Bill, a baggage handler in the Twin Cities, had been skeptical from the start and became even more so when his results became known. For him, highest by far was the gift of faith, defined in the study not as the faith that trusts God for salvation, which we all experience, but as a particularly deep sense of God's continued presence in our lives, as Paul used the word in 1 Corinthians 13. "This can't be right," he snorted. "How could I have the gift of faith?" His wife, a nurse, looked at him in disbelief. "You mean you didn't know that about yourself?" It turned out that it was one of the things she found most endearing about her husband.

Even though the Formula uses the phrase "third use of the law" (law as a guide for the Christian life), this section has less to do with the law and more to do with the nature of good works and whether they are coerced from our flesh or arise spontaneously from faith. In one way the spontaneity of Bill's experience and his very ignorance of the presence of such an amazing good work — strong faith on which others in his life could depend — go a long way in describing how law and works function in the lives of believers.

History

In 1534 Melanchthon introduced the notion of a "third use" of the law into the third edition of his commentary on Colossians. In so doing, he wanted to emphasize two things. First, against the antinomian statements of his opponent from 1527, John Agricola (see article 5), he wanted to make clear that Christians, by virtue of justification by faith, do not somehow escape the law. It reveals God's will, keeps order in this world, and continues to reveal sin. Second, especially in 1534 Melanchthon had begun to enter into discussions with moderate Roman Catholics in the hopes of averting war between Protestants and the Roman Catholic emperor. These theologians defined the "gospel" as including Christ's command to the disciples to love one another as he had loved them. Melanchthon argued that, although this word was clearly spoken to Christians, it was still law and not gospel (defined in the strict sense of the term as free forgiveness of sin). Thus, to distinguish the unconditional promise of the good news in Christ from the law of love, Melanchthon started speaking of a third use of the law — that is, the law, even for the Christian life, was *not* gospel.

From the 1534 commentary or from the 1535 (second) edition of Melanchthon's theological textbook, the *Loci communes theologici,* John Calvin picked up this notion of the law's third use for his famous compendium of theology, *The Institutes of the Christian Religion.* However, Calvin and his followers made this use the chief one and argued especially that it contained laws peculiar to the Christian life. Lutherans, on the other hand, equated "law" in all its uses with the Ten Commandments. The law does not change, but we do. As we shall see, for the concordists the third use of the law was nothing but the first and second uses applied to Christians.

Debates over the third use of the law arose within the Gnesio-Lutheran camp. Two pastors, Anton Otto of Nordhausen in Saxony and Andreas Poach of Erfurt, argued that Melanchthon's notion of a third use of the law would make people think the completion of their

Christian life depended on them and their works. The law ordered life and accused but was not even theoretically a way of salvation. To other Gnesio-Lutherans, these pastors' position sounded as if the law could not even adequately judge human sin in a believer. As the dispute unfolded, Otto also attacked the notion that the law and the repentance it caused had anything to do with the new life of a Christian. The marriage of the believer and Christ by faith did not need a third party, the law, to consummate the union. Although Otto's opponents labeled his arguments "anti-nomian" (against the law), they might better be understood as "pro-evangelical" (in favor of the gospel).

During the same period a similar dispute over the law arose in the principality of Brandenburg at the University of Frankfurt an der Oder between Andreas Musculus and his colleague Abdias Praetorius. Although both could probably be labeled Gnesio-Lutherans for their stands on other issues, Musculus rejected the notion of a third use of the law because it imposed a false necessity on the works of a believer, which he thought should (as Luther had taught in *The Freedom of a Christian*) spring naturally from faith. Praetorius, encouraged by Melanchthon, worried that his colleague's position would eliminate ethical standards from the church and obscure God's will revealed in the law.

Unlike the major disputants in the debates on the first half of the Formula, most of whom had passed from the scene, Musculus was still on hand, and actually helped write this article. In fact, we have Andreas Musculus to thank for its vitality, especially in the final edition of the Solid Declaration, article 6. As the concordists first worked on this dispute, most of those in the room were students of Melanchthon and Johann Brenz (the pious south German reformer). They all accepted the existence of a third use of the law as a matter of course and wanted, like their teachers, to avoid the appearance of lawlessness (antinomianism) among Lutherans. They were understandably highly suspicious of opponents to the third use of the law.

As negotiations proceeded, the church of Brandenburg became involved in the talks, and Musculus, the brother-in-law of Agricola, entered the room. Although related to Agricola by marriage, he had managed to avoid the older man's antinomian perspective without giving up Luther's remarkable insight into Christian freedom. Saint Paul had hinted at this freedom already in Galatians 5:16-24 by distinguishing "works" of the flesh from "fruits" of the Spirit, against which "there is no law." In the section of the Solid Declaration attributable to him, Musculus distinguishes works of the law and works of the Spirit. Behind these two kinds of works are two kinds of people. Human beings, insofar as they are not reborn, keep the law because they are commanded to, and out of fear of punishment or desire for reward. However, "when people are born again through the Spirit of God and set free from the law (that is, liberated from its driving powers and driven by the Spirit of Christ), they live according to the unchanging will of God, as comprehended in the law, and do everything, insofar as they are reborn, *from a free and merry spirit*" (SD V.17, in *BC 2000*, 590, emphasis added). We will say more about that provocative phrase below.

The Heart of the Matter

When people read the parable of the sheep and the goats in Matthew 25, they often miss the point. As some New Testament interpreters remind us, Jesus' parables often had the structure of a good joke, a short story punctuated by a surprise ending that, in jokes at least, is intended to make us laugh. People often think the "punch line" of Matthew 25 is that we meet God in the destitute. As important as this point is, it is hardly unique to Christianity. The rabbis of Jesus' day and even the Egyptian Book of the Dead made the same claim.

A far more surprising point arises from the fact that in Jesus' story the sheep think they are goats and the goats are sure they are sheep. "When did we see you naked, *and not clothe you?*" the latter boast. To these goats, who insist on following the law (and think they get perfect marks in so doing), the king replies, "You missed one! As often as you did *not* do it to one of the least of these, you did not do it to me." Try living by the law, and you will be toast. On the contrary, the poor befuddled sheep, like Bill in our opening story, cannot seem to see their gifts and works at all. "When did we see you naked, etc., and clothe you?" The king answers, "I remember one time." Rather like those poor split-brained disciples of the Sermon on the Mount, whose right hand did not know what the left was doing, these people's good works sneak up on them and remain hidden to them (but not necessarily to others) their whole life long. The only thing Christians truly sense is their desperate need for a Savior, the Good Shepherd, who seeks the lost.

The third use of the law reminds us of two things. First, Christians do not graduate from God's law to a higher form of existence. As long as we are in the flesh (which is going to be for a very long time), we are under the law. It curbs our inveterate addiction to ourselves, drives us to serve our neighbor whether we want to or not, and continues to show our desperate need for a Savior. Moreover, for those ignorant Christians who, having fallen in love with God, would like to know what God enjoys, the law reveals what God loves most: that we trust God and love our neighbor. No wonder Luther's well-known post-communion prayer speaks of "faith toward God and fervent love toward one another." Second, the gospel does not function as law to condemn but as good news to comfort. For the Christian life this means that we serve God not under the burden of rules and regulations but "with a free and merry spirit," with the spontaneity of good fruit from a good tree. What a comfort that is!

The Text of the Epitome

Concerning the Third Use of the Law

Status controversiae

The Chief Question concerning This Controversy

[1] The law has been given to people for three reasons: first, that through it external discipline may be maintained against the unruly and the disobedient; second, that people may be led through it to a recognition of their sins; third, after they have been reborn — since nevertheless the flesh still clings to them — that precisely because of the flesh they may have a sure guide, according to which they can orient and conduct their entire life. In this connection a dispute occurred among a few theologians over the third use of the law.

It concerned whether the law is to be urged upon the reborn Christians or not. The one party said yes, the other no.

Affirmative Theses

The Correct Christian Teaching concerning This Controversy

[2] 1. We believe, teach, and confess that, although people who truly believe in Christ and are genuinely converted to God have been liberated and set free from the curse and compulsion of the law through Christ, they indeed are not for that reason without the law. Instead, they have been redeemed by the Son of God so that they may practice the law day and night (Ps. 119[:1]). For our first parents did not live without the law even before the fall. This law of God was written into the heart, for they were created in the image of God.

[3] 2. We believe, teach, and confess that the proclamation of the law is to be diligently impressed not only upon unbelievers and the unrepentant but also upon those who believe in Christ and are truly converted, reborn, and justified through faith.

[4] 3. For even if they are reborn and "renewed in the spirit of their minds" [Eph. 4:23], this rebirth and renewal is not perfect in this world. Instead, it has only begun. Believers are engaged with the spirit of their minds in continual battle against the flesh, that is, against the perverted nature and character which clings to us until death and which because of the old creature is still lodged in the human understanding, will, and all human powers. In order that people do not resolve to perform service to God on the basis of their pious imagination in an arbitrary way of their own choosing, it is necessary for the law of God constantly to light their way. Likewise, it is necessary so that the old creature not act according to its own will but instead be compelled against its own will, not only through the admonition and threats of the law but also with punishments and plagues, to follow the Spirit and let itself be made captive (1 Cor. 9[:27]; Rom. 6[:12]; Gal. 6[:14]; Ps. 119[:1]; Heb. 13[:21]).

[5] 4. Concerning the difference between the works of the law and the fruits of the Spirit, we believe, teach, and confess that the works performed according to the law remain works of the law and should be so called, as long as they are coerced out of people only through the pressure of punishment and the threat of God's wrath.

[6] 5. The fruits of the Spirit, however, are the works that the Spirit of God, who dwells in believers, effects through the reborn; they are done by believ-

ers (insofar as they are reborn) as if they knew of no command, threat, or reward. In this manner the children of God live in the law and walk according to the law of God — what St. Paul in his epistles calls the law of Christ and the law of the mind. And yet they are "not under the law but under grace" (Rom. 7[:23] and 8[:1, 14]).

[7] 6. Therefore, for both the repentant and unrepentant, for the reborn and those not reborn, the law is and remains one single law, the unchangeable will of God. In terms of obedience to it there is a difference only in that those people who are not yet reborn do what the law demands unwillingly, because they are coerced (as is also the case with the reborn with respect to the flesh). Believers, however, do without coercion, with a willing spirit, insofar as they are born anew, what no threat of the law could ever force from them.

Negative Theses

False and Contrary Teaching

[8] 1. Therefore, we reject as contrary teaching and error, which harm Christian discipline and true piety, the teaching that the law should be preached in the way and extent described above only among unbelievers, non-Christians, and the unrepentant, not among Christians and those who truly believe in Christ.

Commentary

Affirmative Theses (pp. 502-3)

Paragraph 1. Here is a handy definition of what the three uses of the law are (but not how they function). The first use is for external discipline to keep the unruly and disobedient in line. It is what happens after a fifth-grade teacher is called out of the room to talk with the principal in the hallway and the class becomes unruly. In my experience, his mere shadow in the doorway is enough to calm the class down. (It is the same thing that happens when drivers see a police car on the open highway and suddenly obey the speed limit.) The first use maintains order in this world and restrains our evil inclinations. The second use confronts us with our sins and, to use Luther's picturesque language, *drives* us to Christ. The third use of the law is a guide for the Christian life. Faced with certain Roman Catholic claims that the church could also prescribe things necessary for salvation, the reformers always insisted that only God's law, not humanly invented rules, revealed God's true desires. Although, as we shall see, this third use functions in ways not unlike the first and second uses, it does provide Christians with an outline of what God desires.

Rather than view this third function exclusively as threat or condemnation, one can, as Luther does in his 1520 treatise *On Good Works,* imagine how the law functions with the ignorant. Imagine a young lover to whom we must whisper, "Pssst! Daniel! Send Pamela flowers! She loves chocolate, so give her some!" Such words, though commands, are far from threatening and come as relief to the lover ignorant of the beloved's desires. Thus, simple folk may never have realized how much God likes it when, for example, we "pray to, praise, and give thanks to God" or "come to [our neighbors'] defense, speak well of them, and interpret everything they do in the best possible light" (SC, Ten Commandments, 4 and 16, in *BC 2000,* 352, 353). "You mean these things please God?" an ignorant believer cries. "Yup," we respond. "God gets a real kick out of them."

Paragraphs 2-3. We are set free from the "curse and compulsion" of the law. So many pastors, when they inquire about the law's third use, try to justify such "curse and compulsion." The result is a famine of the Word of God — that is, no gospel. "Third use" never justifies beating up on people in a sermon right after announcing the gospel, for fear that they will put nothing in the collection plate or, more seriously, will not "take God seriously." Compulsion is just that: compulsion. And believers are freed from that very thing, insofar as they are believers. At the same time, we cannot wish the law away. God's promises make us *believers* in God, not unbelievers, and they set us in a community of folks who need our prayers and support. Moreover, the law is hardwired into creation itself, because it reveals God's will and desire for all people and for the world God has made. The story in Genesis 1-3 depicts a world in which there are nonthreatening commands: "Be fruitful and multiply; fill the earth and oversee it." "Cling to your spouse." "Take care of the garden." "Trust me!" Redemption gives us back creation and its beautiful order as gifts, in which we may revel. No wonder the believing psalmist in Psalms 1, 19, and 119 looks at the law and sees only blessing and invitation and even sweetness. Thus, there is a place for law in the believer's life of faith, but only as invitation (par. 3). Any threat must be aimed squarely at the flesh and sin.

Paragraph 4. Although the concordists do not use Luther's famous phrase *simul iustus et peccator,* "at the same time righteous and sinner," they do express here in similar terms how the law works on the believer. Chiefly, we need the law because the old creature, drowned in baptism, is (as mentioned above) a good underwater swimmer. We are, as Paul describes in Romans 7, in a continual battle against the flesh.

One of the places that battle is most often joined in believers occurs in what Luther calls in his translation of Colossians 2:23, "self-chosen spirituality." The old creature, hearing the gospel, cooks up the notion that it is now up to it to figure out what God likes, and it is forever dreaming up special "Christian" works. Each age has its favorites. "You have to make a pilgrimage to Rome [or Wittenberg!], or enter a monastery [especially if caught in a thunderstorm]." "You have to go forward in a revival meeting [or: go on a retreat]!" "Every Christian must refrain from drinking, dancing, card playing." "Good Christians are only Republicans [or: Democrats]." The list goes on and on. "You really need to study the Formula of Concord to be a true Christian." Sometimes the motives sound spiritual but result in a destructive dividing up of Christians into good and better, carnal and spiritual, holy and perfect. Thus the law, which simply commands trust in God and love of the neighbor, prevents people from deciding to serve God "on the basis of their pious imagination in an arbitrary way."

Moreover, the old creature needs to be fenced in by the law and, as Luther says in the Small Catechism (Baptism, 12, in *BC 2000,* 360), drowned daily, and die. The continual return to our baptisms in confession and forgiveness, even in simply praying "Forgive us our sins," marks that use of the law in us. Thus, the third use of the law is nothing other than the first use (to order our lives toward what God wants and drive the old creature to do good) and the second use (to reveal our sin daily and thus to drive us to return to Christ and his forgiveness) applied to Christians. Thus, do not be surprised when, listening to a sermon or reading Scripture, we, too, hear the law ordering and restraining, driving and condemning. That is all the law can do, even for Christians.

Paragraphs 5-7. These paragraphs in the Epitome mark the place where Andreas Musculus entered the room (SD VI.15-19, in *BC 2000*, 589-90). Until this point it would still be possible to view the Christian life as strictly a matter of coercion and law — albeit now against the flesh — as if Luther had said that we are *simul peccator et peccator* (at the same time sinner and sinner). However, faith in Christ truly makes all things new, even our relation to the law and works. To be sure, there are "works of the law" (par. 5). There are threats and coercion: "Do this, or else!" The unbeliever and our own flesh must be forced. (Think of how seldom we do things freely and how often we refrain from evil simply because we are afraid we might get caught!)

But think how out of place this coercion sounds in the language of love (par. 6). If the beloved says, "Kiss me!" what kind of answer is "Do I *have* to?" Here Musculus preserves that remarkable freedom of the Christian, a freedom that caused Paul to shout, "Rejoice in the Lord always. Again I will say, rejoice!" Do I *have* to? No! Because the "fruits of the Spirit come as freely, as spontaneously, as inevitably, as good fruit from a good tree." In the Solid Declaration (cited above) Musculus described the Christian doing good works from "a free and merry spirit." The picture this conjures up is of a little boy, fishing pole in one hand and grandfather in the other, walking down the road whistling, hardly able to contain himself for the joy of being with the person he adores, loving every aspect of the day, from the persons he meets who know Grandpa to baiting the hook and waiting for hours in the boat. What better way to spend one's life? Yet this free and merry spirit is the gift to all Christians who, often like Bill, do not even know the gifts they have and the good they do.

To be sure, the law remains the law (par. 7). The Ten Commandments contain enough for us to do to last a lifetime. However, when the law hits the old creature — whether in the unrepentant or in the flesh of the believer — it can only threaten and coerce. But when the believer, as God's new creature of faith, hears the law, all threats drop away, and there remains a willingness that comes not from ourselves (we cannot make ourselves willing), but from God. Then we hear only the voice of the beloved, and there is no coercion, only faith alive in love.

A friend from Iowa, Pastor Irving L. Sandberg, once showed me what a difference this perspective makes in preaching. I expressed my embarrassment with the passage in John (14:14) where Jesus says, "Ask me anything, and I will give it to you." He sent me a sermon on the text, the center of which was a story about how he and his wife, Joyce (also a pastor), love to dance. As I remember it, he told his congregation, "When we are on the dance floor, she may say to me, 'What do you want me to do for you? Ask me anything.' But," he continued, "I am in my lover's arms, and we are doing what we most enjoy. What, indeed, can I ask for but to have another turn around the dance floor, and another, and another?" Then we are, in Charles Wesley's words, "Lost in wonder, love, and praise."

Negative Thesis (p. 503)

Paragraph 8. We cannot rid ourselves of the law by theological legerdemain. There is no question that, as we discovered in article 4, the very unconditional nature of the gospel might trick us into worrying that we should not tell the kids. However, Christians are not idealists, even though Hollywood often portrays them in that light. We need never fool ourselves into thinking that we are not sinners in desperate need of God's grace and mercy or that we can wish away the law from ourselves, our church, or our society. When we do that, far from demonstrating faith, we reveal our original sin, once more believing the snake's line ("You shall not die; you will be like gods"), but in this demonic rephrasing, "You shall no longer sin; you are already divine."

This article implies, among other things, that Christians who commit crimes are always liable to society's judgment, and that divine forgiveness of sins does not protect Christians from civil prosecution. Our underwater swimmer, the old creature, daily needs a new drowning in the font — and for some that may include a term in the slammer. This article also implies that Christians as believers need not fear the law and its accusation but can finally discover there an invitation to life with God and the neighbor — the very thing the law describes but cannot give. Only when we confuse law and gospel (as many folks do who think they are defending the third use of the law) do things get turned upside down and (of course) the gospel disappears.

A Formula for Parish Practice

Placing law and gospel at the center of a congregation's life means that everything changes. For example, what would a stewardship program look like that started with the Christian condition of righteous and sinner at the same time? For the old creature, who would just as soon not share with anyone or who would like to turn giving to a congregation into some sort of superspiritual, meritorious work, the law comes and forces giving with no room for boasting. At the same time, for the new creature there is no coercion but only spontaneous giving to those in need. One seminary professor, reminiscing about the good old days, said, "There was a time when if you just said the word 'mission' in some rural congregations, those old farmers would just start digging in their pockets."

I once experienced something of that spontaneity as a pastor. The brother of a woman in our congregation was an intern in a poor congregation on the Texas-Mexico border. Hearing that the folks there did not have enough winter clothing, she requested that we ask members of our congregation for clothing. I was skeptical, to say the least. I allowed a single, small note in the newsletter and a few halfhearted announcements, and we netted a half-ton of clothing from a congregation of 330 members, about three pounds per man, woman, and child. Some people, having nothing to spare, bought new clothes to give. Given that that rural congregation had no resources to ship so much so far, a trucker got his company to ship it all free of charge. I doubt that congregation had any sense of what it had accomplished — and all without moralistic pleas, pictures of freezing children, or any hint of biblical reward. I suspect that, outside of the intern's sister, most have forgotten and would still say, when asked to give an account to the king (Matt. 25), "When did we see you naked . . . ?" Everything depends not on us but on the Word that kills and makes alive and reveals the heart of God. Anyone care for another dance?

DISCUSSION QUESTIONS

▶ To what extent do our good works come from fear of punishment (or a sense of "we should") or from spontaneous reaction (from "a free and merry spirit")?

- ▶ In what ways do we need to hear the preaching of the "law" in our congregation? How would that make a difference?
- ▶ Are threats and focus on divine judgment and punishment helpful today? What happens when no one really believes that God cares?
- ▶ How does "the law," understood as the will of God, sometimes seem like a wonderful opportunity and blessing in our lives? How does it restrain or convict believers?
- ▶ How do you understand the various "uses" of the law?

Article Seven (Part One)

When Jesus Throws a Party,
He Shows Up (the Real Presence)

She was one of the smartest children I ever confirmed. At the time, however, she was only in fifth grade, daughter of an oil hauler and the town's first-grade teacher. Like almost every other child her age, Michelle was eager to attend classes to learn more about the Lord's Supper in anticipation of receiving the sacrament on Maundy Thursday of Holy Week. It was always a special event. For the first time the children had their pastor as a teacher. We would meet three times and cover worksheets that explained the names for the Eucharist, sample the bread and wine, and, especially, learn what the Supper was. As the Small Catechism states, they discovered that the Sacrament of the Altar "is the true body and blood of our Lord Jesus Christ under the bread and wine, instituted by Christ himself for us Christians to eat and to drink," and that the benefits are "forgiveness of sin, life, and salvation" (Lord's Supper, 2 and 6, in *BC 2000,* 362).

Without fail I would instruct the children that there were two questions one could ask about Christ's presence. First, how do we *know* Christ is present in the Supper? Answer: he promises to show up ("This *is* my body"). The second question — how is Christ present in the Supper? — I explained, is the only question they'll ever hear whose correct answer is "I don't know." After three weeks of instruction I visited each family so that the parents could hear what their children had learned and give their blessing to their children's participation in the Supper. (It was actually simply a sneaky way to instruct the parents. After hearing his daughter Abbie answer my questions to her, her father Dave exclaimed, "She knows more than I do!" — which was the point.)

As one might imagine, Michelle knew all the answers. Six names for the meal, facts about the Last Supper, how Jesus had promised to show up — all these answers and more came tumbling off her lips. Then I asked, "How is Jesus present?" Silence. I prodded (shame on me!), "Come on, Michelle, this is important!" Her fair skin began to redden. Mom and Dad leaned forward. Finally, she blurted out, "Pastor Tim, I don't know!" "Right answer, Michelle," I responded, and she just groaned.

History

What Michelle did not know was that she had (finally) given the same answer Luther gave in his 1529 debate with Ulrich Zwingli. The two reformers, from Wittenberg in Saxony and Zürich in Switzerland, respectively, had been waging a paper war over the presence of Christ in the Supper since 1525. Zwingli had insisted that the words "This is my body" meant "This signifies my body" or "This is a sign of my body," because the finite bread cannot contain the infinite Christ. Paraphrasing John 6:63 (to some degree in line with Platonic philosophy's distinction between matter and spirit), Zwingli argued that "the flesh" of Christ in the sacrament "was of no avail; the spirit makes alive." His colleague from Basel, John Oecolampadius (the Greek form of his German name, Hausschein), added the argument that Christ's body could not be present in the meal because it had ascended to the right hand of God. When the landgrave of Hesse, Prince Philip, in an effort to resolve the conflict and insure a united political front against the emperor, Charles V, summoned the theologians to his castle in Marburg in early October 1529, the debate took place. Zwingli kept asking Luther to explain how Christ was present in the bread and wine. Luther responded, "Don't ask me mathematical (or: geometrical) questions!" That is, to the question "How is Christ present?" Luther responded, "I don't know."

It is not as if Lutherans were unable to dream up responses from physics or philosophy. Although Luther dismissed transubstantiation as too complicated and an unnecessary importation of Aristotle into theology, one could — by his lights foolishly — try to explain Christ's presence in the following way. Aristotle had said that everything is made up of qualities *(accidentia)* that change and quiddities (essences; *substantia*) that do not. In the Lord's Supper the "accidents" or appearance of the bread and wine remains while the "substance" changes into Christ's body and blood (hence: tran*substant*iation). This theory had become the official doctrine of the Roman Church in 1215 at the Fourth Lateran Council. Luther preferred the duck test ("If it looks like bread, tastes like bread, and feels like bread, it is bread") and simply argued that Christ is present "in" the bread or (in language closer to that of Roman doctrine) "under" (the form of) the bread.

At one point, when pressed by Zwingli in writing, Luther did speculate about how one might answer the "how" question using nominalist philosophy, in which he had been trained at the university. God's presence is such that all of God can be in a single walnut shell and leave room for the nut, and yet, at the same time, the entire universe cannot contain God. In any case, as Luther consistently argued, God's "right hand," to which Christ ascended, is not a place. In the Scripture it is always a metaphor for God's power and rule. Human rules of time and place simply do not apply there. The point is that when God makes a promise ("This *is* my body"), God shows up. Leave the physics to God!

Although Zwingli and Luther reached an impasse at Marburg, the prince asked Luther to compose a set of articles of faith. Of the fifteen articles, only the one on the Lord's Supper could not be agreed on. Even there, however, the reformers agreed, in opposition to Roman Catholic teaching, that the Lord's Supper was not a sacrifice to God by the priest, that both bread and wine should be offered to all who commune, and that receiving the Supper in faith was central to the Supper's purpose. Only on the question of Christ's presence was there disagreement.

In 1531 Zwingli and Oecolampadius, the main disputants with Luther, died, and an opportunity arose for rapprochement. One participant at Marburg, Martin Bucer, the reformer in Strasbourg (then a part of the empire, now in France), had been impressed enough with Luther's arguments to contact Melanchthon for further discussion. Bucer worried that the Wittenbergers' insistence on the "real presence" of Christ's body and blood "in" or "under" the elements of bread and wine would lead to a worship of the bread apart from its use in the Supper (Christ trapped *in* the bread) and to a return to the Roman "sacrifice of the Mass." He also thought that while believers might receive Christ's body and blood in the Supper, the ungodly were not worthy to receive it and did not. Negotiations finally led to a dramatic 1536 meeting in Wittenberg between Bucer, accompanied by other pastors from southern Germany, and Luther and his colleagues. After some tense moments, both sides agreed that Christ's body and blood were received "with" the bread and wine and that, in order that our faith might not undermine Christ's promise, all participants, whether worthy or not, received Christ. This Wittenberg Concord was so important that forty years later the concordists quoted it in the Solid Declaration. "With the bread and wine the body and blood of Christ are truly and essentially present, distributed, and received." This does not mean "that the body and blood of Christ are *localiter,* that is, spatially enclosed in the bread or are permanently united in some other way apart from reception." Finally, the power or effectiveness of the sacrament "does not rest upon . . . the worthiness or unworthiness of the one who receives it" (SD VII.12-16, in *BC 2000,* 595-96).

With this agreement relative peace returned to the Protestant side. On this basis both Bucer and an exiled French pastor serving the French-speaking refugees in Strasbourg, John Calvin, were able to subscribe to the Augsburg Confession (albeit an officially altered version that spoke of Christ's presence "with the bread"). To be sure, some Swiss cities, especially Bern and Zürich, refused to accept the Wittenberg Concord and continued to teach that Christ was not present in the meal but that it was a memorial of Christ's death where "Christ's body" was the assembled congregation of believers, which feeds on Christ spiritually by faith. Granted, there were tensions among the agreeing parties. In the 1540s Luther was heard to complain about Bucer's views and seemed even to support transubstantiation in a letter to Christians in Venice, turning his ire toward the intransigent Swiss cities and their pastors in a 1544 tract on the subject. Some questioned Melanchthon's position, which differed somewhat from Luther's. (See the historical section on article 7, part 2.)

After Luther's death real trouble broke out in Hamburg. In 1552 a pastor there, Joachim Westphal, who had studied in Wittenberg under Melanchthon and Luther, became concerned about Calvin's understanding of the Lord's Supper. Three years earlier, in 1549, Calvin had entered into an agreement with the successors to Zwingli in Zürich, notably the chief pastor, Heinrich Bullinger. In this so-called Zürich Consensus, published in 1551, Calvin had moderated his understanding of Christ's effective presence to accommodate the spiritualizing views of the Zürich theologians. In 1552 Westphal collected what he considered suspicious statements from the consensus and other sources, and followed it the next year with a thoroughgoing commentary on the biblical passages, attacking Calvin in the process. Calvin returned the favor with published condemnations of Westphal, calling him a bread worshiper and hoping for a united Lutheran attack on the Hamburg pastor. In private correspondence Melanchthon, too, was contemptuous of Westphal's position, but he never publicly supported Calvin (with whom he also did not fully agree), something his students would do a decade later.

Neither side fully appreciated the other. Calvin held that the person of Christ was present at the Lord's Supper but not trapped in the bread and wine. Instead the Holy Spirit gathered our spirits by faith to God's right hand, where the communicants fed on Christ by faith. Westphal, on the contrary, reproduced Luther's position quite accurately. Christ's body and blood are truly present under the forms of bread and wine. Calvin mistakenly thought Westphal believed in consubstantiation, where the bread's substance is joined to the substance of Christ's body in a permanent manner. Westphal imagined that Calvin denied Christ's presence with the meal, as had Zwingli.

In 1555 a similar dispute broke out in Bremen, another important maritime trading center in northern Germany with close ties to Hamburg. In this case Johann Timann and Albert Hardenberg came into open conflict when Timann published an attack on the Polish-born John à Lasco, a friend of Hardenberg whose theology matched Calvin's. Here the dispute focused more on the christological question (cf. article 8). Was it correct to say that Christ's humanity, by virtue of the union between Christ's human and divine natures, was everywhere (and thus capable of being in the Supper)? Hardenberg thought this destroyed the integrity of Christ's humanity (since a property of human beings is to be in a single place). Like Melanchthon, he deeply distrusted the notion of the "ubiquity" (ability to be everywhere) of Christ's body and blood and the way Timann described how Christ's human and divine attributes were in communion with each other. Timann and his supporters insisted that Christ's body and blood were present in and with the bread and wine, and they felt they were using orthodox Christian distinctions to defend their positions. Among others who later came to Timann's defense were Johann Brenz, the reformer of Württemberg, and Martin Chemnitz, then a pastor in the city of Braunschweig. The latter's views of Christ's presence, arising from his study of the Bible, the church fathers, and Luther, came to shape fundamentally the text of the Formula of Concord.

A third controversy broke out in Heidelberg and involved a former student of Melanchthon, Tileman Hesshus. When the principality of the Rhenish Palatinate accepted the Reformation in the late 1550s, Hesshus, at Melanchthon's recommendation, became chief professor of theology at its university in Heidelberg. Immediately a fight broke out there between Hesshus and several clergy over the nature of Christ's presence in the Lord's Supper. Hesshus, although skeptical about certain claims regarding ubiquity, insisted on Christ's real presence in the Supper, stating at one point that "the bread is the true body of Christ." Melanchthon, when asked by the Palatine elector for an opinion, rejected both the Bremen church's claim that the bread is the substantial body of Christ and Hesshus's position. He preferred the language of 1 Corinthians 10:16, namely, that the bread is the *koinonia* or association with the body of Christ, which happens only in its proper use (see article 7, part 2). He rejected the notion of the ubiquity of Christ's body and criticized Hesshus for rejecting the use of the patristic word "symbol" (as in "the bread and wine are symbols of the body and blood").

As a result of Melanchthon's letter, both Hesshus and his chief opponent were removed from office. However, they were soon replaced by Zacharias Ursinus and Caspar Olevianus, both Reformed (Calvinist) theologians who helped write the important Reformed statement of faith, the Heidelberg Catechism. Melanchthon died in 1560, but when his letter to the elector became public, he was roundly attacked posthumously by many Gnesio-Lutherans. In the 1560s attempts at rapprochement between the various parties, led by Jakob Andreae, a disciple of Brenz, failed, among other reasons because the Reformed theologians of Heidelberg insisted that the finite bread was not capable of bearing the infinite Christ.

Finally, when in the late 1560s the Wittenberg theological faculty started criticizing theologians like Andreae and Brenz for their insistence on Christ's ubiquity, suspicions began to arise regarding the Wittenbergers' fidelity to Lutheran teaching. While someone like Chemnitz thought he was faithfully developing Luther and Melanchthon's eucharistic theology, theologians at Wittenberg began to take Melanchthon's position in a quite different direction. A series of documents produced by the Wittenbergers in the late 1560s and early 1570s revealed these shifts, albeit hidden under an insistence on their fidelity to Lutheran theology. Although earlier scholars labeled the work of these theologians, which included Melanchthon's son-in-law Caspar Peucer, crypto-Calvinist, a more accurate designation may be crypto-Philippist: "crypto" because of the concealed nature of their position, and "Philippist" because they thought they were developing the consequences of Melanchthon's perspective. In essence they denied any real "communication of attributes" between the two natures of Christ (see article 8) and insisted more and more on a spiritualized presence of Christ in the Supper, since Christ's humanity had ascended to the right hand of God in heaven. Initially protected by the Saxon elector, August, who refused to believe they were not Lutheran, they quickly lost favor and were arrested on suspicion of conspiracy in 1574 when a misdirected letter by one of the main supporters of this position, critical of the elector's wife, became public. Two died in prison; Peucer was released after a decade of captivity. With the collapse of crypto-Philippism in Saxony, the stage was set for the development of the Formula of Concord.

The Heart of the Matter

Each year, in the required course on the Lutheran Confessions at the seminary, we spend a good deal of time on the Lord's Supper and the disputes over it during the Reformation. One year two students who had become Lutherans later in life happened to be sitting across from each other in a discussion session. Both admitted that, although they had been members of Lutheran congregations for five and fifteen-plus years, respectively, only in my course on the Confessions had they discovered that Lutherans believe in Christ's real presence in the sacrament.

Now, the first thought of this professor of Lutheran Confessions and editor of *The Book of Concord* was, predictably, to demand the names and addresses of their pastors in order to read them the riot act. That did not happen. However, a second reaction prevailed. Think of the pastoral effect! Imagine receiving the Lord's Supper for all those years and never knowing the comfort of Christ's presence and the gifts of forgiveness, life, and salvation that his presence brings. The heart of Christ's presence is *not* a doctrine, it is a promise: "Here I am for you." Never to hear that promise spoken directly to you personally and communally to the entire group would be the greatest tragedy of all. That is why Lutherans are so adamant about this point in their discussions with other Christians. What matters most to us is just this: Christ promises to show up. His body and blood are truly present with the bread and wine. What could be more glorious, more comforting than that?

Every year, prior to confirmation, the education committee and I would interview each confirmand to determine what he or she had learned. One young woman, unlike Michelle, had clearly not learned very much, or so it seemed, judging from her inability to answer our questions. Perhaps it was nerves (her mother was on the committee), or perhaps she was just not very keen on the subject. Finally, out of desperation, I asked, "Didn't you learn anything, Joanne?" She paused; her eyes filled with tears, and she recounted this one thing. "You told us one time that our altar rail [modeled, as it happened, after those in many Scandinavian immigrant churches] was in the shape of a half-circle because the other half was in heaven, and Christ is in the center both here and there." Tears began to role down her carefully made-up cheeks. "Ever since my grandpa died last February, I remember that." A confession of faith by the Saxon church in 1551 made this very point. The Lord's Supper is both intensely individual ("not just for others, but for you") and intensely communal (it is the church's meal). Perhaps that Scandinavian altar rail in a semicircle, in which a copy of the famous statue of the welcoming Christ in the Copenhagen cathedral often graces the altar, can remind us of that fact. "Here I am, for you all and for you individually." What matters is the presence of the living Christ with the bread and wine, binding us all together in heaven and on earth.

The Text of the Epitome

Concerning the Holy Supper of Christ

[1] Although those who teach Zwinglian doctrine are not to be counted among the theologians of the Augsburg Confession — since they separated themselves from this confession immediately, at the time it was presented — we, nonetheless, want to report on this controversy because they are insinuating themselves and spreading their error under the name of this Christian confession.

Status controversiae

The Chief Issue between Us and the Teaching of the Sacramentarians on This Article

[2] In the Holy Supper are the true body and blood of our Lord Jesus Christ truly and essentially present, distributed with the bread and wine, and received by mouth by all those who avail themselves of the sacrament — whether they are worthy or unworthy, godly or ungodly, believers or unbelievers — to bring believers comfort and life and to bring judgment upon unbelievers?

[3] The sacramentarians say no; we say yes.

To explain this controversy, it must first of all be noted that there are two kinds of sacramentarians. There are the crude sacramentarians, who state in plain language what they believe in their hearts: that in the Holy Supper there is nothing more than bread and wine present, nothing more distributed and received with the mouth. [4] Then there are the cunning sacramentarians, the most dangerous kind, who in part appear to use our language and who pretend that they also believe in a true presence of the true, essential, living body and blood of Christ in the Holy Supper, but that this takes place spiritually, through faith. Yet, under the guise of such plausible words, they retain the former, crude opinion, that nothing more than bread and wine is present in the Holy Supper and received there by mouth.

[5] For "spiritually" means to them nothing other than "the spirit of Christ" that is present, or "the power of the absent body of Christ and his merit." The body of Christ, according to this opinion, is, however, in no

way or form present, but it is only up there in the highest heaven; to this body we lift ourselves into heaven through the thoughts of our faith. There we should seek his body and blood, but never in the bread and wine of the Supper.

Affirmative Theses

> The Confession of Pure Teaching concerning the Holy Supper, against the Sacramentarians

[6] 1. We believe, teach, and confess that in the Holy Supper the body and blood of Christ are truly and essentially present, truly distributed and received with the bread and wine.

[7] 2. We believe, teach, and confess that the words of the testament of Christ are not to be understood in any other way than the way they literally sound, that is, not that the bread symbolizes the absent body and the wine the absent blood of Christ, but that they are truly the true body and blood of Christ because of the sacramental union.

[8] 3. Concerning the consecration, we believe, teach, and confess that neither human effort nor the recitation of the minister effect this presence of the body and blood of Christ in the Holy Supper, but that it is to be attributed solely and alone to the almighty power of our Lord Jesus Christ.

[9] 4. In addition, we believe, teach, and hold with one accord that in the use of the Holy Supper the words of Christ's institution may under no circumstances be omitted but must be spoken publicly, as it is written, "The cup of blessing that we bless . . ." (1 Cor. 11 [10:16]). This blessing takes place through the pronouncement of the words of Christ.

[10] 5. The reasons for our position against the sacramentarians on this matter are those which Dr. Luther set forth in his *Great Confession:* [11] "The first [reason for his position] is this article of our faith, that Jesus Christ is true, essential, natural, complete God and human being in one person, undivided and inseparable. [12] The second, that the right hand of God is everywhere." Christ, really and truly placed at this right hand of God according to his human nature, rules presently and has in his hands and under his feet everything in heaven and on earth. No other human being, no angel, but only Mary's son, is so placed at the right hand of God, and on this basis

he is able to do these things. [13] "The third, that the Word of God is not false or deceitful. [14] The fourth that God has and knows various ways to be present at a certain place, not only the single one . . . , which the philosophers call 'local'" or spatial.

[15] 6. We believe, teach, and confess that the body and blood of Christ are received not only spiritually through faith but also orally with the bread and wine, though not in Capernaitic fashion but rather in a supernatural, heavenly way because of the sacramental union of the elements. The words of Christ clearly demonstrate this, when Christ said, "take, eat, and drink," and the apostles did this. For it is written, "and they all drank from it" (Mark 14[:23]). Likewise, Saint Paul says, "The bread, which we break, is a Communion with the body of Christ" [1 Cor. 10:16], that is, who eats this bread eats the body of Christ. The leading teachers of the ancient church — Chrysostom, Cyprian, Leo I, Gregory, Ambrose, Augustine, and others — unanimously testify to this.

[16] 7. We believe, teach, and confess that not only those who truly believe and are worthy, but also the unworthy and unbelievers receive the true body and blood of Christ, though they do not receive life and comfort, but rather judgment and damnation, if they do not turn and repent.

[17] For though they reject Christ as a savior, they still must, against their will, accept him as a harsh judge, who is just as much present to exercise and visit judgment upon unrepentant guests as he is to bestow life and comfort upon the hearts of those who truly believe and are worthy guests.

[18] 8. We believe, teach, and confess that there is only one kind of unworthy guest, those who do not believe. Of them it is written, "Those who do not believe are condemned already" [John 3:18]. The unworthy use of the holy sacrament increases, magnifies, and aggravates this condemnation (1 Cor. 11[:27, 29]).

[19] 9. We believe, teach, and confess that no genuine believers — no matter how weak — as long as they retain a living faith, receive the Holy Supper as condemnation. For Christ instituted this supper particularly for Christians who are weak in faith but repentant, to comfort them and to strengthen their weak faith.

[20] 10. We believe, teach, and confess that the entire worthiness of the guests at the table of his heavenly meal is and consists alone in the most

holy obedience and perfect merit of Christ. We make his obedience and merit our own through true faith, concerning which we receive assurance through the sacrament. Worthiness consists in no way in our own virtues, or in internal or external preparations.

Negative Theses

The Contrary, Condemned Teaching of the Sacramentarians

[21] On the other hand, we unanimously reject and condemn all the following erroneous articles, which oppose and are contrary to the teaching presented here, the simple belief and confession regarding the Supper of Christ:

[22] 1. The papal transubstantiation, when it is taught in the papacy that bread and wine in the Holy Supper lose their substance and natural essence and thus cease to exist, in such a way that the bread is transformed into the body of Christ and only its outward form remains.

[23] 2. The papal sacrifice of the Mass for the sins of the living and the dead.

[24] 3. That the laity are given only one of the sacramental elements and that against the clear words of the testament of Christ the chalice is kept from them and they are robbed of the blood of Christ.

[25] 4. When it is taught that the words of Christ's testament ought not to be understood or believed simply as they sound, but that they are an obscure expression, the meaning of which must be sought in other passages.

[26] 5. That the body of Christ in the holy sacrament is not received orally with the bread, but only bread and wine are received by mouth; the body of Christ, however, is received only spiritually, through faith.

[27] 6. That the bread and wine in the Holy Supper are no more than distinguishing marks, through which Christians recognize each other.

[28] 7. That the bread and wine are only representations, similes, and symbols of the far-distant body and blood of Christ.

[29] 8. That the bread and wine are no more than a reminder, a seal, or a guarantee, through which we are assured that when faith soars into heaven, it will participate there in the body and blood of Christ as truly as we eat and drink bread and wine in the Supper.

[30] 9. That the assurance and confirmation of our faith in the Holy Supper take place only through the outward signs of bread and wine, and not through the true body and blood of Christ present there.

[31] 10. That in the Holy Supper only the power, effect, or merit of the absent body and blood of Christ are distributed.

[32] 11. That the body of Christ is enclosed in heaven, so that it can in no way be present at the same time in many or all places on earth where his Holy Supper is being conducted.

[33] 12. That Christ could not have promised the essential presence of his body and blood in the Holy Supper, nor could he make that possible, because the nature and characteristics of the assumed human nature would not permit or allow that.

[34] 13. That God, even on the basis of his total omnipotence (a dreadful statement!), cannot possibly make his body to be essentially present in more than one place at one particular time.

[35] 14. That not the almighty words of the testament of Christ, but rather faith, effects and creates the presence of the body and blood of Christ in the Holy Supper.

[36] 15. That believers should not look for the body of Christ in the bread and wine of the Holy Supper but should instead lift their eyes from the bread to heaven and look there for the body of Christ.

[37] 16. That unbelieving, unrepentant Christians do not receive the true body and blood of Christ in the Holy Supper but only the bread and wine.

[38] 17. That the worthiness of the guests at this heavenly meal consists not only in true faith in Christ but indeed also in people's outward preparation.

[39] 18. That those who truly believe, who have and retain a true, living, pure faith in Christ, can receive this sacrament to their judgment, simply because they are still imperfect in their outward way of life.

[40] 19. That the outward, visible elements of bread and wine in the holy sacrament should be adored.

[41] 20. Likewise, we commend to the proper judgment of God all impu-

dent, sarcastic, blasphemous questions and expressions, which we will not recite for the sake of propriety and which the sacramentarians utter in a crude, carnal, Capernaitic, and detestable manner, blasphemously, and with great offense concerning the supernatural, celestial mysteries of this sacrament.

[42] 21. We also hereby completely condemn the Capernaitic eating of the body of Christ. It suggests that his flesh is chewed up with the teeth and digested like other food. The sacramentarians maliciously attribute this view to us against the witness of their own conscience, despite our many protests. In this way they make our teaching detestable among their hearers. On the contrary, on the basis of the simple words of Christ's testament, we hold and teach the true, but supernatural, eating of the body of Christ and the drinking of his blood. Human reason and understanding cannot grasp this, but our understanding must be taken captive by obedience to Christ here as in all other articles of faith. Such a mystery cannot be grasped except by faith and is revealed alone in the Word.

Commentary

The Chief Issue (pp. 503-4)

Paragraph 1. The concordists begin by admitting that the question of Christ's presence in the Lord's Supper is not, strictly speaking, a "Lutheran question," as defined in the introduction to this book. Already in 1530 at Augsburg, Zwingli had presented his own confession of faith, which denied the presence of Christ in the sacrament. Similarly, a consortium of four imperial cities also confessed a spiritual presence of Christ in the meal. The Augsburg Confession, which defines Lutheranism to this day, stated instead that "the true body and blood of Christ are truly present under the form of bread and wine in the Lord's Supper and are distributed and received there" (CA X.1-2, in *BC 2000*, 44). The problem, as the concordists defined it, was what might even be called "crypto-Zwinglianism." Of course, as we have seen, the historical circumstances were far more complicated. Nevertheless, there was a suspicion that any other position was simply not Lutheran at all.

Paragraph 2. This pithy paragraph shows how Lutheran understanding of the Supper had developed by the 1570s. First, as in CA X, the words "true" and "truly" appear twice: the true body is truly present. To underscore the reality of this presence, the concordists then add a second adverb, "essentially," and speak of an oral reception. As we will see in paragraph 5, this contrasts with a purely spiritual presence and a spiritual eating. However, strictly in line with the Wittenberg Concord, the concordists here use the single preposition "with" (not "in" or "under") to describe this presence. Moreover, this presence depends *not* on our faith but on Christ's unshakable promise. Finally, they also touch on the purpose of this sacrament: comfort and life for believers and judgment for unbelievers (see article 7, part 2).

Paragraphs 3-5. Because there is no "internal" opponent to this position, the concordists have no need to stake out middle ground. However, they do recognize that there are several types of opponents: "crude sacramentarians" (par. 3), who believe in the real absence, and "cunning sacramentarians" (par. 4), what are now called crypto-Philippists, who cover up their true opinion (that Christ is only spiritually present) with plausible words that sound Lutheran but in reality are not. "Spiritual," a word that in other circumstances might help people who imagine a carnal (cannibalistic) presence to express the mystery of Christ's presence, had come to mean simply "the spirit of Christ" or the "power of his absent body." To these people Christ was somewhere up in heaven. "To this body we lift ourselves into heaven through the thoughts of our faith." This single phrase introduces the real worry for the concordists: that Christ's real presence depends on us and our faith and not on Christ's trustworthy promise.

Affirmative Theses (pp. 505-6)

Paragraph 6. Again the concordists cannot say the word "truly" (or "essentially") often enough. However, this word begs the question of *how* Christ is present. For them, as for Luther, such a question was a sure invitation to import some philosophy or another into God's Word and to undermine trust in God's promise by putting faith in human explanations instead. As throughout this article of the Epitome, Andreae, echoing the Wittenberg Concord, uses the preposition "with."

SD VII.35-39 (*BC 2000,* 599) discusses all three prepositions: "with," "in," and "under." Later Lutherans mistakenly run all three together ("in, with, and under"), but the concordists — the author of this section of the Solid Declaration was one of Melanchthon's favorite students, David Chytraeus — clearly distinguish them. The reason for using prepositions (instead of simply quoting Jesus himself ["this is my body"] or Paul ["participation in Christ's body"]) is to reject transubstantiation and point to the sacramental union and not to a localized presence inside the bread. Just as Christ's human nature and divine nature are joined in the incarnation (John 1:14), so Christ joins himself with the bread and wine, something to which the church fathers had also attested. These words simply indicate that Christ's words ("This is my body") are unique and define a real, not simply figurative, presence.

Paragraph 7. The concordists will deal with Christ's ascent into heaven in article 8. Here they focus on the simple words describing the Supper: "This is my body." The passing reference to Christ's "testament" is connected to one of Luther's most important tracts on the sacraments, *The Babylonian Captivity* of 1520. There and in a sermon from the previous year he describes the Supper *not* as a sacrifice the priest offers up to God but as Christ's "last will and testament," in which he makes a promise ("My body and blood for you, for the forgiveness of sin") that goes into effect with his death and is distributed to his heirs. Despite Melanchthon's plea that the church fathers' use of the word "symbol" legitimized its use in his day, the concordists reject this word because it may be understood to remove Christ's presence so that the bread merely symbolizes "his absent body." Instead, the bread and wine "are truly the true body and blood of Christ because of the sacramental union."

Paragraphs 8-9. How do we know Christ is present? To this question Lutherans have an answer: when Christ promises to show up, he does so because everything depends on him and his powerful promise, not on human effort or ministerial magic. Here the language links the presence of Christ to the teaching of justification by faith alone. Everything depends on Christ, not on us. This eliminates both the notion that somehow our faith makes Christ present, as the "cunning sacramentarians" imagined, and the notion that the priest, by his words, offers to God an "unbloodied sacrifice" of Christ's body and blood. That is always the danger: turning God's promise into a human work.

This positive statement also points to one of the serious charges of the opponents, who worried that any insistence on such a real presence turned the Supper into a magic trick performed by a priest. Indeed, when the Lord's Supper liturgy is reduced to mere incantation of the Words of Institution or expanded into a production worthy of a Hollywood director, this appearance of ministerial magic may even be heightened. However, this does not mean that the words of Christ's institution should be neglected (par. 9)! That would rather be like a lawyer calling all the members of a family together to distribute the inheritance to the heirs and refusing to read the will and testament of the departed! These are words of proclamation and blessing! Without Christ's promise, clearly stated for all to hear and believe, we simply reduce the meal to an appetizer for the congregation's potluck supper. Everything that takes place around the meal — the songs and prayers, the readings and liturgy — points to Christ crucified, "who on the night he was betrayed took bread. . . ."

Paragraph 10-14. This is one of the few places in the Epitome where Andreae quotes Luther directly, in contrast to the Solid Declaration, which cites him extensively in this article and in article 8. In this case Luther's comments effectively summarize the concordists' arguments. First (par. 11), one dare not divide Christ in such a way as to reduce his presence in the sacrament to the nature that gets around faster. Christ is human and divine in one inseparable, undivided person. Second (par. 12), God's right hand in Scripture is a metaphor for God's power, not a physical place. After all, God does not have "hands" in a literal sense. Therefore the words do not designate a place but picture God's power. Although in other aspects of this debate Luther and Melanchthon may have disagreed, here they were united. Third (par. 13), God's word can be trusted, even if human reason cannot figure out how such a thing could be true. It is such a relief to have someone to trust. "Although everyone is a liar, let God be proved true," Paul says in Romans 3:4. Finally (par. 14), God has more than one way to be in a place. In other words, "Do not ask mathematical questions!" Lutherans do not know how God is present, just that, when Jesus promises to be there, he really and truly shows up.

Paragraph 15. Luther's final point demanded more explanation by the concordists because it refuted one of the charges most often leveled against them by their opponents: that they held to a "Capernaitic" eating of Christ's flesh. This adjective arose from the question of the listeners in Capernaum's synagogue: "How can this man give us his flesh to eat?" (John 6:52). True, the eating is not simply spiritualized (and thus dependent on our spirituality); it is oral, but "in a supernatural, heavenly way." In other words, leave the "how" to God! Because of Melanchthon's penchant to quote 1 Corinthians 10:16, the concordists also explain that passage here. "Communion [Greek: *koinonia*] with the body of Christ" means that to eat this bread is to eat Christ's body. A simple list of patristic sources points to fuller citations that were present in an earlier version of SD VII and later excised. (See *BC 2000*, 603-5 nn. 200 and 203, for details.) Citing these sources was designed to deflect Melanchthon's charge that the church fathers did not teach Christ's real presence as other Lutherans had taught it.

Paragraphs 16-20. This material and the sections in the Solid Declaration to which it refers are the focus of the next chapter (article 7, part 2). Here it is worth noting that the sacrament was not instituted for the strong, and certainly not for the contemptuous, but precisely "for Christians who are weak in faith but repentant, to comfort them and to strengthen their weak faith" (par. 19). This pastoral intention of the sacrament (present already at the Last Supper) must never be lost from view. Even though the concordists had to discuss the issue of worthiness (given their opponents' desire to make Christ's presence depend on our faith or lack thereof), they do not want to lose sight of the fact that nothing dare contradict justification by faith alone. Our "worthiness" consists in Christ's worthiness alone. Even in the sacrament we live by Christ's grace and mercy alone.

Negative Theses (pp. 507-8)

Paragraphs 22-24 and 38-40. The concordists take the opportunity to contrast their view not only with that of their immediate opponents, the crypto-Philippists, but also with that of out-and-out Zwinglians and Roman Catholics. In these paragraphs the ostensible opponent is Roman Catholicism, especially the Council of Trent. However, one of the reasons for stating their opposition to these positions was to refute charges by opponents (including Melanchthon) who accused them of "bread worship" and returning to Rome. Thus, they reject transubstantiation (par. 22), the notion that a priest could offer the Mass as a sacrifice for the sins of the living or dead (par. 23), and the prohibition of the cup to the laity (par. 24; lifted only in the 1960s, after Vatican II). They also attack certain Roman attitudes, such as the necessity of fasting before receiving the sacrament (par. 38), the widespread fear that one's human imperfection could make the sacrament harmful to a recipient (par. 39; see LC, Lord's Supper, 55-57, in *BC 2000*, 472-73, for Luther's own experience), and the adoration of the elements (par. 40). To the concordists, all these things are simply attempts of the old creature to ignore God's promises and build everything on human works.

Paragraphs 25-28. These paragraphs relate especially to Zwingli's original arguments, which the concordists encountered in their close reading of Luther's tracts from the 1520s. Zwingli had argued that the phrase "this is my body" was an *alloiosis* (par. 25), a Greek term he used technically to designate a sentence where subject and predicate refer to essentially different things. The only kind of eating he allowed for was the spiritual eating of faith described in John 6 (par. 26). He also had defined sacraments as equivalent to oaths Swiss soldiers took when swearing allegiance to their cantons, that is, as a sign of a Christian's commitment to God and the church (par. 27). Finally, he described the bread and wine as symbolizing Christ's body and blood, which were in heaven (par. 28). Most of these Zwinglian views were not held by Calvin and other later Reformed thinkers, let alone by the crypto-Philippists.

Paragraphs 29, 30, and 35. Here Andreae characterizes a teaching of Calvin (especially in the Zürich Consensus), Hardenberg, and the crypto-Philippists, who sought to express Christ's presence more fully but (in the case of Calvin) against the backdrop of Zwingli's more radical views. This presence is actualized through faith, which through the power of the Holy Spirit feeds at God's right hand on Christ, "as truly as we eat and drink bread and wine in the Supper." For the concordists, this explanation was not only too complicated, but it made faith itself and not God's promise the guarantee of Christ's presence. Moreover, it easily reduced that presence to a virtual, not a real, event. In the same way, they reject the notion that faith rests on the elements themselves and not on Christ's real presence (par. 30). In his 1528 tract against the Anabaptists, Luther argued that by making faith a prerequisite for baptism people practicing rebaptism had placed their faith in faith rather than in God's promise. Here, too (par. 35), the concordists will not allow anything to come between the believer and God's promise to be present — even the believer's faith.

Paragraph 31. This view of Calvin and the crypto-Philippists attempted to bridge the gap between a completely symbolic understanding of the sacrament and one they regarded as overly realistic by arguing that the real effects of Christ's body, not the body itself, were distributed in the Supper. Although such a position rejected Zwingli's denial of the sacraments as means of grace, for the concordists it still fell far short of Christ's promise to give his body and blood with the bread and wine.

Paragraphs 32-34, 36. Although they will deal with the question of Christ's nature more fully in article 8, the concordists must deal with positions related to Christ's ascension to God's right hand, which appeared in various phases of the debate, especially in the writings of Calvin's successor in Geneva, Theodorus Beza. The first is tied to the notion that God's right hand is a place (par. 32); the second restricts the presence of God on the basis of the restrictions of human nature (par. 33); and the third restricts God's omnipotence (par. 34). Finally, they again take aim at a notion, favored by Calvin, that we "lift up our hearts" from the Supper to Christ in heaven (par. 36). In the concordists' view, all these positions ignored the metaphorical nature of God's right hand and demanded an explanation to the "how" question. Philosophical restrictions on God must yield to God's own comforting promise.

Paragraph 37. This paragraph will be dealt with in detail in the next chapter.

Paragraphs 41-42. During the heat of the debate, the concordists' opponents used some shockingly crude language and made some outrageous exaggerations of the Lutheran position. The crudities (par. 41), detailed in SD VII.67 (in *BC 2000*, 605), described the oral eating of Christ's body and blood in shocking terms, even for an age where gross expressions abounded. But the concordists' point ought not be lost. They view the sacramental presence of Christ as "supernatural, celestial mysteries." Furthermore, their position did not imply a fleshly, "Capernaitic" eating. Instead, such eating was "true, but supernatural" (par. 42). At the end of the article they come to agree with Michelle's "I don't know." "Human reason and understanding cannot grasp this, but our understanding must be taken captive by obedience to Christ here as in all other articles of faith. Such a mystery cannot be grasped except by faith and is revealed alone in the Word."

A Formula for Parish Practice

In the sixteenth century Lutheran churches celebrated the Lord's Supper each week, as long as there were communicants, although no one would have communed weekly. In recent years many congregations have placed the Lord's Supper in a far more prominent place in their common life. Few things touch people as deeply as this simple meal, at which we hear "the body of Christ given for you" and "the blood of Christ, shed for you." This twofold promise, "Here I am" and "for you," gives comfort and assurance that Christ does not abandon us but gathers the entire congregation together and distributes with the elements, to each of us individually, his forgiveness. It is one of the clearest testimonies of justification by grace through faith on account of Christ. The Supper is not a ministerial work of magic nor a work of faith; it is Christ who works with bread and wine in his promise: "Here I am for you."

Many pastors, when leaving a congregation for another ministry, can remember their final Lord's Supper vividly. That certainly was my experience. As each person received Christ's body, there flashed in my mind all my experiences with that person during the previous six years. I remember one couple that had escaped from heartbreaking situations in previous marriages only to find each other and true love and commitment. I had happily performed their marriage several years before. The previous week I confirmed a child from the woman's previous marriage, and only a year before baptized a child from their union. I had come in the middle of the night to comfort them when her brother had tragically died in a fire. Now, if my presence in that setting brought forth in an instant those poignant memories for me, think of what our Lord Jesus considers as we eat his body and blood with the bread and wine. Imagine the forgiveness of sin pouring from his cross. Consider the hope of new life. Here he comes to us, takes upon himself all our burdens, and changes us into himself. Indeed, "such a mystery cannot be grasped except by faith and is revealed alone in the Word."

DISCUSSION QUESTIONS

- ► How important is the Lord's Supper to you and to members of your congregation?
- ► Has the teaching of Christ's presence in the Lord's Supper made a difference in your life of faith? If so, how? If not, why not?
- ► How have "how" questions (for example, *how* is Christ present? *how* did God create the world?) influenced your understanding of Christian doctrine?
- ► If someone from another faith tradition were to ask you, "Why do Lutherans believe Christ is present in the Lord's Supper?" how would you respond?

Article Seven (Part Two)

How Lutherans Receive the Lord's Supper

Consider two practical questions. First, who is worthy to receive the Lord's Supper? She was ninety years old if she was a day, sitting in a wheelchair near the elevator of the Lutheran nursing home in Minneapolis. As a seminarian, I was assigned to field education at the home, and that particular Sunday was helping Chaplain Lloyd Mart distribute the Lord's Supper. After communing those healthy enough to gather in the seventh-floor chapel, we then took the elements — I with the bread; Chaplain Mart with the wine — down the elevator to each floor and communed those who were too frail to leave the floor but who had gathered under the speaker near the elevator to hear the service. As I approached with the bread, she clasped her hand to her mouth and croaked, "Not worthy! I am not worthy!" I stopped dead. I'd never heard of such a thing. The thought crossed my mind that if she wasn't worthy, we were all in a lot of trouble. Chaplain Mart seemed to know just what to do. He crossed in front of me, laid his hand on her head, and pronounced the absolution: "In Christ, I pronounce to you the entire forgiveness of all your sins." Slowly her hand dropped, and I was able to commune her.

Second, what do we do with the leftovers, and what does that say about our views of the Supper? It's amazing how differently Lutheran congregations have answered that question. Nowadays, within the same region, you may find one congregation that saves the consecrated bread in a special place in the sanctuary, another that uses eucharistic ministers to distribute the elements to the sick, still another that sees to it that the bread gets consumed and pours the wine out on the ground, and a fourth that very carefully puts the wafers back in the cupboard for use next time. One congregation I served also poured the wine back into the bottle. When the congregation's council decided to offer grape juice as well, which no one took, people poured that back in the bottle every week, too. Four months later — God having managed to perform the yeasty miracle of transforming grape juice into brandy — someone drank the former grape juice by accident, and we quickly discontinued the practice and began disposing of the grape juice in other ways.

When the concordists dealt with the Lord's Supper, they considered it not only in terms of teaching but also in terms of practice. The two are intimately connected. We profess Christ's presence in the sacrament with our lips, but we also need to consider how that presence affects us and our celebration. Although this chapter will examine only two examples of this practical side of the Supper, there are many other questions that come up in the life of the church: Who should commune? Who should preside at Holy Communion? How often should we celebrate the sacrament? The list goes on and on. Seeing how the concordists dealt with these two problems in their day and age here and in article 10 may help us deal with our practical concerns today.

History

Worthy and Unworthy Communicants

The question of unworthy communicants has plagued Lutherans since the beginning of the Reformation. One of the advantages of a "spiritual" understanding of the Lord's Supper (that is, a view that argues that Christ is present in the Supper among only those who believe) seems to be that there is no such thing as "unworthy" communicants. If faith insures Christ's presence in the Supper and only believers receive the body and blood of Christ, then the unworthy (or unbelievers) receive only bread and wine. The Supper is helpful to those who believe but neutral to those who do not. As we saw in the previous chapter, the problem with this approach is that it makes Christ's promised presence in his meal dependent on our faith — an uncertain matter at best.

So, Luther and later Lutherans insisted that Christ is present to all who commune — regardless of their spiritual state. Moreover, as the Gospels indicate, Christ's presence is never neutral. On the one hand, when Christ shows up, water gets turned to wine, lepers are cleansed, the poor get the gospel preached to them, and tax collectors find forgiveness. On the other, when Christ shows up, Pharisees start complaining, scribes get condemned, and the religious rulers start plotting to get rid of him. In the same way, Christ's presence in the Lord's Supper brings either consolation or condemnation. Add to this the statement of Saint Paul in 1 Corinthians 11:27 ("Whoever . . . eats the bread or drinks the cup of the Lord in an unworthy manner will be answerable for the body and blood of the Lord"), and the stakes grow even higher. Even though Luther pointed out that this verse had to do with the Corinthian congregation's total disregard for their poor fellow Christians (and not necessarily with a faulty doctrine of the Supper), later Lutherans connected this warning to false belief and immoral behavior.

This debate over who receives Christ's body and blood in the Supper arose already in the 1520s, when Luther opposed those who defended Christ's spiritual presence alone in the sacrament. Christ was truly present in the bread and wine. This, of course, implied that all receive his body and blood. The comfort and forgiveness received by believers were never in dispute. But what might an unbeliever or godless person receive? In the 1530s, in an effort to heal the rift among Protestants over the Lord's Supper, Luther and Melanchthon signed the Wittenberg Concord with Martin Bucer. Although dispute arose later over what the agreement meant, it would seem that all agreed that the worthy and unworthy received Christ's body and blood, the worthy to their benefit and the unworthy to their harm, thus assuring that Christ's promise could not be overturned by our faith (or lack of it). (At the same time, some claimed that they had also agreed that truly ungodly persons were *offered* Christ's body but received only bread.)

When once again in the 1570s Lutherans debated the real or spiritual presence of Christ, questions also arose over the unworthy. Then, however, with over forty years of pastoral experience behind them, the concordists realized that the question was not just one of doctrine but also one of comfort. In their zeal to assure people that Christ's presence depended on Christ and not on us (and our faith or lack thereof), they had inadvertently sparked another pastoral crisis: What if the recipients were unworthy? It almost seemed better that Christ should be absent from the meal to (unworthy) unbelievers than that they be terrified by his presence in their unworthy lives. Who wants to eat judgment on themselves?

Leftover Elements and Christ's Presence

Churches in the early Reformation faced different communion issues than we do today. Moreover, Reformation churches were confronted with a problem that had not been dealt with in the church for at least 300 years: what to do with leftover wine. The Lateran IV Council of 1215 decreed that the laity would no longer receive the wine in the Supper. Thus, when Lutherans began to celebrate the Supper in both kinds (bread *and* wine), a problem arose concerning what to do with the leftover wine. People still were required to announce beforehand to the pastor or his assistants their intention to receive the Lord's Supper. Thus, it was easy enough to count out the number of wafers required for each celebration of the sacrament. The wine, however, was a more difficult matter.

The problem came to a head in Eisleben during the early 1540s. At one particular celebration of the Supper, a deacon who had not communed proceeded to drink the remaining wine in the cup, perhaps even mixing some unconsecrated wine with it. While the local church official saw nothing wrong in the practice, others were incensed. The deacon and his pastor were behaving as if the consecrated elements were no different from ordinary wine! An opinion obtained from Melanchthon, who worried about misusing the elements by worshiping them, seemed to support the deacon's behavior. However, when one of the pastors in Eisleben continued to object to treating consecrated elements as ordinary bread and wine, an opponent attacked him from the pulpit for believing in the Roman Catholic doctrine of transubstantiation and challenged him to a debate. The one under attack went to Wittenberg to obtain Luther's opinion. Suddenly, the tables were turned, and Luther upbraided this casual treatment of the elements (and the unchristian public attack upon a fellow pastor). To him it smacked of Zwinglianism — the belief of Ulrich Zwingli (among others) that Christ was not present in, with, or under the elements of bread and wine.

When the attacker sent Luther a copy of Melanchthon's letter, Luther responded by noting that Melanchthon was concerned with the "outside" (unnecessary adoration of the elements outside of the Supper that effectively trapped Jesus in the bread). On the contrary, Luther was concerned with the "inside" (practices within the meal that might leave the impression that Christ is not present at all in the sacrament). Luther insisted that Christ was present in the Supper during the entire "action," that is, from the time the elements were placed on the altar until the benediction. Otherwise, if it were taught that Christ showed up only during the moment of reception, one could get the impression that he was more absent from the meal than present. The final recipient of the cup during the meal, usually the pastor, should simply drain it (a practice that continues in some Lutheran churches to this day).

Later in the sixteenth century, similar disputes came up. In one case Melanchthon accused one overly scrupulous soul of worshiping crumbs. Still later, Johann Saliger, a pastor in Lübeck and Rostock in the 1560s, insisted in his zeal to defend the real presence that the elements remained the body and blood of Christ after their use for the sacrament itself. David Chytraeus, a professor in Rostock and one of Melanchthon's favorite students, who possessed copies of at least one of Luther's letters from the earlier dispute, was called on to mediate the controversy. From there the matter passed into the Formula of Concord.

The Heart of the Matter

As different as these two issues may seem on the surface, they actually arise out of the same concern. What difference does Christ's presence make for us? Is Christ's presence a threat that sends us searching inside ourselves to see if we are worthy? Is Christ's presence so massive that, to use Melanchthon's phrase, he gets trapped in the bread and cannot get out? Or is Christ's presence so ephemeral that we can treat the elements as if he had never shown up at all?

In both instances the concordists' resolution of the matter reveals a remarkable characteristic of Lutheran teaching. What matters most to Lutherans is not so much setting up strict rules for celebrating the sacrament (protecting it from the unworthy or keeping crumbs off the floor) as it is seeing that God's promise achieves its goal: strengthening the weak through Christ's real (not magical or imagined) presence. In other words, the practical, pastoral issues matter as much as the doctrinal. The concordists admonish us that if our doctrine and practice manage to leave false impressions in the minds of the faithful, then we should change them. The point is always to deliver the goods to those who need them most (the weak), not simply getting the rite doctrinally or liturgically right.

Comments on the Text of the Solid Declaration

These two disputes (especially the second) are touched on only tangentially in the Epitome. To see best how the concordists handled them, it is necessary to examine two texts in the Solid Declaration, article 7, especially paragraphs 60-72 (for the worthy and unworthy) and 73-90 (for the consecrated elements).

The Worthy Are the Unworthy!

The pastoral heart of the concordists' answer to the first question becomes especially clear in paragraphs 68-70. First, they provide what we might term a textbook definition of unworthy communicants. "It is essential to explain with great diligence who the unworthy guests at this Supper are, namely, those who go to the sacrament without true contrition or sorrow over their sins and without true faith or the good intention to improve their lives. With their unworthy eating of Christ's body they bring down judgment upon themselves, that is, temporal and eternal punishments, and they become guilty of Christ's body and blood" (SD VII.68, in *BC 2000*, 605). With as strict a definition as this, all communicants should be shivering in their boots! The definition indicates where the pastoral problem will arise. It is a bitter irony that weak souls, when confronted with these strictures (true sorrow, true faith, and good intentions), will immediately count themselves unworthy, while those who consider themselves strong (perhaps the greatest folly of all) will assume they are worthy. Perhaps that nonagenarian who clasped her hand to her mouth was just a serious reader of the Formula!

However, to appreciate what the writers are up to, we need to examine "the rest of the story" — in this case the next three paragraphs. Here it becomes clear that *precisely* the weak, who are most likely to count themselves among the unworthy, are the "worthiest" of all. Instead of taking the legalist's path and defining worthy communicants as those with true sorrow, true faith, and good intentions — which is what one would expect, given paragraph 68 — the concordists take a different, more pastoral route.

> The true and worthy guests, for whom this precious sacrament above all was instituted and established, are the Christians who are weak in faith, fragile and troubled, who are terrified in their hearts by the immensity and number of their sins *and think that they are not worthy* of this precious treasure and of the benefits of Christ because of their great impurity, who feel the weakness of their faith and deplore it, and who desire with all their heart to serve God with a stronger, more resolute faith and purer obedience. (SD VII.69, in *BC 2000*, 605, emphasis added)

There it is! The worthy are the unworthy — that is, those who sense that they are unworthy. Perhaps Chaplain Mart would have done well to read this paragraph to that poor soul — and, in one way, he did! He put his hand on her head — Lutheranism is always such a physical thing — and announced to her the entire forgiveness of all her sins. Nothing works better. Nowadays the unworthy — those burdened by guilt or shame (for example, the recently divorced) — may excommunicate themselves from the Supper by staying home. Perhaps for them we need to include in our "inactive members calling kit" the Lord's Supper, and since their guilt often precludes them coming to us, we should take the reconciling news of God's grace to them visibly in the Supper.

Just to show how serious they are about the gospel and how convinced they are that the gospel of inclusion trumps our laws of exclusion, the concordists then add (in par. 70) quotations from the Gospels and Paul: "Come to me, all you that are weary!" (Matt. 11:28); "Those who are well have no need of a physician, but those who are sick" (Matt.

9:12); "God's power is made mighty in the weak" (2 Cor. 12:9, Luther's translation); and "Welcome those who are weak in faith" (Rom. 14:1; cf. v. 3). The climax comes with the citation and gloss on the gospel in a nutshell, John 3:16: "For 'whoever believes in the Son of God,' whether weak or strong in faith, 'has eternal life'" (SD VII.70, in *BC 2000*, 606).

As if that were not enough, they aim one parting shot at those legalists who exclude the weak by their (correct!) preaching and teaching about human worthiness. "This worthiness consists not in a greater or lesser weakness or strength of faith, but rather in the merit of Christ, which the troubled father with his weak faith (Mark 9[:24]) possessed, just as did Abraham, Paul, and others who have a resolute, strong faith" (SD VII.71, in *BC 2000*, 606). We do not make ourselves worthy at all! Christ does. Now everything is turned on its head, and the good news of a communion table open to all the weak triumphs over all attempts to fence the table to include only the strong and to exclude those who need the Great Physician's "medicine of immortality." No wonder one of Luther and Melanchthon's favorite verses in the Bible was the one to which the concordists' refer here, Mark 9:24: "I believe; help my unbelief!"

The Consecration

The question of the duration of Christ's presence in the Lord's Supper occupies the Solid Declaration in paragraphs 73-90. At first reading it may appear that Chytraeus, the major contributor to this section, tended to take more from Melanchthon's view (Christ is not trapped in the bread) than from Luther's (Christ is not more absent than present during his meal). Several comments, however, reveal just how broadminded and careful the concordists really were. All along the way they provide insight into how we might regard our celebrations today.

"No human words or works create the true presence of Christ's body and blood in the Supper, whether it be the merit or the speaking of the minister or the eating and drinking or the faith of the communicants. Instead, all this should be ascribed solely to the almighty power of God and to the words, institution, and arrangement of our Lord Jesus Christ" (SD VII.74, in *BC 2000*, 606). No surprise here! The concordists refuse to let any "works righteousness" creep into this meal. Yet, how often do people not imagine that the holiness of pastors affects their office in the church! I remember the intern who called me when her supervisor had abandoned spouse and congregation for another woman, and people were inquiring whether their children needed to be rebaptized. The specter of Donatism (an ancient heresy that insisted that the holiness of the minister determined the holiness of the sacraments) continues to haunt churchgoing folk in the United States of America. When it comes to the Supper (or baptism, for that matter), what matters is God's power and promise, not our sin or weakness.

Notice, too, that the Formula refuses to make the Words of Institution into a magic formula. The concordists do not simply say "words," but "words, institution, and arrangement" — a point on which they then expand. When the presider recounts the words of Christ's institution, it is not he or she who makes them effective. Instead, Christ's Word alone continues to sound forth from that first Supper right down to our tables today. For good measure, the writers include a long quote from Chrysostom, the fourth-century bishop in Antioch and Constantinople, who compares Christ's Words of Institution ("This is my body") to God's command at creation ("Be fruitful and multiply"). According to him, Christ's words "are powerful and do their work in our day and until his return, so that in the Supper as celebrated in the church his true body and blood are present" (SD VII.76, in *BC 2000*, 606, citing John Chrysostom, *De proditione Iudae* 1.6). For good measure they also quote Luther to the same effect (SD VII.77-78, in *BC 2000*, 607).

But why such an emphasis on the Words of Institution? By their single-minded concentration on those words, some have, practically speaking, turned them into a special, magical formula that excludes all other prayers, songs, or preparations. That was hardly the concordists' intention. Instead, they give three reasons why these words are so important, all of which relate to — you guessed it — pastoral care. First, we use these words according to Christ's command, "Do this." The congregants need not worry that this might be the pastor's invention; it is *Christ's* institution (SD VII.80, in *BC 2000*, 607). Second, these words are not an incantation but are used instead "so that Christ's words will arouse, strengthen, and confirm the hearers' faith in the nature and benefits of this sacrament" (SD VII.81, in *BC 2000*, 607), namely, Christ's presence for forgiveness.

Finally, these words sanctify and consecrate the bread and wine to be offered as Christ's body and blood. Yet, this is not simply a matter of some narrow construal of these words. Rather, Chytraeus immediately puts them in the wider context of the entire celebration, or action, of the Supper. Quoting from the so-called Wismar Agreement, which he wrote in the controversy with Saliger, he applies the results of the much earlier Eisleben controversy to his own situation. Saying these words, say, over a bakery truck would not somehow create an entire van filled with Christ's body. The point of the sacrament is not to trap Christ in the bread and then carry him around in procession or stick him in a monstrance. "On the contrary, Christ's command, 'Do this,' must be observed without division or confusion. For it includes the entire action or administration of this sacrament: that in a Christian assembly bread and wine are taken, consecrated, distributed, received, eaten, and drunk, and that thereby the Lord's death is proclaimed" (SD VII.84, in *BC 2000*, 607).

Note the order: taken (to the altar or by the presider), consecrated with words spoken or sung, distributed to the guests, and finally received, eaten, and drunk by them. Here Luther's suggestion that Christ remains throughout the meal comes to expression, but not against the Zwinglians, as Luther had intended it, but "against papistic abuses," as Chytraeus felt he had encountered them (SD VII.87, in *BC 2000*, 608). Yet, Chytraeus was not ignorant of the abuse to which the other side could put this rule, "interpreting it so as to deny the true, essential presence and the oral partaking of Christ's body" (SD VII.88, in *BC 2000*, 608). These opponents had reduced the action to a person's faith, claiming that Christ was present with the bread and wine only for those with true faith. Against this position, Chytraeus thunders, "Faith does not make the sacrament, but only the true Word and institution of our almighty God and Savior Jesus Christ, which Word is always powerful and remains efficacious in Christendom" (SD VII.89, in *BC 2000*, 608). Just as with the gospel itself, which is heard by believers and godless alike, the minister's worthiness and the recipients' faith make no difference for the Supper's validity. What comfort to know, when receiving the Sacrament, that what matters is what rings in our ears and is placed in our mouth and on our lips: "The body of Christ, given for you"; "the blood of Christ, shed for you." Christ alone is our worthiness.

A Formula for Parish Practice

Once again the concordists succeed in opening up the Supper and placing it on our tongues and in our hearts. What spiritual revival ensues when these pastoral concerns uncover the heart of this sacrament in our congregations! Suddenly, Sunday worship becomes the weak person's weekly encounter with our Savior, who strengthens us with his presence and excludes no one. Then there would be no more clasping of hand to mouth or self-excommunication by staying home, but a joyful coming to the table. In Luther's words, people "would come on their own, rushing and running to it; they would compel themselves to come and would insist that you [pastors] give them the sacrament" (SC, Preface, 23, in *BC 2000*, 351). What more could sinners, the tired, the oppressed, the broken, the grieving, want than this gracious encounter with their Savior and Liberator?

What would happen, too, if everything we did in our regular celebration of the Supper glorified the One who was born in Bethlehem to the song of angels, who, as in his triumphal entry into Jerusalem, comes in the name of the Lord, to whom the seraphim still sing, "Holy, holy, holy," and who is the Lamb of God who takes away the sin of the world (including the weak in our midst)? As Luther and these early Lutherans knew well, the traditional parts of the Western liturgy, which had been left to the people (later sung aloud by the choir), called believers' attention to Christ's real, saving presence in the Supper. The Gloria in Excelsis begins with the angels' song to shepherds in the fields: "To you is born a savior." And *that* savior comes in this meal. The Sanctus connects Isaiah's vision of God in the temple to the joyful hosannas of the Palm Sunday crowd. Thus, the liturgy places on our lips the confession of Christ's presence. Here, heaven comes down to earth; Christ comes "humble," not mounted on a donkey, but in the lowly forms of bread and wine. Then, as we prepare to approach this mystery (mystery, mind you, not a potluck dinner), we sing the words of John the Baptist, chief preacher of the gospel: "Look, the Lamb of God who takes away the sin of the world!" And we combine his proclamation with the words of every suppliant at Jesus' feet, from the blind Bartimaeus (Mark 10:46-52) to the Syrophoenician woman (Mark 7:24-30): "Have mercy!" (as in the Kyrie Eleison [Lord, have mercy]) and "Grant peace." Once again, the very heart of the congregation's gathering echoes the testimony of the Formula of Concord. "Here is Christ for us!"

DISCUSSION QUESTIONS

Many practical questions revolve around the Lord's Supper. Here are some issues that may merit consideration.

▸ How frequently should we receive the sacrament? How do questions of worthiness factor in? What other issues may be important to consider?

▸ In some services when the Lord's Supper is celebrated — at weddings, first communions, confirmations, and funerals, for example — we offer it to all but treat some as special. In your experience, has anyone been treated as special at the Lord's table? What are the issues involved in knowing what to do in such situations?

▸ In Luther's day, people were especially sensitive to processions with the Lord's Supper, although a few still carried the Supper to the sick. How does your congregation treat the communion of the homebound? What might help reinforce a healthy understanding of the Lord's Supper?

▸ The benefit of the sacrament is not dependent on the quality of the one leading the celebration. Are any criteria appropriate for the one who presides?

▸ Communion is administered with a single chalice and wafers, but also with different cups, different kinds of wine or grape juice, and different kinds of bread. Does all this variety enhance or detract from the gift of Christ in the sacrament? Does it reflect the concern for quality pastoral care?

Article Eight

God Suffers in the Flesh for Us

She seemed young and helpless, this separated mother of four. I had first met her when she and her husband approached me about baptizing their second child. Despite an invitation to join the congregation, they declined and soon moved to another community. But now, years later, she was back with an agonizing story of abuse, abandonment, debt, an eating disorder, and despair. She had the requisite professionals to help her: physician, social worker, counselor, and lawyer. What she wanted to know from me came at the end of her tale of woe: "Pastor, does God still love me?"

What can anyone say to someone who in her own hopeless life is living out Psalm 22, "My God, my God, why have you forsaken me?" Whatever else one may say, there is finally only the remarkable paradox that the God to whom we pray has also prayed that psalm and suffered with us and for us in the flesh. In Christ there is no level at which God does not know and bear our infirmities. In fact, deeply hidden in, with, and under her calamities and ours is the crucified God.

The eighth article of the Formula of Concord, on the person of Christ, while sparked by the controversy over the Lord's Supper, presents for Lutherans in radical language uncharacteristic of the concordists the amazing paradox of God in flesh and blood. As such, it may help not only those whose lives are laments but also the entire church to reground their lives in the wonder of the incarnation: the Word made flesh.

History

The question of who Jesus is has been with Christians from the beginning. According to Mark's Gospel (8:27-30), it stretches back to Jesus' question to the disciples on the road to Caesarea Philippi. Fights over this question also stretch back to the earliest church, so that in 1 John 4:2-3 we read, "By this you know the Spirit of God: every spirit that confesses that Jesus Christ has come in the flesh is from God, and every spirit that does not confess Jesus is not from God."

Even the greatest monument to common Christian confession, the Nicene Creed, was born in controversy and did not finally resolve the question. In part this is because the question stretches the very limits of human language and thought, as we gaze on the mystery of the Word become flesh. In part this question — "But who do you say that I am?" — dare not go away. It is the heart of the Christian faith, extending from Peter on the road ("You are the Messiah!") to the centurion at the cross ("Truly this man was God's Son!") to us. As the French church historian Charles Kannengiesser once remarked, the church is not fully alive unless being forced to confess (and debate) Christology, the nature of Christ's person.

In that light, the sixteenth century was a lively time for the church. Already early in the Lord's Supper controversy between Luther and Zwingli, the question of Christology arose. If Christ in his humanity has ascended to the right hand of God, as confessed in the creed (cf. Col. 3:1), he cannot be truly present in the Lord's Supper, so the argument ran. Luther responded on two levels. First, he demonstrated that in Scripture the designation "God's right hand" is not a place but a metaphor for God's power. (Later the Lutheran theologian John Brenz tried to show the absurdity of such a Zwinglian view of the ascension by calculating how fast Jesus' body could have traveled, arguing that in 1,500 years he still would not have reached heaven.) It was never really clear to Luther how one should speak of God as occupying space and time, as human beings do.

Second, Luther insisted on the fundamental unity of the human and divine natures in the one person of Christ. The humanity and divinity of Christ are so united in the one person of Christ that wherever Christ's divinity is, we encounter Christ's humanity. For Luther this second point was not only a matter of theological speculation. The incarnation, that is, the coming of God into the flesh, was the human be-ing's best protection against encountering the "naked God" *(nudus Deus)*, that is, God's naked power and judgment. God comes in weak-ness so that we need not fear. Any encounter of the divinity without Christ's humanity spelled certain destruction.

Moreover, both Luther and Melanchthon suspected that Zwingli was guilty of Arianism because of his dependence on the Dutch hu-manist Erasmus of Rotterdam. Arius was a priest in Alexandria, Egypt, during the fourth century who had taught that God the Father was the source of all life, even that of God the Son, so that, in Arius's words, "There was [a point] when he [the Son] was not." To counter this heresy the Nicene Creed took shape, confessing Jesus Christ as "true God from true God" and "of one Being with the Father." Over against what they saw as a denigration of Christ's divinity, Luther (and to a lesser degree Melanchthon) developed the doctrine of the *communicatio idiomatum* (the communication of attributes or charac-teristics from one nature of Christ to the other). Thus, an attribute of Christ's divinity (for example, omnipresence) is shared with Christ's humanity, in such a way that Christians encounter the whole Christ in the Lord's Supper.

When the Lord's Supper controversy heated up again in the 1550s and 1560s, the christological question quickly bubbled to the surface. Part of the problem had to do with Melanchthon's later understanding of Christ's presence in the Supper. Whereas Luther could state "that the bread and the wine in the Supper are the true body and blood of Christ" (SA III.6.1, in *BC 2000*, 320), Melanchthon preferred to stick more closely to the biblical expression in 1 Corinthians 10:16, that the cup is "a sharing [*koinonia*] in the blood of Christ" and the bread "a sharing [*koinonia*] in the body of Christ." Even more importantly, Melanchthon did not approve of certain ways in which his contempo-raries were using the communication of attributes. It sounded to him like a mixing of the two natures, so that Christ's humanity seemed dif-fused throughout the universe; he preferred a more dialectical (linguis-tic) interpretation of the term.

Even Lutherans who disagreed with the crypto-Philippists (see article 7, part 1) had reservations about how to use the communication of attributes. Of course, those who held to a spiritualized presence of Christ in the sacrament objected both to the notion of Christ's humanity being present in the bread and wine and to any real communication of attributes between the two natures. For them the term was simply a linguistic turn of phrase, because any real communication of attributes implied the ancient heresy of Eutyches, the fifth-century priest of Constantinople who mixed the two natures of Christ to such a degree that his opponents thought the humanity simply dissolved into the divinity.

As the concordists worked on the Formula of Concord, there was some initial hesitation about whether to discuss Christology at all. However, two of the authors (Jakob Andreae and Martin Chemnitz) had already written extensively on the communication of attributes and the unity of the two natures in the one person of Christ. Thus, it seemed natural to them to include an article on this topic. As they examined the teachings of the crypto-Philippists, they discovered there such a separation of the two natures in Christ that they accused their opponents of repristinating the ancient heresy of Nestorius. (That patriarch of Constantinople in the fifth century held that the two natures were conjoined but not united in Christ's person.) They also realized that they needed to avoid certain interpretations of the communication of attributes that seemed to turn Christ's humanity into a kind of diffused gas spread throughout the universe.

In particular, Chemnitz distinguished three principles of sharing Christ's divinity and humanity. First is the principle of attributes, which holds that attributes of either nature are in fact shared in the one person of Christ. Everyone in these disputes agreed with this. Second is the principle of actions within Christ's office, where some things may be attributed to Christ's divine nature (for example, miracles) and other things to his human nature (for example, touching). Here again the disputants were in agreement. Third, however, is the principle of majesty, which holds that within the personal union the divine nature shares its characteristics (especially omnipresence) with the human nature. This, of course, was the heart of the dispute. Underlying this claim, however, is the remarkable theological principle that in Jesus Christ (and, by extension, in the bread and wine) the finite bears the infinite. The union between the humanity and divinity of Christ is not an imaginary one but a real one, just as Christ's presence in the Lord's Supper is not simply metaphorical or theoretical but real.

The Heart of the Matter

Christology, study of the person of Christ, must navigate between two extremes. On the one hand, some have emphasized the unity of the humanity and divinity of Christ in such a way that the divinity overwhelms the humanity and simply absorbs it into the divine nature. On the other hand, efforts to take seriously the two natures of Christ — human and divine — have led to such a separation between them that, as the Formula says, they are not much more than two boards stuck together with nothing in common.

Luther, Melanchthon, and their supporters emphasized and reinvigorated an ancient formula that the two natures, while remaining distinct, share intimately their characteristics by a "communication of attributes" *(communicatio idiomatum)*. When Christians confess that Christ is one person, they do not mean it abstractly or theoretically, but in reality. Thus, this "communication" is not simply a linguistic trick — where we *say* the one nature shares with the other, when in fact they do not. Instead, it is a reality that reflects the mystery of the incarnation: "The Word became flesh."

The reason for this insistence is not however just for the sake of "pure teaching" *(reine Lehre)*. It makes a tremendous difference for every aspect of pastoral care and ministry. It means that we receive Christ's body and blood in the Lord's Supper, and not just his divinity or spirit. As close as the bread comes to our teeth and the wine to our tongue, so close is the whole Christ present for us. Because of the communication of attributes, we can also know for certain that in our suffering the God to whom we pray knows our anguish, even our death, intimately. This is no mere theoretical matter for God. Christ's suffering on the cross means that God suffered. In a world filled with sin, evil, death, and oppression, there is no greater, better news. Some theologians talk about "God's preferential option for the poor," but in some ways this does not go far enough! God does not just prefer the poor; God became poor for us (2 Cor. 8:9). God does not just *prefer* those who suffer, who are weak, who are dying; God suffered, became weak, and died for them and us.

Article Eight

The Text of the Epitome

Concerning the Person of Christ

[1] Out of the controversy regarding the Holy Supper there arose a disagreement between the theologians of the Augsburg Confession who teach purely and the Calvinists (who also led some other theologians astray) over the person of Christ, the two natures in Christ, and their characteristics.

Status controversiae

Chief Issues of Disagreement in This Dispute

[2] The chief question was whether on the basis of the personal union the divine and human natures — and likewise the characteristics of each — are intimately linked with each other within the person of Christ, in reality (that is, in fact and in truth), and to what extent they are intimately linked?

[3] The sacramentarians contended that the divine and human natures are united in the one person in such a way that neither nature in reality (that is, in fact and in truth) shares with the other what is unique to that nature. Instead, they have only the name in common. For they say that *unio* simply "causes the names to be held in common," that is, the personal union results in nothing more than the sharing of their names. That is to say, God is called a human being and the human being God. In other words, they claim that God has nothing to do with humanity, and humanity has nothing to do with the divinity or with its majesty and characteristics in reality (that is, in fact and in truth). Dr. Luther and those who supported him defended the opposite position against the sacramentarians.

Affirmative Theses

> The Pure Teaching of the Christian Church
> on the Person of Christ

[4] To explain and settle this dispute according to the guidance of our Christian faith, we teach, believe, and confess the following:

[5] 1. That the divine and human natures in Christ are personally united, and therefore, that there are not two Christs (one the Son of God and the other

142

the Son of Man), but one single Son of God and Son of Man (Luke 1[:31-35]; Rom. 9[:5]).

[6] 2. We believe, teach, and confess that the divine and human natures are not blended together into one essence. Neither is one transformed into the other. Rather, each retains its own essential characteristics, which never become the characteristics of the other nature.

[7] 3. The characteristics of the divine nature are: that it is almighty, eternal, infinite, present everywhere (according to the characteristics of the nature and its natural essence, in and of itself), all-knowing, etc. These never become the characteristics of the human nature.

[8] 4. The characteristics of the human nature are: being a bodily creature, being flesh and blood, being finite and circumscribed, suffering, dying, ascending, descending, moving from one place to another, suffering from hunger, thirst, cold, heat, and the like. These never become characteristics of the divine nature.

[9] 5. Since both natures are personally united (that is, united in one person), we believe, teach, and confess that this union is not a connection or association of the sort that neither nature shares things with the other personally (that is, because of the personal union), as if two boards were glued together, with neither giving the other anything or receiving anything from the other. Instead, here is the most complete Communion, which God truly has with this human being; out of this personal union and out of the most complete and most indescribable communion that results from it flows everything human that can be ascribed to and believed about God and everything divine that can be ascribed to and believed about the human Christ. The ancient teachers of the church have explained this union and communion of the natures using similes of a glowing iron and of the union of body and soul in the human being.

[10] 6. Therefore, we believe, teach, and confess that God is a human being and a human being is God. That could not be if the divine and human natures had absolutely no communion with each other in fact and in truth. [11] For how could the human being, Mary's son, be called, or be, the Son of the most high God in truth if his humanity was not personally united with God's Son, in reality, that is in fact and in truth, but instead shared only the name "God" with him?

[12] 7. Therefore, we believe, teach, and confess that Mary did not conceive and give birth to a child who was merely, purely, simply human, but she gave birth to the true Son of God. Therefore, she is rightly called and truly is the Mother of God.

[13] 8. Therefore, we also believe, teach, and confess that no mere human being suffered, died, was buried, descended into hell, rose from the dead, ascended into heaven, and was exalted to the majesty and almighty power of God for us, but rather it was a human being whose human nature has such a profound, indescribable union and communion with the Son of God, that this human nature is one person with the Son of God.

[14] 9. Thus, the Son of God truly suffered for us — to be sure, according to the characteristics of the human nature, which he had assumed into the unity of his divine person and made his own, so that he could suffer and be our high priest for our reconciliation with God, as it is written, "They crucified the Lord of glory," and, "With God's blood we have been redeemed" (1 Cor. 2[:8]; Acts 20[:28]).

[15] 10. Therefore, we believe, teach, and confess that the Son of Man in reality, that is, in fact and in truth, was exalted to the right hand of the almighty majesty and power of God according to his human nature, because he was assumed into God, when he was conceived by the Holy Spirit in the womb of his mother and was personally united with the Son of the Almighty.

[16] 11. According to the personal union he always possessed this majesty, and yet dispensed with it in the state of his humiliation. For this reason he grew in stature, wisdom, and grace before God and other people [Luke 2:52]. Therefore, he did not reveal his majesty at all times but only when it pleased him, until he completely laid aside the form of a servant [Phil. 2:7] (but not his human nature) after his resurrection. Then he was again invested with the full use, revelation, and demonstration of his divine majesty and entered into his glory, in such a way that he knows everything, is able to do everything, is present for all his creatures, and has under his feet and in his hands all that is in heaven, on earth, and under the earth, not only as God but also as human creature, as he himself testifies, "All authority in heaven and on earth has been given to me" [Matt. 28:18], and St. Paul writes: He ascended "above all the heavens, so that he might fill all things" [Eph. 4:10]. As present everywhere he can exercise this power of his, he can do everything, and he knows all things.

[17] 12. Therefore, he is able — it is very easy for him — to share his true body and blood, present in the Holy Supper, not according to the manner or characteristic of the human nature, but according to the manner and characteristic of God's right hand, as Dr. Luther says in [his explanation of] our Christian creed. This presence is not an earthly nor a Capernaitic presence, but at the same time it is a true and essential presence, as the words of his testament say, "This is, is, my body," etc.

[18] Through this our teaching, faith, and confession the person of Christ is not divided, as Nestorius did. (He denied the *communicatio idiomatum,* that is, the true communion of the characteristics of the two natures in Christ, and thus divided his person, as Luther explains in his book *On the Councils and the Church.*) Nor are the natures with their characteristics mixed together with each other into one essence, as Eutyches falsely taught. Nor is the human nature denied or destroyed in the person of Christ, and neither nature is transformed into the other. Rather, Christ is and remains for all eternity God and human being in one inseparable person, which is the highest mystery after the mystery of the Holy Trinity, as the Apostle testifies [1 Tim. 3:16]. In this mystery lie our only comfort, life, and salvation.

Negative Theses

Contrary False Teaching concerning the Person of Christ

[19] Accordingly, we reject and condemn the following erroneous articles as contrary to God's Word and our simple Christian creed, when it is taught:

[20] 1. That God and the human being in Christ are not one person, but there is one person, the Son of God, and another person, the Son of Man, as Nestorius foolishly asserted.

[21] 2. That the divine and human natures are mixed together with each other into one essence and that the human nature is transformed into divinity, as Eutyches fantasized.

[22] 3. That Christ is not true, natural, and eternal God, as Arius held.

[23] 4. That Christ did not have a true human nature, with body and soul, as Marcion contrived.

[24] 5. That the personal union creates only common titles or names.

[25] 6. That it is only an expression or *modus loquendi,* that is, only a matter of words or a way of speaking, when it is said: God is a human being, a human being is God; for the deity has nothing in common with the humanity, and the humanity nothing with the deity in reality, that is, in fact.

[26] 7. That it is merely a *communicatio verbalis,* that is, nothing more than a figure of speech, when it is said that the Son of God died for the sins of the world or that the Son of Man has become almighty.

[27] 8. That the human nature in Christ became an infinite essence in a manner like that of the deity and is present everywhere in the same way the divine nature is present, on the basis of some sort of essential, shared power and characteristic, which has been separated from God and poured out into the human nature.

[28] 9. That the human nature has been made the same as the divine nature in its substance and essence or in its essential attributes and has become equal with it.

[29] 10. That the human nature of Christ is spatially extended into all parts of heaven and earth (an idea that should not be applied to the divine nature either).

[30] 11. That it is impossible for Christ, because of the characteristics of the human nature, to be in more than one place at the same time — much less to be bodily present in all places.

[31] 12. That only the mere humanity suffered for us and redeemed us, and that the Son of God in fact had no communion with the humanity in the suffering, as if it had not affected him at all.

[32] 13. That Christ is present with us on earth in Word, in the sacraments, and in all times of need only according to his deity, and that such presence has absolutely nothing to do with his human nature; and that after he redeemed us through his suffering and death, he has nothing more to do with us on earth according to the human nature.

[33] 14. That the Son of God, who assumed the human nature, after he laid aside the form of a servant does not perform all the works of his omnipotence in, through, and with his human nature, but only a few and exclusively in the place in which his human nature is spatially present.

[34] 15. That he is not at all capable of exercising his omnipotence and other characteristics of his divine nature according to his human nature, contrary to the express words of Christ, "All authority in heaven and on earth has been given to me" [Matt. 28:18], and St. Paul: "In him the whole fullness of deity dwells bodily" (Col. 2[:9]).

[35] 16. That to him [Christ] has indeed been given greater power in heaven and on earth, that is, greater and more than all angels and other creatures, but he does not share in the omnipotence of God; moreover, such divine power has not been given to him. In this way they invent a *media potentia*, that is, a kind of power between God's almighty power and the power of other creatures, which is given to Christ according to his humanity through the exaltation, and which is less than God's almighty power and greater than the power of other creatures.

[36] 17. That according to his human spirit Christ has a fixed limit on how much he can know, and that he cannot know more than is appropriate and necessary for him to know in the exercise of his office as judge.

[37] 18. That Christ does not yet have perfect knowledge of God and all his works, although it is, of course, written, that in him "are hidden all the treasures of the wisdom and knowledge" [Col. 2:3].

[38] 19. That it is impossible for Christ, according to his human spirit, to know what has existed from eternity, what is happening at the present time everywhere in the world, and what will be in the future in eternity.

[39] 20. When anyone teaches and so interprets and blasphemously perverts the passage in Matthew 28[:18] ("All authority . . . has been given to me") that in the resurrection and his ascension all power in heaven and on earth was restored or again returned to Christ according to the divine nature — as though in the state of humiliation he had laid it aside and forsaken it even according to his deity.

Such teaching not only perverts the word of Christ's testament but prepares the way for the return of the accursed Arian heresy, that finally denies the eternal divinity of Christ. In this way Christ is completely lost, along with our salvation, if such false teaching is not contradicted on the basis of the firm foundation of God's Word and our simple Christian creed.

Article Eight

Commentary

The Controversial Issue (pp. 508-9)

Paragraph 1. The reason this question even arose has to do exclusively with the controversy over the Lord's Supper. Otherwise, Lutherans are content to confess with the ancient councils concerning the natures of Christ. Here they name the culprits "Calvinists," although the actual opponents could hardly be called followers of the Genevan reformer, since they disagreed on questions of election, free will, and many other things. In fact, even Calvin's understanding of the Lord's Supper differs from the position the concordists are attacking.

Paragraph 2. Here the concordists lay out two problems: whether the characteristics of each nature are intimately linked in reality (that is, in fact and in truth), and to what extent. The Latin word *realiter,* "in reality," receives the German gloss "in fact and in truth" to make clear that the kind of communication being described is not merely a linguistic trick for making paradoxical statements. The addition of the second question, "to what extent," indicates that the concordists will try to exclude any and all christological heresies, especially the charge of mixing the two natures, as Eutyches had.

Paragraph 3. Here the concordists express their fears regarding the linguistic claims of the "sacramentarians," as they prefer to call their opponents, the crypto-Philippists. If *"communicatio idiomatum"* is merely a theological play on words, then what does this imply for the union of Christ's natures? What difference does it make merely to *call* Christ human and divine in one person, if there is no true union. Here, almost unlike any other article in the Formula, the concordists do not pretend to stake out a middle ground. Instead, they make clear that they stand with "Dr. Luther" and opposite the "sacramentarians."

Affirmative Theses (pp. 509-12)

Paragraphs 4-8. The first thing the concordists address is the serious charge that their position implies that the two natures are blended in the one person of Christ. All sides recognized this as a heresy. There is, first of all, a single person of Christ (par. 5). However, these natures are

148

not blended together, nor is one transformed into the other (par. 6). One cannot say that Jesus Christ "used to be" truly human but now is some sort of divine figure. He was and is 100 percent human being and 100 percent divine. The uniqueness of each nature is spelled out more fully in paragraphs 7-8. However much one nature may communicate its characteristics to the other, those characteristics never become the properties of the other nature. Of course, here we find ourselves on the edge of the mystery of the Christian gospel itself.

Paragraph 9. Here Andreae summarizes the heart of the matter in positive terms. The union of the two natures is not a matter of plywood: two boards glued together with nothing in common. "Instead, here is the most complete Communion, which God truly has with this human being." To this union everything ascribed to the human being, including suffering and dying, can be ascribed to God, and vice versa. Rather than invent their own analogies for this union, the concordists stick with traditional ones: glowing iron and the unity of soul and body.

Paragraphs 10-14. In the following paragraphs they then fill out the implications for this kind of union "in fact and in truth." "God is a human being and a human being is God." Here the translator and editors of *BC 2000* reached the limits of their own desire to use inclusive language, rephrasing "Gott ist Mensch, und Mensch ist Gott" (old versions: "God is man, and man is God"). In a few cases in the sixteenth century, even German authors render the traditional Latin phrase, "God is *this* human being, and *this* human being is God." This is one of the most startling, stunning truths of the Christian faith. As the British theologian J. B. Phillips once wrote, "We live on a visited planet." Or, as the ancient church insisted and the concordists conclude (par. 12), Mary is not simply the bearer of Christ *(Christotokos)* but the bearer of God *(theotokos)*. Moreover, the suffering, death, and resurrection of Christ were not simply actions of a human being, but by an indescribable "union and communion" involved God (par. 13). Thus, Christ's suffering is, by the communication of attributes, "assumed into the unity of his divine person" (par. 14). Now we have an answer to the sufferer's question, "Does God still love me?" Yes, enough to die with you and for you.

Paragraphs 15-17. The final conclusions to the assertion in paragraph 9 move the Formula to the christological issue underneath the Lord's Supper controversy. First, the concordists explain that the claim of Christ's ascension, far from meaning that the humanity must be in some sense separated from the divinity in Christ, points, as the very metaphor of "God's right hand" implies, precisely to the place of God's majesty and power (par. 15). Second, although during his time on earth Christ "dispensed with" (laid aside) this majesty (Phil. 2:7), with the resurrection he picked it up again. When Jesus himself says in Matthew 28:18 that he has been given "*all* authority," and when Ephesians (4:10) says the purpose of his ascension is so that "he might fill *all* things," this means that Christ can truly live up to all his promises for us (par. 16). This includes showing up with his true body and blood in the Lord's Supper, not because of any human characteristic but precisely because of the characteristic of God's right hand (par. 17).

Paragraph 18. This final paragraph of the affirmative theses brings to light one of the most consistent aims of all Lutherans in the sixteenth century: to bear witness *with* the ancient church to the truth of the gospel. They refuse to divide the two natures, as Nestorius did, and they refuse to mix them destructively, as Eutyches did. Yet, their purpose for holding to this is not simply because of its truth as "the highest mystery after the mystery of the Holy Trinity," but, as the opening story indicates, because "In this mystery lie our only comfort, life, and salvation." God suffered and died with us and for us in the flesh!

Negative Theses (pp. 512-14)

Paragraphs 19-23. The opportunity to confess "our simple Christian creed" (par. 19) first gave the concordists leave to reject the pertinent heresies of the ancient church. Thus, they reject Nestorius's division of the two natures (par. 20), Eutyches's mixing of the two natures (par. 21), Arius's diminution of Christ's divinity (par. 22), and Marcion's rejection of Christ's humanity (par. 23). (Marcion, a second-century thinker, was associated with those who viewed Christ as little more than a spirit with a human appearance.) The concordists' view of church and theology was never limited to their own era and its problems, but encompassed all who confess Christ. Christians never graduate to a higher plane beyond their forebears in the faith, but always build on the ancient confessions to form their own.

Paragraphs 24-26. The concordists then hone in on the actual dispute and reject any notion that the union of Christ's natures is somehow just a matter of names (par. 24), wordplays (par. 25), or figures of speech (par. 26). This temptation to reduce things to words arises directly from our human hankering to control God and what God is capable of doing. Here, in Luther's words, human reason must be taken captive to Christ's word (LC, Lord's Supper, 12-14, in *BC 2000*, 468). At stake is our salvation. When we say the Son of God died for the sins of the world, we can really mean it!

Paragraphs 27-29. There were some Lutheran theologians (Tileman Hesshus being the most well-known) who, while not crypto-Philippists, nevertheless had grave misgivings about the use of the communication of attributes to explain Christ's presence in the Lord's Supper. To try to meet their objections (many of which Melanchthon had raised), the concordists included these three paragraphs. The human nature does not somehow become "an infinite essence" or, as I like to put it, a diffused gas spreading throughout the universe (par. 27). That is, the divine characteristic of ubiquity remains the divine nature's characteristic alone, even when shared with Christ's humanity. The human nature also does not become essentially divine (par. 28), nor does it extend spatially throughout the universe (par. 29). This last mischaracterization of Lutheran Christology misses the point by reducing even God's power and presence to mere human physics and geometry.

Paragraphs 30-32. These theses address the problem of the *extra Calvinisticum*, as it is sometimes called, inaccurately, by the way, since other theologians (including Zwingli and Albert Hardenberg) held this view and Calvin may not have. This was the notion that outside Christ's humanity, one could encounter Christ through his naked divinity. Paragraph 30 rejects the notion that the metaphor of God's right hand traps Christ's humanity some place in heaven. Paragraph 31 insists on a true union of divine and human natures in Christ so that not just the human nature suffered for us (a position held by Francesco Stancaro; see article 3). Finally, paragraph 32 takes aim directly at the notion of the *"extra"*: that outside of (Latin: *extra*) the humanity of Christ we can encounter his divinity. For Luther this was a terrifying thought, since it is precisely Christ's humanity that protects us from any encounter with God's naked power and wrath.

Paragraphs 33-38. Here the other chief objection to the implied Christology of the crypto-Philippists gets addressed. In Christ, God's humanity never acts outside the divinity (par. 33). The whole Christ truly has the authority claimed for him (par. 34), not just some part of Christ (the divine nature) that gets around better. Similarly, some sort of middle position — that allows Christ more power than human beings or angels but less power than God — fails to take this union seriously (par. 35). Thus, the concordists reject the notions that Christ now has limited knowledge of human affairs (par. 36), of God (par. 37), or of all times and places (par. 38). A crude analogy might be this: if you or I could scale the heavens in an attempt to take a picture of the second person of the Trinity, God the Son, we would be disappointed to find that Jesus always gets in the way.

Paragraph 39. After one last look at Matthew 28:18, in which the concordists reject any notion that the authority given back to Christ pertains to his divinity, they turn to the motivation behind their christological concerns. They refuse to back away from the central mystery and confession of the Christian faith throughout the ages: that Jesus Christ is truly divine and truly human *in one person.* Again, it is not simply doctrine that is at stake for them, but salvation itself. "In this way Christ is completely lost, along with our salvation, if such false teaching is not contradicted on the basis of the firm foundation of God's Word and our simple Christian creed."

A Formula for Parish Practice

On the day of my ordination my mother gave me a hug and told me, "When you preach, comfort the people." This very Lutheran attitude toward preaching the gospel — namely, to comfort the distressed — permeated the very heart and soul of the concordists' approach to Christology. All is truly lost when we lose a direct encounter with Christ, human and divine, in the manger, on the cross, at the resurrection, or in the Lord's Supper. Thus, this article of the Formula touches not only on preaching sermons filled with comfort for the terrified but also on seeing that every encounter with God's Word in the parish brings consolation. The question, "Pastor, does God still love me?" is on more lips and in more hearts than we may at first imagine.

At first blush, given our concentration on the important psychological tools for listening and understanding the human condition, it might seem surprising to claim that Christology could provide resources for pastoral care. However, the facts are that, as important as human resources can be for addressing human problems, pastoral problems also involve deep spiritual crises. The grieving child, the abused spouse, or the anxious parent can hear from Christians alone the comforting news of God in the flesh, suffering with us and for us. Even when we do not know or cannot fathom another's suffering (which is often the case), we do know the One who has suffered and does suffer, Jesus Christ crucified. No wonder the concordists, in one of their final recensions of the Solid Declaration, included these stirring words (par. 20 and 25, respectively, in *BC 2000, 619-20*).

> Because of this personal union . . . not only the bare human nature (which possesses the characteristics of suffering and dying) suffered for the sins of the entire world, but the Son of God himself suffered (according to the assumed human nature) and, according to our simple Christian creed, truly died — although the divine nature can neither suffer nor die.

> This [exercise of God's power] was true even in death, when he did not die merely as another human being but in such a way that by and in his death he overcame sin, death, the devil, hell, and eternal damnation, which the human nature alone would not have been able to do, had it not been united with the divine nature personally and had communion with it.

We can teach and learn no more comforting message from the Christian gospel than this!

DISCUSSION QUESTIONS

► "The finite bears the infinite." How might you use this truth of Christ's incarnation to provide comfort?
► Often we separate the comfort of the gospel message from the truths it contains. The concordists defend the *communicatio idiomatum* (communication of attributes). What does this mean, *and* how might it be good news for you?

Article Eight

▶ What does it mean to you that *God* died on the cross? How might you best communicate that good news to others?
▶ Were other aspects of this chapter news to you? If so, in what ways were they also good news?

154

Article Nine

Lutherans Don't Have All the Answers
(Just the One That Matters)

It happens to me all the time. I wander into an adult forum somewhere, and people immediately think I'm an expert. I throw around a few Latin or German phrases. Cite the Bible from memory. Rattle off a few dates and unfamiliar names. Then someone comes up to me and says, "I'm not sure about this. Can you tell me if I'm thinking right?" More often than not I succumb and tell the adoring listener what he or she ought to think. Would that I behaved more like a wise teacher I encountered as an undergraduate, studying for a year in Germany. A student asked him a question to which he did not know the answer, and he answered her, "Ich bin überfragt," literally, "I am overquestioned." Even in theology, despite the authorities of Scripture and tradition, we, too, may be "overquestioned." In theology, it is a gift of the Holy Spirit to admit it.

One of the problems facing teachers and pastors in the church is the widely held conviction that Christians (or at least pastors) ought to have all the answers. In public discourse and in internecine strife, Christians seem to know it all. Despite the fact that we know how frustrating it is in other parts of our lives when we encounter people who think they know everything, we seem unable to appreciate what a devastating effect our know-it-all attitude has on others inside or outside the church.

Now, often when Christians are faced with such self-assurance, they quickly race to the opposite extreme and proclaim that no one has any answers. Quite frankly, a know-nothing is scarcely better than a know-it-all. Moreover, this know-nothing position is tinged with a peculiar kind of know-it-all attitude. After all, we at least know for certain that no one has any answers! This attitude is also widespread in American churches, where we have learned the dangers of holding religious views publicly. By imagining that faith is a private matter, we consign all matters of faith to personal conjecture and consider it bad form when someone actually asserts some theological principle in the open.

Such commonly held views may explain why some people seem so doctrinaire: hanging on to religious positions with such tenacity and condemning opponents so harshly. People, especially religious people, feel a particular need to be sure. "Blessed assurance, Jesus is mine," the song goes, and it expresses the genuine desire for certainty — a desire many folks experience at some time in their religious life. It is easy to imagine Christian teaching as a precariously constructed house of cards: take out one support and the entire edifice comes crashing to the ground. Thus, if we do not know the right answer about one thing, it calls into question everything else we do know about a topic.

Into this predicament article 9 on Jesus' descent into hell comes as a breath of fresh air. Although by far the briefest article in the Formula of Concord, it contains within it one of the most helpful principles for theological conversations the church can have: there are limits to what we know and need to know in matters of theology. Therefore, sometimes we must own the mystery and concentrate instead on what really matters: Christ crucified and risen again.

History

There were actually several separate fights over Christ's descent into hell. The last, involving a criticism of the (Reformed) Heidelberg Catechism by the (Lutheran) clergy of the county of Mansfeld during the 1560s, linked this question to the Lord's Supper controversy and may explain how it ended up where it is in the Formula, immediately after articles 7 and 8. As with the ascension of Christ, Lutherans argued that we always encounter the whole Christ, even in the descent into hell. In this they rejected, as another example of importing Aristotle's philosophy into Christian theology, the Heidelberg Catechism's view that only

Christ's soul descended into hell. The Mansfeld theologians preferred putting up with the physical difficulty of having the whole Christ in two places at once (in the grave and in hell) to dividing the person of Christ. Let God figure out the geometry; our comfort is in the whole Christ's victory over all evil, even hell itself.

Melanchthon played an important mediating role in an earlier dispute, which broke out in the late 1540s in Hamburg. At first he was reticent to resolve controversy over this issue because already in 1531 he admitted that he did not understand certain biblical texts on this issue (1 Pet. 3:18ff. and 4:6) and that he and Luther disagreed with the interpretation of Wittenberg's pastor, Johannes Bugenhagen. In any event, already in June 1546 there were rumblings of a dispute, initially between the superintendent (bishop) of Hamburg's church, Johannes Aepinus, and a chaplain, Tilemann Epping.

Three years later, in 1549, the fight was still on. Melanchthon's responses allowed various positions to coexist. One side, led by Aepinus, taught that it was necessary to believe that Christ's soul separately suffered the pangs of hell. He argued that the creed did not mean (as Calvin had taught) that Christ suffered in hell before he died because the creed said, "He descended." It also did not mean (as Luther had taught) that Christ was victor, because of the phrase "into hell." Psalm 16:10 (Vulgate: "You will not leave my soul in hell") proved that Christ's soul suffered (our) punishment in hell.

The other side, represented not only by Epping but also by Johannes Garcaeus, pastor of Saint James Church in Hamburg, argued that although the phrase "he descended into hell" was not in the oldest versions of the creed, later versions nevertheless accepted the article. However, they argued that the phrase could still refer to Christ's suffering on the cross, since that suffering alone was sufficient for all, as noted in Philippians 2:8. Moreover, the phrase "he descended" did not exclude the possibility that he descended as victor either in his soul or, after the resurrection, in soul and body, to reveal to the souls there the truth about his incarnation and victory, as in 1 Peter. (In his account of the fight, Melanchthon also mentioned that Nicholas von Amsdorf "cut the Gordian knot" by observing that Scripture nowhere speaks of the separation of soul and body in either Christ or anyone else.)

Melanchthon's advice to the warring parties and to the Hamburg city council contained the kernel of the concordists' response. He noted the differences between Bugenhagen and Luther on Psalm 16 and other texts. He called this a dispute about "arcane matters" and urged that there be no public debate, since most people would not understand the sources. When Bugenhagen and Melanchthon wrote a joint letter to the city council in September 1550, they referred directly to Luther's comments about Christ's victory in his Genesis lectures and in his sermon at the Torgau Castle (see below), and again begged the two parties simply to avoid public dispute. Neither side should be forced to lose its ecclesiastical position over this matter, provided no one debated the issue in public. Similar disputes broke out later, first in Augsburg and then in Mecklenburg, but they never caught the imagination of other theologians and died down long before the writing of the Formula of Concord.

The Heart of the Matter

"He descended into hell" or (in the modern, more accurate rendering of the Latin) "He descended to the dead." Surely, something that ended up in our creed, that gets recited Sunday in and Sunday out, should not be up for grabs. Yet, there it is. The concordists refused to decide. They found Luther's comments sufficient and also admitted that there is no final answer to this theological issue. This article "cannot be comprehended by reason or understanding, but must be grasped alone by faith" (par. 2).

This phrase comes as close as the Formula can to expressing Luther's famous "theology of the cross." This theology, far from being a mere description or explanation of Christ's death on the cross (as its name seems to indicate), asserts that God is revealed "under the appearance of the opposite," that is, in the last place we would reasonably look. (See, especially, Luther's Heidelberg Disputation [*LW* 31:52-53] and his Explanation to the Ninety-five Theses [*LW* 31:125-30, 224-28].) This theology asserts that reason is not always a helper in theology but is many times the culprit. When we try to make up our own reasonable answers to such mysteries, the gospel itself suffers. Many years later the question of the millennium (Christ's 1,000-year reign on earth) arose for Lutherans in America. Leaders in the Iowa Synod, as it was then called, objected to other Lutherans' certainty that such a reign would not happen by arguing that some doctrines are "open questions" that do not require a final answer. This concept of open questions, based in part on this article in the Formula, later passed into the constitution of the original American Lutheran Church (1930-60).

Luther's Sermon

Along with the contrast of reason and faith comes the idea of simplicity. Thus, the concordists cite "Dr. Luther of blessed memory" because of his simple explanation from a series of catechetical sermons delivered in 1532 in Torgau and published the following year. "Christ descended into hell and destroyed hell for all believers," write the concordists in this article. This unabashedly warlike metaphor, which also figures in Luther's famous hymn "A Mighty Fortress," is simple even to the concordists' ears because they, too, recognized its picturesque nature. This childlike approach comes directly from Luther's sermon, which they refer to in this article and we quote here.

> The customary way of depicting how Christ descended into hell on church walls represents him with a cape and with banners in his hand as he makes his descent and stalks and assaults the devil, as he storms hell and rescues his own people from it. The children's play presented at Easter depicts it in a similar way. It seems better to me that you depict, act out, sing, and recite the story in a very simple way and let it remain at that and not concern yourself with sublime and precise ideas about how it actually took place. For it did not happen in a physical manner, since he indeed remained three days in the grave. (*Sources and Contexts,* 246)

In this sermon Luther showed his uncanny ability to focus on what matters, or rather, *who* matters. While other theologians fought over whether and how this descent took place, Luther allowed it to remain a "spiritual" picture and was far more concerned about what it communicated: Christ's victory over sin, death, and the power of the devil.

Luther's narrow focus may come as a surprise to us. In fact, today's churches are much more likely to debate whether a verse or teaching in the Bible is literal or figurative. Moreover, people on both sides of modern debates may agree that "literal" texts are more trustworthy than figurative ones. For Luther, such fights and worries miss the point. Whether the Bible uses figures or facts, parables, poems, or prose, the point of it all is the point God wants to make. Thus, Luther said, "For such paintings [of the descent into hell] show well how powerful and useful this article is, why it took place, why it is to be preached and believed that Christ destroyed hell's power and took all his power away from the devil" (*Sources and Contexts*, 247).

In a similar way we can view the story of creation as answering not *how* but *who* created the heavens and the earth. Those who read Genesis 1–2 literally will view the world as created in six twenty-four-hour days. Those who read the same text figuratively will not. However, when the former spend so much time defending their creationist theories or the latter spend so much time disparaging them, and when either group anathematizes the other, then everyone loses. The point of the creation stories is to confess, as we do in the creed, that *God* created heaven and earth and everything in them. Applying Luther's comments on Christ's descent into hell, we can say with him, "That I should be able to grasp how it actually happened in such a way that I can speak about it or perceive with my senses is far above what is possible in this life" (*Sources and Contexts*, 247). By his own admission, Luther dealt with these matters "because I see that the world still wants to be smart in the devil's name and to establish and master everything in the articles of faith according to its own head" (248).

What, then, really matters? For Luther it is Christ's resurrection, through which God assures us of victory over sin, death, and the devil. Thus, in the same sermon he reminded his listeners that "It is characteristic of a strong faith to make this article of faith strong and sure and to write these words, 'Christ is risen,' with large letters onto the heart and make them as large as heaven and earth. As a result, our hearts will be able to see, hear, think, and know nothing else than this article, as though there were nothing else written in all creation. Faith should submerge itself totally in this article and live from it alone, as St. Paul was accustomed to say; he was a true master at setting forth this article" (251). In this connection Luther and modern Christians may use the creed as a handy guide to where the truth lies. And Luther's explanation of the creed in the Small Catechism, which is an explanatory paraphrase, provides even more help in focusing the entire

Scripture on what matters: "I believe that God has created me. . . ." "I believe that Jesus Christ . . . is my LORD. . . ." "I believe that by my own understanding or strength I cannot believe in Jesus Christ . . . but instead the Holy Spirit has called me . . ." (SC, Creed, 2, 4, and 6, in *BC 2000*, 354-55).

Luther's single-minded approach to the descent into hell and Melanchthon's gentle admonitions to Hamburg's disputants demonstrated to his successors, including the concordists, how to approach the articles of Christian belief: not with reason, demanding explanations, but by faith alone. Later in the sermon Luther noted that the promise of our resurrection is equally beyond our senses and reason. "For we cannot have thoughts of anything else but death when we see a corpse lying there. . . . But when you grasp the word in faith, you get another point of view. It can see through this death into the resurrection and form nothing but thoughts and images of life" (*Sources and Contexts*, 253).

It is this article of faith — that Christ defeated the devil and rose from the dead — that makes all the difference for Christians. Thus, Luther concluded, "Where this article remains, everything remains. It grants us assurance, and in it we have the correct foundation for speaking about all other matters and living" (255). All of us have faced and will face the reality of death. Only in Christ's resurrection do we experience the promise of life thrown into death and evil's very face, so that we may come to trust in God.

The Text of the Epitome

Concerning Christ's Descent into Hell

Status controversiae

The Chief Issue regarding This Article

[1] Among some theologians committed to the Augsburg Confession there has been some dispute regarding this article: when and in what manner the Lord Christ descended into hell, according to our simple Christian creed, and whether it took place before or after his death. Also, whether he descended only in his soul, or only in his deity, or with body and soul, bodily

and spiritually. Also, whether this article of faith belongs to the suffering of Christ or to his glorious victory and triumph.

[2] Since this article, as is true of the previous article, cannot be comprehended by reason or understanding, but must be grasped alone by faith:

[3] It is our unanimous counsel that there should be no dispute over this issue but it should be believed and taught on the simplest level as Dr. Luther of blessed memory explained this article in a most Christian manner in his sermon at Torgau in 1533. There he cut off all unprofitable, unnecessary questions and admonished all godly Christians to a simple Christian faith.

[4] For it is enough that we know that Christ descended into hell and destroyed hell for all believers and that he redeemed them from the power of death, the devil, and the eternal damnation of hellish retribution. How that happened we should save for the next world, where not only this matter but many others, which here we have simply believed and cannot comprehend with our blind reason, will be revealed.

Commentary

Paragraph 1. Here the concordists sketch a few of the issues that had come up. When did Christ descend into hell, before or after his death? (The former position was that of John Calvin, among others.) Did the whole Christ descend or only those parts that get around faster? (Here there are echoes of the debate in article 8 over the relation of Christ's human to his divine nature.) Was this descent part of Christ's suffering for sin or victory over sin? (Here we can see echoes of the debate in Hamburg.)

Paragraph 2. Here is the key to this and all other disputes: faith alone. Reason always derails faith by seeking control, not understanding. We treat Christian doctrine rather as if it were Rumpelstiltskin's name: to know the gnome's name was to control him; to know the intricacies of Christian doctrine is to control the very mind of God!

Paragraph 3. Next to faith, the concordists cherish simplicity. Rather than looking for answers in the complexities of theology, they turn to a simple sermon, delivered for the Saxon court. That sermon itself, in its very refusal to speculate about Christ's descent into hell, shows us an entirely different way to do theology, as we have seen in the excerpts quoted above.

Paragraph 4. Here the concordists tip their hand, so to speak, and in fact eliminate certain answers to the questions in paragraph 1. Christ's descent was triumph over sin, not simply satisfaction for it. Our picture of the atonement (God in Christ reconciling the whole world to God) must be large enough to allow the richness of the biblical images to speak to us. Otherwise we wait for the last day, when we shall know even as we are known. That was what Melanchthon himself hoped for. So, at the end of his life, one of his last written statements was a list of why death was not to be feared — among other reasons because we would understand how Christ's divinity and humanity are united.

A Formula for Parish Practice

My mother once told her pastor that when she got to heaven, she was going to have a lot of questions God would have to answer. "Perhaps, Janet," he replied. "But maybe our questions will no longer matter." Many of us are obsessed about getting the answers to all our theological questions. Sometimes entire adult classes in congregations have collapsed because of the dogged insistence of a single participant to obtain a definitive answer for his or her query. Others of us fall into the trap of trying to provide answers even when we should know better. Sometimes we even fall into the trap of basing our faith not in God but in our ability to give or receive answers to our questions.

The Formula of Concord comes to our rescue and provides a way out of our constant questioning and answering. There are some questions that God indeed does answer unequivocally, regarding the depth of human sin (articles 1-2), the breadth of Christ's righteousness (articles 3-4), and the lengths to which God will go to get the good news out (articles 5-8). The old creature prefers to dominate God and the good news either by knowing everything or by making everything relative. Faith adores the mystery and, in not "knowing," catches a sure glimpse of God's salvation in Jesus Christ, the one who alone matters. In the meantime, we wait for that last day and sigh with the hymn writer,

"When he shall come in trumpet sound, O may I then in him be found."

DISCUSSION QUESTIONS

▶ Do you believe in hell? If so, describe it. If not, why not?

▶ In light of "the heart of the matter" above, what might it now mean to you to recite in the creed that Christ "descended into hell" or "to the dead"?

▶ As evidenced by the popularity of television shows about forensic science, today's society is enamored by scientific certainty in response to questions of life and death. What does it mean to not be able to explain Christ's descent into hell? How does the lack of a reasoned answer impact your faith?

▶ When have you encountered sin, death, and the devil in your life? For Luther, what mattered in this article was not the *how* but the *who* — that Christ's descent into hell meant victory over sin, death, and the power of the devil. In what situation does this make a difference in your life and give you comfort?

▶ What do you want to ask God when you get to heaven?

Dealing with Congregational Conflict:
Neutral Things in a Polarized World

Lutheran congregations (like congregations of every other stripe) often fight, not just over the "Lutheran questions" examined throughout the other articles of the Formula of Concord but over other, less earth-shaking matters. Many such questions have to do with worship. At what age should persons receive the Lord's Supper? How often should the Supper be celebrated? Do we use white wine or red wine? What language should we use in worship? Should a pastor wear a white robe or only a black one, a chasuble or only a surplice, or must he or she wear no vestments at all? Where should we place the baptismal font? Should a congregation sing only contemporary songs or may it also use ancient hymns? Other questions touch on administration. Who should be the president of a congregation, the pastor or a layperson? Who should vote at congregational meetings? How should money be raised? I was once the pastor of a congregation where there was serious debate over whether and how to provide meals for children who came to church on Wednesday evenings for Christian instruction.

All these questions and others like them are very significant to the parties involved, even if they seem trivial to outsiders. Some of the questions can have at their heart substantive theological issues. In certain circumstances these questions touch on issues on which the church stands or falls. For the rest, big or small, the Formula of Concord gives a set of guidelines for determining their importance and, in some cases, for reaching lasting peace among the disputants. Even if congregations used no other part of the Formula, implementing this article in their lives could be, as the saying goes, worth the price of admission or, at least, of the book.

History

Two events shook the internal peace of evangelical (Lutheran) congregations in the late 1540s. The first was the death of Martin Luther in February 1546. The second was the outbreak of full-scale war in mid-1546. The Smalcald War, as it was called, involved the emperor, Charles V, and his allies (including some evangelical princes) on one side and the Smalcald League, comprised exclusively of evangelical princes, on the other. Along with religious issues, there were other things at stake. Most importantly, Duke Moritz of Saxony, although a Lutheran, sided with the emperor in the hopes of defeating his cousin, the elector of Saxony John Frederick, and wresting from him both the electoral dignity (legally tied to the city of Wittenberg) and a substantial portion of his lands. (In the sixteenth century there were seven princes [three archbishops and four secular princes] who held the title of elector, because under the Holy Roman Empire's constitution they had the responsibility of electing a new emperor upon the death of the old. These were the archbishops of Mainz, Trier, and Cologne, the Count Palatine [centered in Heidelberg], the king of Bohemia, the margrave of Brandenburg [centered in Berlin], and the duke of Saxony.)

The evangelical forces were finally outgunned and outmaneuvered by the emperor's Spanish troops and his allies and suffered a crushing defeat on Easter 1547 at the battle of Mühlberg. John Frederick was captured and led away in chains. Wittenberg, which had been under siege, capitulated, and Moritz soon received the electoral dignity he had been promised. The triumphant Charles V called for an imperial diet to meet in Augsburg in 1547-1548, where the religious issue was to be settled in the interim, that is, before a general council of the church could settle things once and for all. The result was a decree, promulgated in May and nicknamed the Augsburg Interim, that had the approval of the victorious imperial party. This agreement, although supported by John Agricola, Lutheran theological adviser to the elector of Brandenburg, Joachim II, was tantamount to a death sentence for the Protestant Reformation, allowing evangelicals the right to married priests and communion in both kinds (bread and wine), but little else.

The new Saxon elector, Duke Moritz, thought he had a separate understanding with the emperor that allowed him free hand for religious matters in his own, newly won territories, but it quickly became clear that he did not. Threatened with the reinstatement of Roman bishops in his territories, Moritz sought advice from the theological faculty of his newly reconstituted university in Wittenberg. This included Luther's close associate Philip Melanchthon, who wrote one of the earliest attacks on the Augsburg Interim (published without his consent in the summer of 1548). Throughout the summer and fall of 1548, they worked feverishly on drafts of a compromise document, in part assisted by Julius Pflug, the reform-minded, reinstated Roman bishop of the area. The basic thrust of this document was clear: in theological matters electoral Saxony would remain clearly Lutheran; in matters of worship not directly related to the gospel, its churches would reinstitute old practices. Because the gospel's message neither commanded nor forbade these practices, they were labeled *indifferentia* (Latin for, in this case, undifferentiated things) or, using a Greek term, *adiaphora*. The German was *Mitteldinge* (things in the middle). These included reciting fixed prayers and psalms during the day (the hours) and the wearing of certain vestments, especially the chasuble (a ceremonial cape worn by the priest when celebrating the Lord's Supper). In December the electors of Brandenburg and Saxony tentatively agreed on a document, which Agricola then proclaimed was in line with the hated Augsburg Interim. When Moritz presented it to his own princes meeting in Leipzig, they did not approve it, but its opponents quickly labeled it the Leipzig Interim.

There were many reasons for this fight. Evangelical pastors in Berlin, struggling against the machinations of Agricola and the Augsburg Interim, felt betrayed. Pastors and teachers in Magdeburg, the one city still under siege, to which many of the most ardent "genuine Lutherans" (Gnesio-Lutherans) had fled, felt under theological attack from the Wittenberg faculty, now under control of their military enemy, Moritz. But there was also a serious theological question lurking in the background: Is there a point when neutral matters of liturgy and organization *(adiaphora)* are no longer neutral?

The political resolution to the religious problems in the empire came in the next seven years. Moritz of Saxony changed sides, rallied the evangelical princes, and defeated the emperor's troops (forcing the poor man to flee over the Alps in his nightshirt). By 1555 the historic Peace of Augsburg had been signed, bringing to central Europe its longest time of peace in the modern era (until 1618). Lutherans, that is, those who held to the Augsburg Confession, were given legal (though second-class) status in the empire. The Augsburg Interim was officially overturned, and with the exception of the city of Constance, which had been completely absorbed into the Austrian lands of the imperial family (the Hapsburgs), all formerly Protestant cities and territories returned to their Lutheran convictions.

The theological end to the battle over *adiaphora* was much longer in coming. As we have seen, other theological issues quickly took center stage, including original sin, free will, justification, good works, and the relation between law and gospel. Nevertheless, the question of *adiaphora* still remained. What about these important but, relatively speaking, neutral matters in practice? How would Lutherans navigate between capitulating to an enemy under the threat of force and unduly restricting Christian freedom in matters that, finally, do not directly limit the gospel?

Perhaps it was because so many years had elapsed between these fights and the writing of the Formula, and because the nature of the dispute was more theoretical after 1555, but the concordists came up with a solution to the question of *adiaphora* rather easily, and in the process provided their descendants with a handy guide to solving all manner of disputes in church life. They managed to express some of the chief concerns of the Gnesio-Lutherans while at the same time not limiting Christian freedom in matters of *adiaphora*.

The Heart of the Matter

The Reformation started by Martin Luther was concerned not with changing church practice but with finding ways to announce the good news of Jesus Christ to hurting souls, to comfort and console them, and to bring meaning to their lives. That is, at the heart of Luther's approach to things was the care of the weak. One can see this even in the famous Ninety-five Theses, where Luther complains about bad preaching that misleads people and bad theology that will confuse them. Even in his letter to the archbishop of Mainz, Albrecht, dated 31 October 1517, Luther emphasizes his and the bishop's responsibility to the weak, whom the indulgence preachers were misleading.

After the imperial diet, or parliament, in the city of Worms condemned Luther, he was whisked away to the Wartburg Castle for ten months. Upon his return to Wittenberg in 1522, Luther faced the problem of *adiaphora* head-on. In his absence his colleague Andreas Bodenstein von Karlstadt had led the charge to bring the liturgy in line with evangelical theology: bread and wine for all; no vestments for clergy; the elements taken in the hand, not placed in the mouth; worship in German, not Latin. Luther arrived to find Wittenberg in chaos, with the city council pitted against the more conservative elector of Saxony, the university faculty divided, and weak souls, who did not know why the changes were happening, confused. He preached against the changes for eight days straight, with one basic message: this may sound like good theology, but it is terrible pastoral care and therefore bad theology at heart. Christian freedom means that we do not have to change things so quickly that we hurt the weak! Melanchthon then took Luther's insights and imbedded them in the Augsburg Confession (CA XV), which allowed for wide diversity of practice among the evangelical churches.

Twenty-six years later, in the struggle over the Interim and *adiaphora*, the Lutheran question debated on both sides was simply this: How do we best avoid hurting the weak? Melanchthon, seeing how evangelical churches were being devastated in areas where the Spanish soldier held sway, looked for a way to protect the vulnerable pastors, preachers, and teachers of Saxony by reaching a compromise on *adiaphora* with his Roman opponents. The Gnesio-Lutherans, too, looked to protect the weak: those who, seeing liturgical practices reverting to what they had been before the Reformation, would automatically assume that people are saved not by grace through faith alone but also through human works and rites. They also raised the question of the relation between the institution of the church and the power of the princes. To what extent could the church criticize the government and seek to prevent it from persecuting believers? The authors of the Formula passed over this political issue in silence.

The concordists, understanding the strength of the arguments on both sides, allowed churches the freedom to change and adapt practices to fit their situation, but not in such a way as to affect the weak. However, in times of true persecution, when the enemy's troops are at the door, then changes in practice cannot be tolerated, because being under the threat of force from a true enemy of the gospel means that nothing is a matter of indifference.

The Text of the Epitome

Concerning Ecclesiastical Practices
Which Are Called Adiaphora or Indifferent Matters

[1] A dispute also occurred among theologians of the Augsburg Confession over ceremonies or ecclesiastical practices that are neither commanded nor forbidden in God's Word but that were introduced in the churches for the sake of good order and decorum.

Status controversiae

On the Chief Controversy regarding This Article

[2] The chief question concerned a situation of persecution, in a case in which confession is necessary, when the enemies of the gospel refuse to come to terms with us: the question was whether, in that situation, in good conscience, certain ceremonies that had been abolished (as in themselves indifferent matters neither commanded nor forbidden by God) could be revived under the pressure and demand of the opponents, and whether compromise with them in such ceremonies and indifferent matters would be proper? The one party said yes, the other said no to this question.

Affirmative Theses

The Proper, True Teaching and Confession
concerning This Article

[3] 1. To settle this dispute, we unanimously believe, teach, and confess that ceremonies or ecclesiastical practices that are neither commanded nor forbidden in God's Word, but have been established only for good order and decorum, are in and of themselves neither worship ordained by God nor a

part of such worship. "In vain do they worship me" with human precepts (Matt. 15[:9]).

[4] 2. We believe, teach, and confess that the community of God in every place and at every time has the authority to alter such ceremonies according to its own situation, as may be most useful and edifying for the community of God.

[5] 3. Of course, all frivolity and offense must be avoided, and special consideration must be given particularly to those who are weak in faith.

[6] 4. We believe, teach, and confess that in a time of persecution, when an unequivocal confession of the faith is demanded of us, we dare not yield to the opponents in such indifferent matters. As the Apostle wrote, "Stand firm in the freedom for which Christ has set us free, and do not submit again to a yoke of slavery" [Gal. 5:1]. And: "Do not put on the yoke of the others; what partnership is there between light and darkness?" [2 Cor. 6:14]. "So that the truth of the gospel might always remain with you, we did not submit to them even for a moment" [Gal. 2:5]. For in such a situation it is no longer indifferent matters that are at stake. The truth of the gospel and Christian freedom are at stake. The confirmation of open idolatry, as well as the protection of the weak in faith from offense, is at stake. In such matters we can make no concessions but must offer an unequivocal confession and suffer whatever God sends and permits the enemies of his Word to inflict on us.

[7] 5. We also believe, teach, and confess that no church should condemn another because the one has fewer or more external ceremonies not commanded by God than the other has, when otherwise there is unity with the other in teaching and all the articles of faith and in the proper use of the holy sacraments, according to the well-known saying, "Dissonantia ieiunii non dissolvit consonantiam fidei," "Dissimilarity in fasting is not to disrupt unity in faith."

Negative Theses

False Teaching concerning This Article

[8] Therefore, we reject and condemn as incorrect and contrary to God's Word:

[9] 1. When anyone teaches that human commands and prescriptions in the church are to be regarded in and of themselves as worship ordained by God or a part of it.

[10] 2. When anyone imposes such ceremonies, commands, and prescriptions upon the community of God with coercive force as if they were necessary, against its Christian freedom, which it has in external matters.

[11] 3. Likewise, when anyone teaches that in a situation of persecution, when public confession is necessary, one may comply or come to terms with the enemies of the holy gospel in these indifferent matters and ceremonies. (Such actions serve to damage God's truth.)

[12] 4. Likewise, when such external ceremonies and indifferent matters are abolished in a way that suggests that the community of God is not free at all times, according to its specific situation, to use one or more of these ceremonies in Christian freedom, as is most beneficial to the church.

Commentary

Preliminary Remarks (p. 515)

Paragraph 1. The introductory sentence tells us several important things about this debate. First, it involved "ceremonies or ecclesiastical practices." These are important because they are so visible. You can tell a lot about a congregation by watching how it conducts itself in worship. Second, these practices are different from, say, the Lord's Supper, baptism, preaching, or praying, because in them we have no direct Word of God to tell us whether or not to do a particular thing. Third, although the title calls these things *adiaphora* or "indifferent" (better: undifferentiated), they are not frivolous. They were introduced into church life "for the sake of good order and decorum." The worship practices in some congregations are so ragged that one might want to introduce a little more order and decorum. One sometimes gets the impression from slipshod liturgical practices that it is not God and God's promises that are at the center of the congregation's life, but the congregation, its pastor, and their good feelings.

Paragraph 2. The controversial issue *(status controversiae)* for this article is sometimes misunderstood. In major church fights sometimes people feel "persecuted" if they "lose the vote." Then suddenly something that is *adiaphora* becomes "church dividing" or "congregation dividing." The concordists are very clear concerning the circumstance about which they are speaking. It is one "of persecution," in which "confession is necessary" and "the enemies of the gospel refuse to come to terms with us." Luther, too, understood the difference between honest disagreements among Christians and persecution. In the controversy in Eisleben over what to do with leftover communion wine (see above, article 7, part 2), he rebuked a pastor for attacking another pastor as if that pastor opposed the very gospel itself. So, before we imagine that some "indifferent matter" suddenly matters, we must look very carefully at our situation. Are we dealing with enemies of the gospel who are using real (not imagined) force? Are the imperial troops at the door? If the answer to these questions is yes, then we are on the same page as the concordists and can ask the second question: Could certain ceremonies (otherwise *adiaphora*) be revived "under the pressure and demand of the opponents"? Can one reach compromise with them on such undifferentiated matters?

One of the reasons we should be so hard on ourselves about this issue is because some believers actually have been persecuted for being Christian. From the 1950s through the 1980s, it was people in Eastern Europe and South Africa. In more recent times it has been Christians in some Islamic states (especially the Sudan). In some places in our nation, self-appointed Christian judges have publicly vilified Christians with practices that differ from their own. In other places, where a more secular society holds sway, that culture itself can put enormous pressure on Christians. So, the first question to ask is this: Are we truly under attack from true enemies of the gospel? If not, then even if we do not like a particular practice, the concordists would urge us to concord!

Affirmative Theses (pp. 515-16)

Here are the ground rules for disputes in the church. They are remarkably simple, and if people agree to them *before* the shouting begins, they may actually help congregations, synods, and perhaps entire church bodies avoid strife. There are, of course, many other things involved in our fights (personalities, histories, sin, the devil, etc.). However, these paragraphs point us in some helpful directions.

Rule 1 (Par. 3): *Adiaphora* Exist

This may seem a rather odd rule. Yet, some churches and some brands of theology argue that *adiaphora* are only theoretically possible, or possible only if some authority (like a pastor or bishop or congregation) allows it. It is rather like a mother sending her child off to the playground with the warning, "You can do anything, as long as I approve." Not much real freedom there! Moreover, some people reduce *adiaphora* to the point where they are no longer an important category. They find unbreakable "rules" in the Scripture for everything imaginable. (To concoct even more rules, they use what might be called a "sectarian approach" to the Bible: what is described there is commanded and what is omitted is forbidden.)

Against this the concordists are clear. We do some things in the church not because they are commanded by God, but simply to keep "good order and decorum." Order is important — in fact, God demands that we do things in an orderly fashion. (Imagine if a congregation never knew when they were going to worship — how would they assemble?) But the particular order (9:30 A.M. every Sunday, or we will quit the church!) is *adiaphora*. The question a congregation and its leaders need to ask is not what time of day has God commanded that we worship, but rather what best serves the needs of this place and time. We dare not confuse that "good order" with direct service to and worship of God (in the German text the word for both worship and service is the same). How easily people confuse their "human precepts" for divine worship and service! Jesus faced it over the Sabbath; Paul dealt with it on circumcision; and we deal with it, too.

Rule 2 (Par. 4): Times, People, and Places Change

"But we've always done it this way!" Oh, please! When a person talks to me this way, I ask him or her, "How long is 'always'?" Usually it is the amount of time that has elapsed from when the person's favorite pastor left the congregation to the present. Divine institutions (preaching the Word, baptizing, celebrating the Lord's Supper) do not really change and have marked the Christian church from its beginning. But everything else is really under our control. "The community of God in every place and at every time has the authority to alter such ceremonies."

There are three reasons (and only three!) to change things, and they are indicated by the phrases "according to its own situation," "as may be most useful and edifying," and "for the community of God." First, each situation is different. Lutherans from North America may worship differently than those in Europe. An urban congregation may worship differently than a rural one; a Spanish-speaking congregation than a German-speaking or an English-speaking one. Even Luther and Melanchthon recognized this principle. Thus, in Wittenberg there were early services for household servants; late afternoon services for children and others to learn the basics of the faith; a main service of the Lord's Supper in German, for the general populace, or exclusively in Latin, especially for foreigners and the university community.

Second, the measuring stick is usefulness and edification — what works (that is half of it) and what "builds up" (that is the other half; cf. 1 Cor. 8:1-3). It can never be "change for the sake of change" or "change because people need to be shaken up" or "change because this is what my seminary professor taught me." It must be useful (that is, it must serve the gospel) and edifying (it must help the people).

Third, it is not for the pastor's sake, the leaders' sake, or the squeaky wheel's sake, but "for the community of God." Now that is a surprise. When we change things, we must always be thinking about the community — those gathered around Word and sacrament who belong neither to the pastor nor to the leaders nor even to themselves (!) but to God.

Rule 3 (Par. 5): Watch the Weak

This rule really comes out of the preceding one. It begins with a warning about "frivolity and offense." Change is no laughing matter. We live in a culture that revels in change, and we must be careful that we do not so closely mirror our culture that we lose the heart of our purpose as Christian communities. Madison Avenue may think there is always room for "new and improved" toothpaste or laundry soap, and we may quickly want to bring in the wrecking ball and start over from scratch, but much of what passes for important and lasting in our world (and in many churches) turns out to be a passing fancy. In fact, one reason our children seem to lose interest in worship and church may *not* be that congregations do not change but that, when they return from their time away as prodigals, they discover that the waiting father has sold the house and moved to the Riviera!

The real concern here, however, is for the weak. This is the pastoral concern. This is also the heart of the gospel itself and, as we said above, of the Reformation. We must be concerned for those who, if we changed something, will lose faith because they are too weak in faith to separate the certain things of faith from the freedom we have in practice. This means that at the onset of any change (or any dispute about change) the most important question must be "Who is the weak person here?" Paul in Romans 14-15 and in 1 Corinthians 8 offers us loads of help. When this question is asked at the *beginning* of a fight, often people will discover that there are loads of weak people on all sides of an issue. In fact, we all have our weaknesses when it comes to matters of *adiaphora*. Discovering what those weaknesses are and what to do about them is the heart of the gospel and true pastoral care. Our approach cannot simply be, "How do we win them over to our side?" Instead, we must ask things like, "How do we strengthen the weak *in their faith?*" "How do we unite around the gospel?" "How do we listen to those who sound strong (but may in fact harbor weaknesses known only to God)?" "How do we distinguish weakness from stubbornness?"

Rule 4 (Par. 6): What to Do When Hell Breaks Loose

What happens when there is true persecution and our persecutors demand changes? Here again, we need to notice that the concordists have a very serious situation in mind (and not just some trivial problem in church politics). It must be a situation when "unequivocal confession of the faith is demanded of us," that is, when all hell breaks loose. Then undifferentiated matters suddenly matter. In fact, everything matters.

Bodo Nischan, a premier late twentieth-century historian of early modern Europe, describes in his book *Prince, People, and Confession: The Second Reformation in Brandenburg* (Philadelphia: University of Pennsylvania Press, 1994) what happened when in the early seventeenth century the (Reformed) elector of Brandenburg forced on the solid Lutherans in Berlin pastors who denied that Christ was truly present in the

Lord's Supper. Now, all the pastor did was to use regular bread and to break it while reciting the Words of Institution, two things many congregations now do without a second thought. But in those days this meant without a doubt that the pastor rejected the real presence of Christ in the Lord's Supper. So those Berliners got mad, went on a rampage through the streets, and drove the poor man out of town (urged on, according to court records, by shouts of encouragement from the palace — the electress herself was a Lutheran). Now, this is somewhat extreme, but it shows how sometimes *adiaphora* are no longer *adiaphora*.

Rule 5 (par. 7): How *Not* to Judge Others

We sometimes forget how varied worship and congregations were during the sixteenth century. In Württemberg, the duchy around Stuttgart in southern Germany, the service was very plain and had little ceremony. In Brandenburg, on the other hand, they still used exorcisms in baptism, spoke Latin in worship, and held elaborate processions. In 1536 a south German from Augsburg wrote home from Wittenberg that he was shocked at how traditional the service was, complete with bells ringing at the consecration and the elevation of the bread during the Sanctus. Thus, this rule was not theoretical, since among the concordists were Nicholas Selnecker (from Wittenberg), Jakob Andreae (from Württemberg), and Andreas Musculus (from Brandenburg).

Our unity does not consist in the way we worship but in the message proclaimed from our pulpits and celebrated in Holy Baptism and the Lord's Supper. Now, there is something to be said for unity in practices. I still remember as a child hearing from my father on his return from four months in India as a governmental adviser how lonely he felt for Christian companionship. So, one Sunday in New Delhi he went off to the local Anglican (Episcopal) church, and although he could not understand a word, he could tell where they were in the service and recited to himself the English while standing among a Hindi-speaking congregation. Good old Bishop Irenaeus of Lyons (ca. 130–ca. 200) said it best: "Dissimilarity in fasting [or any other matter of *adiaphora*, the concordists and we might add] is not to disrupt unity in faith."

Negative Theses (p. 516)

Here, the concordists' condemnations (par. 8-12) are straightforward. Do not confuse your way of doing things with worship commanded by God. When someone uses coercive force (the troops at the door), this destroys Christian freedom. When someone complies with the demands of this force, the results "damage God's truth," because in such situations no one can distinguish practice from theory.

The final paragraph (12) harkens back to Luther's original point when he came back from the Wartburg: change, even for good reasons, must not destroy Christian freedom. Lutherans need never worry that a particular practice is "too [Roman] Catholic" and therefore must be eliminated. We are free to keep or even add whatever ceremony is most beneficial to the community. Some in the Reformed camp were complaining that Lutherans, having failed to rid themselves of all practices from the medieval church, had not quite taken the final step toward true reformation. There is no such thing as a perfect, Christian (read: scriptural) ceremony. We Lutherans can wait for such things in heaven. In the meantime, we simply respect good order and decorum, build up the congregation, and take special care for the truly weak ones in our midst. Start forcing us to give up practices under false or coercive pretenses, however, and remember what those Berliners did!

A Formula for Parish Practice

In the 1840s United States citizens were called to arms with the slogan Remember the Alamo! Perhaps in the midst of congregational fights we need similar slogans calling us to peace: Remember the Wartburg! Remember the Smalcald War! Remember Those Feisty Berliners! Or perhaps most important of all, Remember the Weak! We, after all, are very often the strong ones in such controversies. We know all the right debating tricks, all the appropriate Bible passages (or even passages from *The Book of Concord!*), all the best political maneuvers. But when Saint Paul faced similar discussions over very serious issues — whether one could eat meat sacrificed to idols — he took a much different approach, one mirrored in this article of the Formula. "Knowledge puffs up, but love builds up" (1 Cor. 8:1). "But take care that this liberty of yours does not somehow become a stumbling block to the weak" (8:9). "Therefore, if food is a cause of their falling, I will never eat meat, so that I may not cause one of them to fall" (8:13). And the point underneath it all? Perhaps Paul said it best in Romans 14:8: "If we live, we live to the Lord, and if we die, we die to the Lord; so then, whether we live or whether we die, we are the Lord's." So why do we pass judgment on our brother or sister? "We who are strong ought to put up with the failings of the weak, and not to please ourselves. Each of us must please our neighbor for the good purpose of building up the neighbor" (Rom. 15:1-2). "Welcome one another, therefore, just as Christ has welcomed you, for the glory of God" (v. 7). At the heart of this controversy beats, once again, the sweet words of the gospel, that we are justified by faith alone and therefore have nothing in which to boast, save in our Lord Jesus Christ.

DISCUSSION QUESTIONS

▶ What issues have caused conflict within your congregation?
▶ What might cause a person to leave a congregation? Does this relate to justification by faith or *adiaphora*?
▶ What is Christian freedom?
▶ What in your worship practices are things on which you will not compromise, and why? Which are matters of *adiaphora*?
▶ Think of the conflicts that occurred in your church. Were they over gospel issues or *adiaphora*? Did the weak persons in the congregation have a voice in the conflict? Did the resolution of the conflict build up the faith in the "body of Christ" or diminish the faith in the community?
▶ How do you feel about acquiescing to the "weak" in a congregational dispute?

Article Eleven

"You Did Not Choose Me; I Chose You" — the Comfort of Election, Even When Faced with Unbelief

My late father-in-law, as dear to me as my own father, was a conundrum in my life. Brought up as a Quaker, he had had, except for a brief involvement with an Episcopal congregation, very little contact with organized Christianity. When I first heard in seminary that Lutherans believed in a doctrine of election (horrors!), I used him as a counterargument. "Are you saying that God chose my father-in-law for hell?" I asked defiantly. "No," came the response. "Lutherans are saying that our salvation is not in our hands but in God's. Is it more comforting to you to blame your father-in-law for not becoming a believer on his own power, or to place him in the hands of God, who is able to raise the dead and make believers out of unbelievers?" Years later, as he lay dying, he asked me to conduct the memorial service, and it was indeed infinitely more consoling for me and my late wife to commend him to the wounded hands of God than to lament his defective personal decisions.

When we deal with the question of election, perhaps most important is to realize that our concerns almost invariably have a human face. We have children, parents, siblings, other relatives, or friends who have heard the same message of salvation that we have and yet appear for all intents and purposes to have completely rejected God's good news. Sometimes that rejection is born of bad experiences within a Christian congregation or home. Often, however, it leaves us wondering why we believe and others do not. One source of consolation on

180

this comes from Saint Paul himself, who in speaking of this issue in Romans 9 expressly mentions his "kindred according to the flesh." Even for him this was not a theoretical issue but a personal and pastoral one. No wonder the concordists called election "an article of comfort when properly treated."

History

From the very beginning of the Reformation, the question of predestination and election arose in connection with the unconditional grace of God. Already in the debate over the freedom of the will with Erasmus, Luther insisted that our salvation depended on God's grace, not on human activity. Only in the light of glory would we understand God's fairness. Somewhat in contrast, Melanchthon, first in his commentary on Colossians of 1527 and later in the Augsburg Confession (XVIII, in *BC 2000,* 48-51), emphasized human freedom in this life and the necessity of God's grace in matters of salvation. God alone is the cause of our salvation; our alienation, however, is our fault alone. Melanchthon developed this stance to avoid charges of Manichaeanism (the fatalistic belief that the universe was divided between forces of good and evil) by his opponents, who charged that Lutherans taught that everything happened as a matter of fate. After 1529 he even applied all comments in Scripture about predestination, especially in Romans 9-11, to God's election of the church. In the 1530s both Luther and Melanchthon insisted that the doctrine of election could under no circumstances undermine the certainty of God's mercy in Christ, proclaimed in the Word and celebrated in the sacraments.

This insistent emphasis on the effectiveness of God's Word set Lutheran views on this topic apart from the position of John Calvin and his followers. They took Luther's comments on human bondage to their logical conclusion and insisted on what is commonly called "double" predestination (that God's choice included both those God saves and those God does not). While this position assured God's sovereign grace in all things, it also, especially among later Calvinists, seemed to undermine the reliability of God's promises. From the 1540s on, Melanchthon objected to this view and privately likened it to the fatalism of Stoic philosophy, nicknaming Calvin after its founder, Zeno.

Two later skirmishes over this doctrine, both tangentially involving future writers of the Formula, guaranteed its inclusion in this document. In 1563 Jakob Andreae and others were called in to arbitrate a dispute in Strasbourg between the Lutheran pastor, Johann Marbach, and an Italian refugee, Jerome Zanchi, who taught in Strasbourg's academy and was far more Reformed than Marbach in his orientation on the Lord's Supper and predestination. Zanchi insisted that the elect could not fall away from grace and that any teaching to the contrary made salvation a work of the human will. Believers must place their faith in God's a priori decision to save them. Marbach, a onetime student in Wittenberg, found Zanchi's position too speculative and emphasized the effectiveness of the law to condemn sinners and of the revealed promises of God to save. Andreae and his colleagues easily reasserted the Wittenberg Concord of 1536 to end the dispute over the Lord's Supper, but found the dispute over predestination more difficult to resolve. They developed what scholars call a "broken" view of predestination. God prepares no one for destruction, because the cause of sin rests with humankind (see already CA XIX, in *BC 2000*, 52-53). However, God chose the elect before the foundation of the world (Eph. 1:3-4). Yet even this election must not be considered outside of Christ and the gospel. Teaching double predestination can lead either to false security or to despair.

The second impulse for the inclusion of this doctrine in the Formula came from the work of an ardent follower of Matthias Flacius, Cyriacus Spangenberg, who published a tract on predestination in 1567 based in large measure on Luther's *Bondage of the Will*. Saxon theologians strenuously objected, and even the pious elector of Saxony, August, took offense. Two years later, in 1569, Martin Chemnitz prepared a catechism for students who had mastered Luther's Small Catechism. He even incorporated into it comments from a sermon of his on Matthew 20:16. He acknowledged Melanchthon's concern about Stoic fatalism but insisted that salvation depended alone on God's grace, not on human cooperation. He also emphasized the trustworthiness of God's revealed promises and the comfort they bring. Thus, like Andreae, he was willing to "break" the logic of double predestination by insisting on the reliability of God's promises and sacraments for all people.

The Heart of the Matter

As he sat at table one evening in 1532, Luther pondered the question of predestination.

> We now have the Word, therefore we ought not doubt our salva-
> tion. This is the way to debate the question. . . . I am baptized; I
> have the Word. Therefore I should have no doubt about salvation,
> as long as one stays with the Word. As soon as you let Christ out of
> your sight, then one encounters predestination and debates it.
> Thus, God says, "Why don't you believe me? Don't you hear me
> when I say to you that you are accepted and your sins are forgiven?"
> We are always so skillful at running away from the Word. (Table
> Talk, no. 365 [WA TR 1:156-57])

In other words, Luther refused to allow our theoretical imagination
about God's secret will to cloud the assurance that comes in the Word
and sacraments. At the heart of the Lutheran understanding of election stands the conviction that nothing — not the reasonableness of
our arguments nor the legal correctness of our judgments — can erode
the certainty of God's love in Christ expressed in Word and sacraments.
Nothing dare undermine the reliability of God's promises to us in
Christ.

When we discuss the doctrine of election, there are two things we
must realize from the outset. The first has to do with what I call question 9. When people first hear about the depth of human sin, the bondage of the will, and the unconditional grace of God in Christ (see
above, articles 1-3), they almost always ask one of two questions: question 6 or question 9 (from Rom. 6 and 9). The concordists address question 6 in article 4: Is grace just license to do whatever we please? Or, in
the words of Romans 6:1, "Should we continue in sin in order that
grace may abound?" (Just don't tell the kids!) Question 9 is posed in
Romans 9:3, What about "my kindred according to the flesh"? In a
sense, when people pose these two questions, I know I am on the right
track as a teacher of the gospel. After all, when one teaches that faith is
a matter of our choosing God and not of grace alone, Paul's questions
will not be posed seriously.

There is a second issue that arises here. It has to do with our questions themselves. "Why does my loved one not believe?" we ask, to which we must first gently ask ourselves, "Why do I ask that question?" Our questions are themselves never neutral. They always imply something about us. Sometimes we ask this particular question out of anguish and sorrow. But at other times we ask it to assert some control over the course of our lives (and our loved ones' lives) and over God. When Paul later in Romans 9 writes, "Who indeed are you, a human being, to argue with God?" he puts his finger on our deep desire to be gods, deciding good and evil. In the end, all Christians who wrestle with this question are forced to exclaim with Paul in Romans 11:33-34, "O the depth of the riches and wisdom and knowledge of God! How unsearchable are his judgments and how inscrutable his ways! 'For who has known the mind of the Lord? Or who has been his counselor?'" We are not God, and even in the midst of our anguish we must commit our questions, our loved ones, and our lives to Christ's wounded hands. Because faith is not our work for God but God's work in us through the Word, we can only blurt out with Peter, "Lord, to whom shall we go? You have the words of eternal life."

Election is a doctrine of supreme comfort, not only for our loved ones but also for us. In my own faith I scarcely see anything except my doubts and failings. Luther's explanation of the third article of the Apostles' Creed in the Small Catechism fits me to a T: "I believe that by own understanding or strength I cannot believe in Jesus Christ my LORD or come to him" (Apostles' Creed, 6, in *BC 2000*, 355). I not only believe this, I experience it on a daily basis! Election takes things out of my hands and places them squarely in God's lap. "But instead the Holy Spirit has called me through the gospel. . . ." What a relief! My life is in God's hands from all eternity. As Ephesians 1:4 says, before the world was made, God had already chosen us. This comfort stands at the heart of this article. As one writer put it, "Election is justification by faith alone seen from God's perspective." Moreover, this choice of God may be found not by speculating about God's secret intentions but by looking to the Word and to Christ. There we discover a merciful, compassionate God, who draws us and through his Word fills us with faith.

The Text of the Epitome

Concerning the Eternal Predestination
and Election of God

[1] On this article there has been no public conflict among the theologians of the Augsburg Confession. However, because it is an article of comfort when properly treated, it is also explained in this document so that no offensive dispute may arise in the future.

Affirmative Theses

The Pure, True Teaching concerning This Article

[2] 1. First of all, the difference between *praescientia* and *praedestinatio*, that is, between God's foreknowledge and his eternal election, must be carefully noted.

[3] 2. God's foreknowledge is nothing else than that God knows all things before they happen, as it is written, "God in heaven reveals mysteries. He has disclosed to King Nebuchadnezzar what will happen in future times" (Dan. 2[:28]).

[4] 3. This foreknowledge extends equally over godly people and evil people, but it is not a cause of evil. It is not the cause of sins, when people act wrongly (sin proceeds originally from the devil and the wicked, perverted human will), nor of human corruption, for which people are responsible themselves. Instead, God's foreknowledge provides order in the midst of evil and sets limits to it. It determines how long evil can continue and determines also that everything, even if it is evil in itself, serves the welfare of God's elect.

[5] 4. *Praedestinatio,* however, or God's eternal election, extends only to the righteous, God-pleasing children of God. It is a cause of their salvation, which God brings about. He has arranged everything that belongs to it. Our salvation is so firmly grounded on it [cf. John 10:26-29] that "the gates of hell will not prevail against it" [Matt. 16:18].

[6] 5. This election is not to be probed in the secret counsel of God but rather is to be sought in the Word, where it has also been revealed.

[7] 6. However, the Word of God leads us to Christ, who is the "Book of Life" [Phil. 4:3; Rev. 3:5], in whom are inscribed and chosen all who shall be eternally saved, as it is written, "He chose us in Christ before the foundation of the world" [Eph. 1:4].

[8] 7. This Christ calls all sinners to himself and promises them refreshment. He is utterly serious in his desire that all people should come to him and seek help for themselves [cf. Matt. 11:28]. He offers himself to them in the Word. He desires them to hear the Word and not to plug their ears or despise his Word. To this end he promises the power and activity of the Holy Spirit, divine assistance in remaining faithful and attaining eternal salvation.

[9] 8. Therefore we are to make judgments regarding our election to eternal life neither on the basis of reason nor on the basis of God's law. Such a course of action would lead us either into a wild, irresponsible, Epicurean life, or into despair — and would awaken harmful thoughts in human hearts. Whenever people follow their reason, they can hardly escape such reflections as these: "As long as God has chosen me for salvation, I cannot be condemned no matter what I do!" or, "I have not been chosen for eternal life, so it does not help when I do good; everything is really in vain."

[10] 9. Instead, the true meaning of election must be learned from the holy gospel of Christ. It clearly states, "God imprisoned all in unbelief that he may be merciful to all," and that he wants no one to be lost but rather that everyone repent and believe on the Lord Christ [Rom. 11:32; 1 Tim. 2:4; cf. Ezek. 33:11; 18:23].

[11] 10. This teaching is useful and comforting for all those who are concerned about the revealed will of God and follow the order which St. Paul observed in the Epistle to the Romans. There he first of all points people to repentance, acknowledgment of their sins, and then to faith in Christ and obedience to God before he speaks of the mystery of God's eternal election.

[12] 11. That "many are called and few are chosen" [Matt. 20:16]* does not mean that God does not want to save everyone. Instead, the reason for condemnation lies in their not hearing God's Word at all or arrogantly despising it, plugging their ears and their hearts, and thus blocking the Holy

---

*Some ancient authorities add this sentence to Matt. 20:16. See also Matt. 22:14.

Spirit's ordinary path, so that he cannot carry out his work in them; or if they have given it a hearing, they cast it to the wind and pay no attention to it. Then the fault lies not with God and his election but with their own wickedness [cf. 2 Pet. 2:9-15; Luke 11:47-52; Heb. 12:15-17, 25].

[13] 12. A Christian should only think about the article of God's eternal election to the extent that it is revealed in God's Word. The Word holds Christ before our eyes as the "Book of Life," which he opens and reveals for us through the preaching of the holy gospel, as it is written, "Those whom he has chosen, he also called" [Rom. 8:30]. In Christ we are to seek the Father's eternal election. He has decreed in his eternal, divine counsel that he will save no one apart from those who acknowledge his Son Christ and truly believe in him. We should set aside other thoughts, for they do not come from God but rather from the imagination of the evil foe. Through such thoughts he approaches us to weaken this glorious comfort for us or to take it away completely. We have a glorious comfort in this salutary teaching, that we know how we have been chosen for eternal life in Christ out of sheer grace, without any merit of our own, and that no one can tear us out of his hand [John 10:28-29]. For he has assured us that he has graciously chosen us not only with mere words. He has corroborated this with an oath and sealed it with the holy sacraments. In the midst of our greatest trials we can remind ourselves of them, comfort ourselves with them, and thereby quench the fiery darts of the devil.

[14] 13. Along with this we should strive as diligently as possible to live according to God's will and to "confirm our calling," as Saint Peter admonishes [2 Pet. 1:10]. We should especially abide by the revealed Word that cannot and will not fail us.

[15] 14. This short explanation of God's eternal election gives God his honor fully and completely. On the basis of his pure mercy alone, without any merit of ours at all, he saves us "according to the purpose of his will" [Eph. 1:11]. In addition, no one is given reason either for faintheartedness or for a reckless, wild life.

Antitheses or Negative Theses

False Teaching regarding This Article

[16] Accordingly, we believe and maintain that those who present the teaching of God's gracious election to eternal life either in such a way that trou-

bled Christians cannot find comfort in it but are driven to faintheartedness or despair, or in such a way that the impenitent are strengthened in their arrogance, are not preaching this teaching according to the Word and will of God but rather according to their own reason and at the instigation of the accursed devil, because (as the Apostle testifies) "whatever was written was written for our instruction, so that by steadfastness and by the comfort of the Scriptures we might have hope" [Rom. 15:4]. Therefore, we reject the following errors:

[17] 1. When it is taught that God does not want all people to repent and believe the gospel.

[18] 2. Likewise, that when God calls us to himself, he does not seriously intend that all people should come to him.

[19] 3. Likewise, that God does not desire that everyone should be saved, but rather that without regard to their sins — only because of God's naked decision, intention, and will — some are designated for damnation, so that there is no way that they could be saved.

[20] 4. Likewise, that the cause of God's election does not lie exclusively in God's mercy and the most holy merit of Christ but that there is also a cause in us, because of which God has chosen us for eternal life.

[21] These are blasphemous, horrible, and erroneous teachings, which take away from Christians all the comfort that they have in the holy gospel and in the use of the holy sacraments. Therefore, these errors dare not be tolerated in the church of God.

[22] This is the brief and simple explanation of the contested articles which for a time theologians of the Augsburg Confession taught and discussed in ways that contradicted each other. From this every simple Christian can recognize, according to the direction of God's Word and the simple catechism, what is correct and incorrect. For here we have set forth not only the pure teaching but have also exposed and rejected contrary, erroneous teaching. In this way the offensive divisions that had arisen are completely resolved. May the almighty God and Father of our Lord Jesus grant the grace of his Holy Spirit, that we may all be one in him [John 17:20-21] and steadfastly remain in this Christian and God-pleasing unity.

Commentary

Introduction (p. 517)

Paragraph 1. As pointed out above, there were some minor skirmishes over this issue. However, like justification and the distinction of law and gospel (and directly related to both), the concordists cannot wait to talk about election because, as gospel, it is "an article of comfort." In fact, that comfort is not simply the goal of their exposition; it is the cause of it. In other words, at the center of God's revelation in Christ is consolation ("Come to me, all who labor . . ."), and nothing can undermine that assurance, not even what appears to be a logically correct doctrine.

Affirmative Theses (pp. 517-19)

Paragraphs 2-4. The easiest way around the notion of predestination is to assume that what we are really talking about is God's foreknowledge. God knows everything, the argument runs, therefore, inasmuch as God knows what is going to happen and allows it to take place, we can say that is his predestination. However, as those who have wrestled with catastrophe in their lives know, this offers little comfort. It is, one angry widower once wrote in a letter to a local newspaper, like imagining that God stands on the side of the pool where a person is drowning and does nothing about it.

The German of the sixteenth century did not contain theologically precise terms. Thus, Andreae uses Latin terms: *praescientia* (foreknowledge) and *praedestinatio* (predestination), where he defines the latter term as God's "eternal election" (par. 2). God knows everything (par. 3), but that does not mean that God is the cause of evil (par. 4). We are truly responsible for the mess we are in, and no fancy theological footwork can get us out from under that fact. However, the concordists do not leave it at that. God's foreknowledge is not simply neutral with respect to evil. Instead, even this attribute of God inclines toward the good, since it "provides order in the midst of evil" and "sets limits to it." When evil things happen to believers, these two things (order and limits) come as gifts of God. So often when tragedy strikes, it appears as though everything is out of control and chaos reigns. The fact that God, too, knows the chaos we face offers comfort. God is not sleeping and will bend even this evil to serve good order. Moreover, God's foreknowledge of evil also implies for the concordists that God knows our limits and accordingly limits evil. Paul's comments in Romans 8:28, "All things work together for good," offer not an excuse for Stoic resignation but a hope-filled promise. My mother quoted this passage so often while we were growing up that, in the end, all she had to say was "all things" to get her point across.

Paragraph 5. In contrast to foreknowledge, there is God's eternal election. The concordists' view of predestination is broken, that is, God's election extends only to the righteous. This position makes no logical sense. After all, the rational argument goes, if God chooses some for salvation, surely God, by passing over others, has ipso facto chosen those others for damnation. Yet, as we will see below, reason has nothing to do with election and only confuses the issue. The concordists' point is rather that for believers God's choice alone is "a cause of their salvation, which God brings about." Why? God's choosing is the ground of our trust in God. Once it becomes clear that faith and salvation are in God's hands alone, then that faith itself would be undermined if God were not finally reliable. We need something against which hell itself cannot prevail, namely, God's sovereign, gracious choice. Thus, the brokenness of election in Lutheranism — as foolish as it appears to human wisdom — already contains great comfort. We can thereby announce this electing promise to anyone and everyone ("God chooses you") and watch as that declaration acts as law and gospel in justifying the sinner. As law, God's choice destroys and puts an end to all our choices. As gospel, we can finally relax and let God's grace truly carry the day. No wonder Jesus could comfort his disciples in John 15:16 by saying, "You did not choose me but I chose you."

Paragraphs 6-8. Melanchthon worried that the doctrine of predestination tended to draw us away from God's promises in Jesus Christ. Even Luther reacted against this "legally correct" way of talking. If, when thinking or teaching about predestination, anyone comes to the conclusion that he or she is not or might not be elect, then the very thing that teaching is meant to preserve — the gospel of God's grace — has been destroyed. Grace disappears and faith becomes impossible when God's will becomes arbitrary or uncertain. Thus, election comes back to God's direct address to us in the Word. Do you want to know about God's eternal election? Do not look for it in your own speculation about God but only in the Word (par. 6). Moreover (par. 7), that Word is not a conundrum but an open book. It leads us to (in Luther's terms) "the Father's heart," Jesus Christ, called here "the Book of Life." All who are saved are chosen "in Christ," not outside of Christ in some secret list of God. Christ does not glower over us and threaten us ("I've chosen some of you, but I am not saying who"). Instead, Christ calls sinners "and promises them refreshment" (par. 8). No one is excluded. He offers himself to us in the Word, wants us to hear and believe. To accomplish this, he sends his Holy Spirit.

The concordists want nothing but comfort to gush from this doctrine, because election, as one of my teachers, Gerhard Forde, wrote, is not the language of logic but the language of love. That is why lovers can be so hard to take. They will sit there for hours recounting how their love just *had* to be, how their meeting was such a stroke of good fortune, how their relationship was "made in heaven." In the same language of love, believers cannot imagine a time when God did not have them in mind, did not love them. Their salvation was truly made in heaven, "before the foundation of the world" (Eph. 1:4). To the (rational) question, "What about so-and-so, who does not believe?" the response can only be, "Give me that person's name and address and I'll go tell him or her the great news. God chooses that person." At the same time, this does not mean Lutherans are universalists — far from it! Grace is not about quaint theories that preserve our logic. The promise of God is universal, but the whole point is particular. It is to bring God's unconditional love and grace to bear on people in such a way that they fall in love and live in faith. Salvation or election is not about some general theory about God, it is about delivering God's actual choice in Word and sacrament, so that we trust God alone.

Paragraphs 9-10. Election is not a matter of reason or law (par. 9) but of gospel and Christ (par. 10). The old creature takes reason, a perfectly good gift of God's creation, and twists it. "I am elect, so I can make whoopee," it crows. Or, in moments of anxiety, it cries, "I am not elect. All is lost!" Then election, rather than being good news, becomes law and judgment only. Then we turn God into a robot, constrained by our laws of logic and fairness. Again, the language of love is lost in legalism. Imagine saying "God chooses me as the beloved, so now I can commit adultery with other gods." Or: "God could never choose me; I am unlovable. Therefore I must despair." As hard as it is to imagine, some people who hold most fiercely to double predestination have often despaired of their own salvation. Then where is the gospel? On the contrary, the gospel is about God's unconditional, all-encompassing grace. The very thing Melanchthon most wanted to preserve, that God wants *all* to be saved, comes to fullest expression here.

Paragraph 11. Paul deals with the question of predestination most extensively in Romans. What the concordists insist on is not isolating God's choice (election) from God's call. Otherwise, the whole point of this teaching — namely, to comfort those who are uncertain about their standing before God — is lost. Paul starts with law and repentance (Rom. 1:18–3:20) and moves to gospel and faith (3:21–8:39) before ever tackling the mystery of God's eternal election (Rom. 9–11). Best we stick with what we know best (law and gospel; repentance and faith), rather than viewing our salvation from God's perspective (election).

Paragraph 12. The extended discussion of Matthew 20:16 points to this article's origins in Martin Chemnitz's sermon on this text and his subsequent catechism. In many ways this original venue shaped this doctrine in its appropriate, comforting direction. To be sure, logic would demand that a verse like "Many are called, but few are chosen" mean that God chooses to save some and to damn others — end of story. However, in the context of Jesus' parable, where a man arrives without a wedding garment, it becomes clear that the problem with the wedding guest was *not* that he owned no garment but that he did not wear it. As shocking as it may seem, having been invited to a wedding, the man dressed as though he were going to the barn to milk the cows. That is, he simply refused to believe that he was invited to a wedding at all! The point in election is not to delve into the mysteries of God but to trust that very call, in which one's election is indeed revealed. We have been invited to the Lamb's wedding feast; let's get the tux out and iron the evening gown. Anything less would deny the invitation and reveal our unbelief!

Paragraph 13. This paragraph is one of the most lyrical in the entire Epitome. Election is nothing other than the comfort of the gospel itself, pouring over our ears in all its richness. Look how the concordists use the phrase "glorious comfort." For Lutherans, the point is not getting the logic of election right or figuring out the laws by which God elects. Instead, it is always about letting nothing stand in the way of the glorious comfort of the gospel. Our election centers in Jesus Christ alone. You want to know whether you are chosen? Look at the Lamb's Book of Life, that is, Christ in the gospel. Here the order of Matthew (many called, few chosen) is reversed by Paul (those whom he chose, he also called). Thus, in the face of doubts we do not have to plumb the mysteries of God but can look precisely where God reveals heart and soul: in Jesus Christ.

All other thoughts come from the evil one, not only thoughts such as "I am not elect" but also speculation about people who have not heard the gospel or loved ones who show no signs of faith. "What about Hindus, Buddhists, cavemen, and my uncle Fred?" we logically ask. "Why do you want to know?" one must respond. "Stick with the One you know, who brings comfort for you in Word and sacrament, and leave the rest in God's hands, where they (and we) belong." We forever want to go where Paul finally refuses to venture in Romans 11, when he cries, "O the depth."

Instead, we can focus our lives and conversation on this "glorious comfort." This is so important when we are crushed by anxiety and riddled with doubts. God has chosen you, and no one falls from our Savior's hands. No one! Whether living or dying, whether filled with faith or bowed down with doubts, whether weak or sinful, the Good Shepherd will not allow anyone to be lost. This is why, at the Lord's Supper and in sermons, pastors actually proclaim your election and mine. "God has chosen you from all eternity," they shout, and then, just to prove it, they give you the unfailing sign of that election, Christ's body and blood for you. The meal itself is a sign of your election in the midst of whatever sorrow or anxiety — big or small — that assails you. "We have been chosen for eternal life in Christ out of sheer grace, without any merit of our own." Here is the "blessed assurance" about which the hymn speaks.

Paragraphs 14-15. In the Reformed churches' struggle with a much more stringent doctrine of election in the seventeenth century, they often pointed struggling souls to their works. Since "good trees bear good fruit," the existence of such fruit surely proved one's election and brought some assurance. The problem is that such an approach could easily devolve into a form of works righteousness, where we imagine that the more works we do, the more likely we are to be elect.

The concordists, too, know about the importance of "confirming our calling," but even then they are rather wary. It is true; the surprising existence of good works in our lives is reason to rejoice. However, perhaps more appropriately, we can confirm our calling simply because we are saved from endless speculation about our election. God chooses us in Christ! That very fact frees us to worry about other things — chiefly, our neighbor and his or her needs. Meanwhile, we leave election where it belongs, in God's revealed Word. (Paragraph 15 merely summarizes the preceding and keeps us focused on the comfort God brings to us.)

Negative Theses (p. 519)

Paragraph 16. This lengthy introduction to the negative theses contains one of the most profound insights of Lutheran theology: The bottom line of any doctrine is not its correctness but its effect, its results. If what we teach on this article leads to despair or arrogance, then we must change the teaching, no matter how "right" it sounds to us. We dare never lose sight of why Christ came and what the gospel is all about. As my mother told me (article 5), "When you preach, comfort the people." This is the criterion by which to measure every doctrine, not just this one. No wonder Paul could write, as he was drawing to a close his magnum opus, the epistle to the Romans, "So that . . . by the comfort of the Scriptures we might have hope" (15:4). In the light of such consolation, the concordists could then criticize the positions of other churches.

    Paragraphs 17-19. Here the concordists take aim at the strict, "double-predestinarian" position of theologians like Theodorus Beza. They criticize the way such theology undermines the loving and gracious will of God (par. 17). They point out that (most seriously) it undermines the gospel and call of God (par. 18), as if one would have to add this caveat to every promise in the gospel: "If and only if you are chosen." Where is the comfort there? Finally (par. 19), they reject what the Solid Declaration calls equating election with a "military muster" (XI.9, in *BC 2000,* 642): "Cooper-White to the right; Rajashekar to the left. Wilson to heaven; Hoffmeyer to hell."

    Paragraph 20. The concordists realize that, having rejected such a stringent view of predestination, they dare not leave the impression that they give any foothold to works righteousness. Despite the logical conflict, they still insist that there is no cause for salvation in human beings. The unconditional grace of God really means grace *alone*. There is no cause in us or in God foreseeing our faith or works. When God makes a promise (namely, that we are saved by grace alone), God keeps it.

Paragraph 21. The point of predestination rests in the gospel, the good news, and in the comfort that news brings. When God names us in baptism, feeds us in the Lord's Supper, or speaks forgiveness to us in public proclamation, such promises can never be undermined by some secret decision of election or by any human work. The heightened language ("blasphemous, horrible, and erroneous") shows how central God's faithful, trustworthy promise is. God has in mind to comfort us. That fact alone, and not some secret fate hidden until the end of time, is the heart of the gospel.

A Formula for Parish Practice

What can Lutherans do in the face of God's gracious election and our loved ones' seeming rejection of it? First, we can with Paul remember that "It is not as though the word of God had failed" (Rom. 9:6). The seed is good and bears fruit, even when we cannot witness it and see only weeds and stony ground and hungry birds before the harvest (Mark 4). Second, we can pray, especially the second petition of the Lord's Prayer, which, Luther reminds us, is a prayer for the Holy Spirit and faith (SC, Lord's Prayer, 8, in *BC 2000*, 357). God has promised to hear our prayers on behalf of our loved ones, just as God had to hear Jesus' cries over Jerusalem. Third, we can remember that our neighbor's faith in God often remains hidden to us. God alone sees into the heart, and we best leave God to judge such things. Finally, we may be called to speak God's unconditional gospel to that person. To be sure, sometimes family dysfunction affects our effectiveness as bearers of the Word to those we love the most but who often can hear only law and judgment in even the most gracious of words. In that case we may pray all the more for someone else to bring "a word fitly spoken." We may, after all, be the one to bear that word for someone else's loved one. In all things, we can content ourselves with the Pauline comfort: "So it depends not on human will or exertion, but on God who shows mercy" (Rom. 9:16).

DISCUSSION QUESTIONS

- ▶ How might Calvinists critique the Lutheran doctrine of election?
- ▶ How and why do Lutherans distinguish between predestination (election) and foreknowledge? Where is the comfort for them in each doctrine?
- ▶ Though natural disasters are not evil, they do bring bad things. In light of God's foreknowledge, where might Lutherans say that God is in these natural disasters?
- ▶ The Lutheran doctrine of election stresses both the universal character of God's grace for all and the particular workings of the means of grace on each person. How might this differ from "universalistic" or "exclusivistic" understandings?
- ▶ Baptism is central for Lutheran teaching and practice. What might Lutherans say about those who are not baptized? How does this article help you to reconcile Lutheran understanding of the Word and sacraments and election?

Baptized Christians, Following Their Lord into Politics (and Other Messy Things)

He did not see me walking my greyhound some forty yards behind him in that well-to-do Houston neighborhood. He simply picked up a newspaper lying on the sidewalk, walked up to the door of the house, and placed it on the front stoop. In light of the Golden Rule, it was a rather simple good deed — made vastly more significant for me because I knew who this man was: homeless, sometimes mentally confused, and the product of a grim childhood. This was even more powerful a scene than the widow's mite in Mark 12, where the widow's behavior demonstrated how religious institutions make rich hypocrites or impoverished believers of us all. This man simply did for others — people whom he did not know and who certainly did not know him — what he would want them to do for him.

Imagine how this contrasts to a Lutheran Sunday school study book for teens published some years back. The point of the study was to give teenagers some sense of what living the Christian life entailed. Each chapter introduced a different historical personage for their consideration, including Francis of Assisi, Johann Sebastian Bach, Dr. Livingston (the missionary Stanley found in Africa), Elizabeth Fedde (founder of Lutheran deaconesses), Dietrich Bonhoeffer, and Martin Luther King, Jr. All of them were Christian "pros," whose idealized lives had no clear connection to the daily life in family, church, school, and society that teens in the 1980s faced every day. Too bad they couldn't have included in the study book that fellow carrying the newspaper or even my plumber, who sometimes brought his profoundly mentally challenged son with him to work on a job and allowed the boy to carry his tools.

When it comes to Christian ethics, the biggest danger and greatest lies arise for us when we trade in the real world and its messiness for an idealized Christian paradise on earth. The Formula of Concord wrestles with this issue in its twelfth and final article, addressed ostensibly to Anabaptists and others, who were in no way counted as Lutherans. Although the writers confronted a myriad of teachings that opposed Lutheranism in this article, the chief problem these Lutherans had with such groups was their idealized view of Christian life, which strove to take believers (and Christ!) out of this world and put them into some perfect Christian community. Such ideas flew in the face of one of Martin Luther's most important discoveries, that daily life — replete with family ties, political and social responsibilities, work, sin, and imperfection — *is* the Christian life. As surely as Christ came into the flesh but is not of the flesh, so Christians are truly "in the world but not of the world." For Christians, trying to escape from everyday life is simply immoral, to say nothing of impossible.

History

"Anabaptists," a nickname given to them by their opponents and meaning "rebaptizers," and other radical groups were never part of a coherent movement in the sixteenth century. Most of those advocating rebaptism were pacifists; a few were bloody revolutionaries. Some held to traditional understandings of the Trinity; others revived ancient heresies and are counted among the spiritual ancestors of present-day Unitarians. Some were scarcely more than lone thinkers; others formed communities that, despite persecution, have survived to this day as Mennonites, Hutterites, Amish, or Schwenckfelders. The best description of these groups is still George H. Williams, *The Radical Reformation,* 3rd ed. (Kirksville, Mo.: Sixteenth Century Journal Publishers, 1992). Here we will simply touch on the groups that come in for criticism in the Formula itself.

The first rebaptisms took place in Zürich, Switzerland, in January 1525, when a group known as the Swiss Brethren rejected Ulrich Zwingli's leadership of the Reformation there in favor (so they

thought) of a radical return to the Christianity of the apostles, especially as described in the Sermon on the Mount and Acts. As similar
small groups arose in other parts of the Holy Roman Empire of the
German Nation, they often espoused pacifism, adult baptism (including the rebaptism of those baptized in Reformation or Roman congregations), and strict, often communitarian life enforced by the ban and
shunning. With the exception of a bloody and short-lived revolution in
Münster, Germany, in the mid-1530s, these groups wanted little or
nothing to do with the wider community, sometimes refusing to take
oaths of allegiance and pay taxes to the constituted authorities.

Luther and Melanchthon, like some modern scholars, saw in such
rejections of sixteenth-century social and political life a return to medieval monasticism on a communal scale. Indeed, many Anabaptist
movements owed far less to Reformation theology, with its insistence
on justification by grace through faith alone, than to other strains of
late medieval piety and practice. Monastic reforms, too, had started as
returns to the *vita apostolica* (apostolic life). Monks and friars, too, practiced various forms of communalism, eschewed some social responsibilities, and tried as much as possible to separate themselves from the
world. Thus, it was not surprising to the reformers that these new
groups also rejected salvation by grace through faith alone, since they
seemed convinced that the purity of their works and communities especially counted in their relation to God.

Antitrinitarians first came to light in the late 1520s and continued
sporadically to show up in subsequent years. As in the cases of John
Campanus and Michael Servetus, the latter best known for his trial and
execution in Calvin's Geneva, sometimes they held views similar to
those of Arius (ca. 250–ca. 336), whose theories that Jesus was a second,
lesser God were rejected in the Nicene Creed. Others, especially followers of Laelius and Faustus Socinus, whose ideas had more influence on
the nineteenth and twentieth centuries than on the sixteenth, rejected
any triune understanding of God.

Caspar Schwenckfeld (1489-1561), a Silesian nobleman, moved
quickly in the 1520s from accepting Luther's theology to developing his
own highly mystical views. He rejected the real presence of Christ in the
Lord's Supper and formulated an understanding of Christ's spiritual
flesh after his resurrection that in the view of many Lutheran contem-
poraries contradicted the incarnation itself.

Luther and Melanchthon both wrote searing indictments of the Anabaptists in the 1520s. Melanchthon also interviewed several imprisoned Anabaptists in the 1530s and, with Luther, strongly rejected the revolutionaries in Münster. Antitrinitarians received somewhat less attention, although in later editions of the *Loci communes theologici,* Melanchthon's textbook on theology, several sections in the chapter on God refer to them. Melanchthon continued to attack both groups in confessional documents (including CA I, V, IX, XVI, and XVII) and other theological works. Schwenckfeld also became the target of the reformers' criticism, especially for his eucharistic theology and its concomitant teaching about Christ. Both referred to him in derogatory terms as "Stenckfeld" (a stinking field). For them, his notion of Christ's heavenly flesh violated the church's common teaching about the incarnation and his views of Christ's spiritual presence in the Lord's Supper seemed far too Zwinglian.

An article on these groups was included in the Formula for several reasons. First, the fact that already in 1530 John Eck had mixed the reformers' teachings with those of Anabaptists necessitated clear demarcation of Anabaptist and Lutheran teaching. Second, in confessional documents by Gnesio-Lutherans these groups had been condemned. Finally, Jakob Andreae himself included discussion of Anabaptists, Schwenckfelders, and antitrinitarians in his *Six Christian Sermons,* which formed the earliest direct source for the Solid Declaration. To underscore the importance of Christian vocation in the world, he organized his comments against the Anabaptists in particular according to the traditional three arenas of Christian activity: *ecclesia* (church), *politia* (society), and *oeconomia* (household, an institution that in the sixteenth century included the workplace). Already Luther had used these medieval divisions in his "Household Chart" (Table of Duties) in the Small Catechism (in *BC 2000,* 365-67) to encompass all Christian walks of life.

The Heart of the Matter

Daily life is the Christian life! This pill is sometimes as hard for today's Christians to swallow as it was for some in the sixteenth century. The powerful myth that one can only truly lead a Christian life by withdrawing from society and family — either permanently in a monastery or commune or for a short time on retreat in the wilderness or to the local Bible camp — continues to seduce Christians. Equally problematic are notions of "congregational monasticism," where people imagine that their Christian life can only truly be led within the four walls of the local church, or of "salvation by turning pro," where people dream that only entering the public ministry will fulfill their Christian life.

Daily life, by contrast, encompasses the true messiness of human existence: in church, society, and household. It ranges from breathing, sweating, and other bodily functions on the one hand to works of art, organization of society, and scientific inventions on the other, and everything in between. Nowadays people sometimes speak disdainfully (idealistically?) of "charity," insisting that real good work with the poor involves seeking social change. Not only does this boozy idealism ignore the fact that early Lutherans never limited doing good works to charity alone, but it also attributes a higher status to certain works on the basis of social theory (liberal or conservative), which sometimes can do greater harm in the name of the greater good than short-term charity. It is hard to imagine a more devastating view of the Christian life than one that tries to impose grand ideals on believers, forcing them to trust not in God but in their own abilities to shape their social world for the higher good.

In contrast, Lutherans ask a basic question: How may I best help my neighbor in this situation? Sometimes this involves picking up a newspaper. Sometimes it involves teaching one child to brush his teeth or another child to say her prayers. Sometimes it involves supporting one's pastor and defending him or her from malicious attacks. Sometimes it may involve working for better working conditions, preventing governmental intervention into household life, or preaching higher taxes to support public schools (in line with Luther's support of education, as in SC, Preface, 19-20, in *BC 2000,* 350). In all cases the neighbor's welfare in the real world is at stake. Christians may disagree *how* best to act in a given situation (after all, our reason is not perfect), but they all agree that help must be given, sometimes in the form of individual acts of kindness, sometimes in forms of simple palliation, and sometimes by reforming laws and institutions. In all cases such help is best delivered within our callings (by God!) in the household, the workplace, the society, and the church.

The Text of the Epitome

Concerning Other Factions and Sects
That Never Subscribed to the Augsburg Confession

[1] So that such heretical groups and sects may not tacitly be associated with us because we have not taken notice of them in the previous explanation of our teaching, we wish here at the end to list only the simple statements of doctrine in which they err and teach contrary to our Christian faith and confession, as we have presented it in detail.

The Erring Articles of the Anabaptists

[2] The Anabaptists are divided among themselves into many different factions, and some advocate many errors, others few. In general, however, they proclaim the kind of teaching that cannot be tolerated or permitted either in the church, in public affairs and temporal government, or in domestic life.

Intolerable Teachings in the Church

[3] 1. That Christ did not receive his body and blood from the Virgin Mary but brought them with him from heaven.

[4] 2. That Christ is not true God but merely has more gifts of the Holy Spirit than any other holy person.

[5] 3. That our righteousness before God rests not only upon the merit of Christ but also in our renewal and thus in the godliness of our own way of life. This rests for the most part upon our own special, self-selected spirituality [Col. 2:23] and is fundamentally nothing else than a new monasticism.

[6] 4. That children who are not baptized are not sinners in God's sight but instead are righteous and innocent. In their innocence, because they have not yet come into full exercise of their reason, they are saved without baptism (which in their opinion children do not need). They reject therefore the entire teaching of original sin and everything connected with it.

[7] 5. That children should not be baptized until they attain the use of reason and can confess their faith themselves.

[8] 6. That the children of Christians, because they are born to Christian

and believing parents, are holy without and before baptism and are God's children. This is also the reason why the Anabaptists do not regard infant baptism as important, nor do they encourage it, against the express words of God's promise, which only extends to those who keep his covenant and do not despise it (Gen. 17[:4-8, 19-21]).

[9] 7. That a congregation in which sinners are still found is not a true Christian congregation.

[10] 8. That no one should attend worship or hear a sermon in the houses of worship in which papal Masses were previously held and recited.

[11] 9. That no one should have anything to do with the ministers of the church who preach the gospel according to the Augsburg Confession and condemn the preaching and errors of the Anabaptists; that no one should serve these ministers or do any work for them, but should flee and avoid them as perverters of God's Word.

Intolerable Articles in Public Affairs

[12] 1. That service in government is not a God-pleasing walk of life in the New Testament.

[13] 2. That a Christian cannot fill or carry out functions in the government with a good, clear conscience.

[14] 3. That a Christian may not make use of the functions of government against the wicked in appropriate situations, nor may the subjects of the government call upon it to use the power it possesses and has been given by God for protection and defense.

[15] 4. That Christians may neither swear an oath with good conscience nor pay homage with an oath to their prince or lord.

[16] 5. That in the period of the New Testament, governmental authority may not execute criminals without harming its conscience.

Intolerable Articles in Domestic Life

[17] 1. That a Christian may not own or possess private property with a good conscience, but rather is bound to surrender all to the community.

Article Twelve

[18] 2. That a Christian may not be an innkeeper, merchant, or arms-maker with good conscience.

[19] 3. That married people may divorce for the sake of faith and abandon the other marriage partner, and then marry another who shares the same faith.

Erroneous Articles of the Schwenckfelders

[20] 1. That all those who hold that Christ is a creature according to the flesh have no correct knowledge of the reigning king of heaven, Christ.

[21] 2. That the flesh of Christ assumed all divine attributes through the exaltation in such a way that in status and essential dignity he, Christ, as a human being, is equal to the Father and the Word in all respects: in power, might, majesty, and glory, that from now on the two natures in Christ share one essence, one set of characteristics, one will, and the same glory, and that the flesh of Christ is a part of the essence of the Holy Trinity.

[22] 3. That the church's ministry, the Word as it is proclaimed and heard, is not a means through which God the Holy Spirit teaches human beings the saving knowledge of Christ and effects conversion, repentance, faith, and new obedience in them.

[23] 4. That the water of baptism is not a means through which God the Lord seals our adoption as children and effects new birth.

[24] 5. That bread and wine in the Holy Supper are not means through which and with which Christ distributes his body and blood.

[25] 6. That a Christian, who is truly reborn through the Holy Spirit, can keep and fulfill the law of God perfectly in this life.

[26] 7. That a congregation which does not practice public exclusion [of sinners] or has no regular process for excommunication is not a true Christian congregation.

[27] 8. That a minister of the church who is not personally and truly renewed, reborn, righteous, and godly may not effectively teach other people or distribute a proper, true sacrament to them.

Errors of the New Arians

[28] That Christ is not true, essential God by nature, of one eternal divine essence with God the Father and the Holy Spirit, but that he is merely adorned with divine majesty under and alongside God the Father.

Errors of the Antitrinitarians

[29] This is a completely new sect, never before heard of in Christendom. It believes, teaches, and confesses that there is not a single, eternal, divine essence of the Father, the Son, and the Holy Spirit, but as God the Father, the Son, and the Holy Spirit are three different persons, so each individual person also has its own distinct essence, separated from the other persons of the Godhead. Either all three — like three different human beings who in all other ways are completely separate from each other in their essences — would have equal power, wisdom, majesty, and glory; or, they are in essence and characteristics not equal, so that only the Father is the real, true God.

[30] These and articles like them and whatever other further errors are attached to these and follow from them, we reject and condemn as incorrect, false, heretical, and opposed to the Word of God, the three creeds, the Augsburg Confession and its Apology, the Smalcald Articles, and the Catechisms of Luther. All godly Christians, of higher or lower social station, should avoid them if they hold the welfare of their souls and their salvation dear.

Commentary

Introduction

Paragraph 1-2. Andreae states the reason for this article: to prevent confusion between these other sects and Lutheran teaching. Although preferring to concentrate simply on what they themselves "believe, teach, and confess," the concordists recognize that they must also from time to time define themselves over against other groups. They are merely saying, in effect, "These questions are not our questions and are opposed to our questions." Moreover, especially in the case of the Anabaptists, they also are expressing an important aspect of Lutheran ethics: daily life is the Christian life. Thus, Andreae specifically lists the three realms of human activity as defined in the sixteenth century: church, government (society), and household (par. 2). (In today's world household and work are generally separate arenas of living; only farmers and the self-employed may actually live and work in the same place.) Andreae also realizes that the term "Anabaptist" lumps together a broad array of groups. In modern encounters with the heirs of the Anabaptist traditions, we may find that they do not hold to any of the doctrines condemned here.

Intolerable Teachings of Anabaptists in the Church

Paragraphs 3-5. Here Andreae discusses basic Christian doctrine. The first intolerable teaching denies the humanity of Christ (par. 3). This is the christological equivalent of the idealism that marks much of Anabaptist ethics, a drive to escape the world. The second simply marks a low Christology that makes Jesus a good model for such human ethical striving (par. 4). The notion is that if Jesus could achieve holiness, so can human beings who similarly exercise their more limited spiritual gifts. The third links the entire enterprise to justification by grace through faith (par. 5). The use of Colossians 2:23 ("self-selected spirituality") and the charge of a new monasticism are in fact standard Lutheran criticisms since the 1520s and again attack ethical idealism.

Paragraphs 6-8. The most obvious difference between Lutherans and these groups comes on the question of so-called believer's baptism. First, such a view denies original sin (par. 6). (See the discussion of the connection between infant baptism and original sin in article 1 above.) Second, it implies that human beings have a free will and may use their reason to confess their faith (par. 7). Already in his tract *On Rebaptism* Luther had said that this was little better than placing one's faith in faith (and human abilities to attain faith) rather than in God's promises. (See the discussion in article 2 above.) Finally, the concordists reject the notion that Christian parents can pass on their holiness to their children (par. 8). Although this may not describe the thinking among the heirs of such groups, it again underscores the danger of idealizing Christian family life. We are all sinners who need God's grace and cannot inherit faith from our parents.

Paragraphs 9-11. Here the idealized view of the Christian community comes in for criticism. Already in Augustine's time, groups of Christians (Donatists) arose in North Africa claiming that the Christian community and especially its clergy had to be pure in order for its sacraments to be effective. Later, the Puritans in this country would often argue similarly against the impure Anglican Church. Even among Lutherans, criticisms of the church often assume that immoral behavior simply destroys God's work in a congregation. Lutherans can reject such idealization of the Christian congregation (par. 9). As Luther once said, "There are greater sinners in Wittenberg than in Rome." Moreover, there is no such thing as an intrinsically unholy place, just because something unholy was once done there (par. 10). God's Word, not human action, declares us forgiven and makes us holy. Finally, charges leveled at Lutheran pastors simply destroy Christian community (par. 11).

To apply this last point to our contemporary setting, one must watch out for the Lone Rangers — self-appointed Christian know-it-alls who form their own little groups and take potshots at teachers, pastors, and bishops. These people are accountable to no one except themselves and very often destroy congregations, synods, and entire church bodies simply by innuendo and unproved charges. Even today Christians "should flee and avoid them as perverters of God's Word." To idealize life in Christian community simply destroys the real community God establishes among sinners by grace alone.

Intolerable Articles in Public Affairs (p. 521)

Paragraphs 12-13. In short order the concordists attack an idealized view of the world. When 1 Timothy 2 enjoins prayer for the emperor and Romans 13 counsels paying taxes and giving honor to governing authorities, Christians are granted freedom to live in the messy world we actually encounter. More to the point, Christians can work in government. No politician or governmental official or police officer ever need feel like a second-class citizen in the church. Those who withdraw from society (and then criticize it from their lofty mountain retreats or ivory towers) simply increase the burdens for the rest of us who live in this world with all our neighbors (Christian and non-Christian alike).

Paragraphs 14-16. Probably the most destructive notion to creep into Christian ethical discussions these days is the widespread assumption that true Christians must be pacifists (par. 14). This view simply ignores the fact that there are real evils in the world and that Christians who do not defend their weaker neighbors against such evils (when they are able) are as guilty of the resulting crimes as the perpetrators! Sometimes such defense involves punishment and the use of force. Note well, however, that Andreae limits the work of government severely by using words like "in appropriate situations," "given by God," and most importantly, "for protection and defense."

Lutherans, like medieval Christians and many Christians today, speak about "just war." However, unlike many other groups, Lutherans follow Luther's lead and insist that for a war to be just it must also be strictly defensive. Luther even went further and argued that for the elector Frederick to defend his own people in religious matters, he must act like a *"fremder Freund"* (a disinterested party; literally, "a foreign friend"). Self-aggrandizement and manifest destiny are never options. At the same time, the concordists do not argue against the death penalty *on religious grounds* (par. 16). Today one may imagine some very good *practical* reasons for abolishing the death penalty (or for not going to war), but we dare not take the "higher" (read: idealized) moral ground and imagine that Christians could never in their right minds argue for retaining it.

The matter of oaths (par. 15) touches on the glue that held late medieval society together. Unlike modern society in the United States, where only new citizens, politicians, and soldiers take oaths of allegiance, everyone in medieval societies was bound to princely or urban governments by oaths. The equivalent in our day might be arguing that driver's licenses, passports, or other means of identification were sinful. These, too, involve basic commitments to society and government.

Intolerable Articles in Domestic Life

Paragraph 17. We need not live as monks. Whatever the practices of the Jerusalem community in Acts, they are not commanded for all Christians. Instead, we may simply live in the world with money and credit cards and all the rest. The danger of abuse, of course, is always there. But such is the case in any social system. The good news for Christians is that they do not have to run off and form their own system before they can truly live the Christian life. The ethical issue is not whether we *have* property but what we actually *do* with the property we have. If we worship money or financial security, ignore our neighbors' needs, try to shelter our wealth from paying our fair share of taxes to support the poor and other governmental functions, then we are in trouble no matter what the economic system.

Paragraph 18. Innkeeper, merchant, and arms-maker are not quite standard professions today. Yet they represent areas of life that many today still consider shady. Less than 100 years ago Prohibition banned the sale of alcohol. Merchants and malls, national chains and international conglomerates also come in for criticism. But what sense would it make to condemn people just for being involved in trade? Christians can handle money and pour beer. And they can sin both in doing those things and in refraining from doing such things. Of course, arms-makers (the profession of Philip Melanchthon's father) give us the worst time ethically. But what is the concordists' perspective? One could pour blood on the gates of arms manufacturers to demonstrate revulsion for the ill such arms may cause, or one could admit that having arms (and far too many of them) may bring down oppressive regimes or prevent them from acting unilaterally. Both "theories" must be measured not by the ideals they espouse but by the neighbors actually helped. In any case, one may not simply say that weapons are in themselves evil or good. Lutherans always ask a second practical question: To what end? How are they actually used? The same may be said of all professions and walks of life.

Paragraph 19. Here the concordists confront a form of idealism that strikes at the very heart of Christian life: that purity demands leaving the impure behind, in this case the impure spouse. This paragraph does not approve forcing a Christian to stay with an abuser or persecutor, but it does allow that the Christian may live deeply in the flesh, intimately connected with an unbeliever, without having to run away to find greater purity somewhere else or with someone else. There are plenty of real reasons for divorce (and even more reasons for faithfulness) without our making up idealized versions of "true" Christian marriage.

Article Twelve

Schwenckfelders, New Arians, and Antitrinitarians

Paragraphs 20-27. Here a real but minor opponent of Lutheranism is rejected. Indirectly the concordists had already in article 8 rejected Schwenckfeld's position on Christ, who, according to him, started out as an ignorant man but then had his flesh assumed into the Trinity (par. 20-21). Christ is true God and true human being; in him alone the finite contains the infinite. This principle also spills over into the concordists' understanding of Schwenckfeld's rejection of the means of grace (par. 22-24). The Holy Spirit uses the actual words coming out of the preacher's mouth, the actual water and word of baptism, and the actual bread, wine, and word of the Supper. The final three statements (par. 25-27) reject the same thing, but in connection with the church. We are at the same time righteous and sinner; all forms of fanatic moral purity imposed on the individual (par. 25), on the congregation (par. 26), or on the pastor (par. 27) have no place in the Christian faith.

    Paragraphs 28-30. Arius, a fourth-century heresiarch, had plenty of imitators in the sixteenth century, especially John Campanus and Michael Servetus. Their condemnation is fairly perfunctory in paragraph 28. Paragraph 29 takes on the Socinians. Their alternatively tritheistic or unitarian views have no place in Lutheran theology. Finally, in an omnibus paragraph (par. 30), the concordists point their theological heirs to Scripture and the other documents contained in *The Book of Concord* as a sure way of combating other errors. The concordists are not simply obsessed with theological correctness. Instead, for godly Christians in all walks of life, they view this as a matter of "the welfare of their souls and their salvation."

A Formula for Parish Practice

God has placed us on earth to serve our neighbors in their needs, not to earn our way into heaven. This means that the opportunity for good works is nearly endless. Every breath we take is a good work. Every time a parent changes a baby's diaper, it is a good work. Every time spouses embrace in love, another good work is committed. Every time we pay for a loaf of bread or earn a decent wage — those things, too, are good works. Have you ever driven on the correct side of the road? That is a good work, too, where, as with many other human activities, the goodness becomes clear only in the face of the opposite. (Try driving against the traffic, and see how much havoc you wreak!) Paying taxes, serving in the military or as a member of a police force, voting, running for office — the list of societal good works is also endless. Rescuing children from despair, reclaiming the environment, serving as a crossing guard — all these qualify, too. The list goes on and on.

Despite the cries of many moralists, on the right or left side of the political spectrum, the problem lies not with the *works* — all human beings do them, whether Christian or not. The problem for Christians lies with *faith*. We do not have the faith to see our mundane lives from the perspective of God, who is forty yards behind us all the time, ready to be amazed by random acts of kindness, by deeds that change lives for the better individually or corporately, and by good in whatever form it takes.

Simply consider the people you know and what they are doing. The only trouble is that what they are doing is so individualized that it is hard to fathom the richness of daily life and infinite examples of doing good works for the neighbor. When I look at my immediate family, for example, and examine only their vocations in this world (their callings in the household, society, or church would require an even longer list), I am simply amazed. There I find a grandfather who, as district attorney of Milwaukee County in the 1920s, made headlines by summarily dismissing an underling for improper behavior with women. There is a grandmother who helped care for her severely handicapped grandson with her daughter-in-law. There is my mother, who spent a lifetime as a nurse, nursed her own husband in his struggle with Alzheimer's, and continued to advise folks in her retirement community. My father, a political scientist, spent five months away from home in 1959 serving on a team advising Prime Minister Nehru on India's food shortage. My sister is a counselor in an elementary school in the toughest neighborhood in Los Angeles. (When I ask her why she bothers, she always responds with the story of the little girl throwing beached starfish back into the sea. When someone points out that the girl's efforts will make no difference because there are simply too many that need help, she picks up a single starfish, throws it back in the ocean, and calmly says, "For that one, it makes a difference.") My brother's work on drying wood increased dramatically the amount of wood that may be successfully harvested from a single tree. My late wife worked as chief cataloguer of a township library in the Philadelphia area; her faith in the face of certain death moved her colleagues beyond description. My daughter often writes articles for medical trade journals and told the story of a burn unit treating a survivor of the 11 September 2001 attack on the Pentagon. My son works for an AIDS foundation and also takes time to tutor disadvantaged children. My second wife is a pastor. And these are simply the closest relatives! It leaves out the nephews — the emergency room doctor, the lawyer for the Government Accounting Office, the Peace Corps worker now in banking — and the nieces trained in social work and business. To say nothing about all my third cousins who are Iowa hog farmers at or around the family's homestead!

Now, of course, being in the world, they also sin, make mistakes, back the wrong solution to a social or political problem, get their priorities wrong, neglect other callings, forget Whose they are, etc., etc. Sometimes what they did may have seemed right at the time but turned out to be wrong. In that case, in the words of Pastor Franklin Fry from New Jersey, they, and we, are well advised to take our "reverent best guess" and move on, admitting the limitations of our reason. Think of what would have happened to all the people whose lives these people touched if they had for some reason decided that the *only* way truly to be Christian was to spend all their time at church, or to turn pro, or to go on perpetual retreat! Instead, they just bumble on in this world, doing more good than they could ever imagine. Would that God would grant them the eyes to see their work in the light of faith!

What, then, is the difference between Christians who do such things and non-Christians? Not the work but faith alone! Externally, the works all look alike, and thus we need not invent "anonymous Christians" among the non-Christians to explain how they can do moral things. After all, God wants to take care of all people and see that all receive their daily bread. The only difference regarding good works is not the works at all but the faith that allows us to see these works for what they are: good and holy in God's sight. Only by faith do we hear the angels singing for joy when a child's diaper is changed, a just tax paid, a spouse kissed, or a worker paid a decent wage.

As a translator, I do not like to criticize translations, but I think the NRSV translators could have done better on Ephesians 2:10. After the stirring words of the previous two verses ("For by grace you have been saved through faith, and this is not your own doing; it is the gift of God — not the result of works, so that no one may boast"), I would render the next verse as follows. "You are God's work of art, created in Christ Jesus for good works, which God has ordained beforehand for us to walk in." Later in the same book (4:28), the author suggests that a thief should stop stealing and work with his hands, so that he has something to give to those in need. This is not an ideal world being described here but the real one, filled with former crooks and needy people. At its center is not, finally, some special set of Christian works for the perfect Christian community but the real world of needy people and the time and energy God has given for us to walk among them. God has prepared for us — we who are God's very own works of art — an entire lifetime of good works in which to walk *by faith alone*. All God "requires" us to do is wake up in the morning, put our feet on the ground, and keep them there by faith alone. *Soli Deo gloria!*

DISCUSSION QUESTIONS

- ► In your daily life, did you witness someone being a Christian today as described above? What was that person doing? Why did you notice?
- ► Have you ever longed to be "more holy" or wanted your community of faith to be more spiritual? What would they have to "do" to achieve such a goal? What would be done to those who "fail to measure up"? If you are a pastor, have you ever longed for "a more faithful" congregation? How does that differ from the Lutheran proposal for daily Christian life?
- ► How do people serve in your congregation? Why do they do it? How has God surprised you even when you felt forced into serving?
- ► Make a list of the work vocations of members of your congregation. (Do not forget to include the "home work" and "volunteer work" of retirees and others.) What would it mean to include specific prayers on Sunday for specific vocations when appropriate? How might this expand your congregation's notion of vocation? How would you feel to hear your work being prayed for?
- ► In a Christmas sermon, Luther admonished his listeners not to

boast about how willingly they would have helped Mary, because Christ is the needy neighbor in their midst whom they neglect. Who has treated you as Christ? Whom have you treated as Christ?

▶ Some consider politics "too dirty" for Christians. But what happens when Christians stand aloof? How can one remain a faithful Christian and be a politician too?

▶ In a world of competing interests, how do we determine which neighbor to help? How do we help especially the poor?

▶ According to Ephesians 2:10, "You are God's work of art, created in Christ Jesus for good works." What work of art is God creating in your life?

Glossary

accidents A technical term in Aristotelian philosophy describing the qualities or external characteristics of a thing (as opposed to its substance or essence); used in the Middle Ages to explain Christ's presence in the Lord's Supper as transubstantiation.

adiaphora A Greek term, used in Stoic philosophy to denote things that are ethically neither right nor wrong but used in Lutheran theology especially for practices that are not specifically commanded or forbidden in Scripture.

Agricola, John (1494-1566) Luther's student and later opponent on the issue of the law; accused of antinomianism. As adviser to the court of Brandenburg after 1540, he also helped draft and supported the Augsburg Interim.

Amsdorf, Nicholas von (1483-1565) A close colleague of Luther and erstwhile bishop of Naumburg; opposed the Philippists, especially Major.

Anabaptists Literally, rebaptizers; a general term for a variety of groups from the sixteenth century that opposed the baptism of infants and, in the early stages of their development, practiced rebaptism.

Andreae, Jakob (1528-1590) A professor at the University of Tübingen and author of the Epitome, as well as portions of the Solid Declaration; a student of Brenz.

antinomianism Literally, belief opposed to the law; a disparaging term for theology that denigrated the law completely or argued that it did not apply to Christians but only to unbelievers or in worldly affairs.

Apology of the Augsburg Confession Melanchthon's defense of the Augsburg Confession, originally written to be delivered to the emperor Charles V in Augsburg in 1530 but subsequently expanded and published first in May 1531 and in a final form in October 1531.

Apostles' Creed The expanded, ancient baptismal creed of the Roman Church used throughout Western Christianity and, in the sixteenth century, thought to have been written by the twelve apostles.

Aristotle (ca. 384-322 B.C.) A philosopher whose rediscovery in the Middle Ages led to the blossoming of scholastic Christian theology (e.g., Thomas Aquinas).

Arius (ca. 250–ca. 336) A presbyter in Alexandria, proclaimed a heretic for his strict view of the subordination of Christ to God the Father.

Athanasian Creed A Latin profession of faith, probably from fifth-century Gaul, written to profess the faith against certain forms of Arianism and hence ascribed to Athanasius, bishop of Alexandria.

Augsburg Confession The basic Lutheran confession of faith, first presented to Emperor Charles V at the Diet of Augsburg on 25 June 1530 and signed by several imperial princes (including John of Saxony and Philip of Hesse) and cities.

Augsburg Interim An interim solution to the religious strife in the Holy Roman Empire; first promulgated by Charles V in June 1548, it was supposedly to remain in effect until the calling of a council of the church. It allowed evangelicals little more than married clergy and communion in both bread and wine.

August, elector of Saxony (1526-1586) Saxon elector from 1553 and staunch supporter of Lutheran theology; purged the University of Wittenberg of crypto-Philippists and supported the development of the Formula of Concord.

Augustine, bishop of Hippo (354-430) Influential theologian and teacher of the Western Church in northern Africa.

Basil of Caesarea. *See* Eusebius of Emesa

Beza, Theodorus (1519-1605) Successor to Calvin and leader of the church in Geneva after Calvin's death in 1564.

Biel, Gabriel (ca. 1420-1495) A late-scholastic theologian whose textbooks were extremely influential in the early sixteenth century and read by Luther.

Book of Concord   The collection of Lutheran confessions of faith, published in 1580, which included the Augsburg Confession and its Apology, Luther's catechisms, and his Smalcald Articles. Its Formula of Concord, written by later Lutheran theologians, provided unity for about two-thirds of the Lutherans in the Holy Roman Empire.

Brandenburg   A principality in the Holy Roman Empire whose capital was Berlin.

Brenz, Johann (1499-1570)   The south German reformer who after the Smalcald War was the chief religious adviser to Duke Christopher of Württemberg.

Bucer, Martin (1491-1551)   The reformer of Strasbourg (then an imperial city) and signer of the Wittenberg Concord in 1536, who fled to England in the aftermath of the Smalcald War.

Bugenhagen, Johannes (1485-1558)   Chief pastor in Wittenberg and colleague and confessor for Luther.

Calvin, John (1509-1564)   French refugee in Strasbourg in the 1530s and later reformer of Geneva. He subscribed to the Wittenberg Concord but later came under attack for his views on the Lord's Supper by Lutherans, including Westphal.

Capernaitic   A derogatory term for those who held to a doctrine of the real presence, implying a physical, cannibalistic eating of Christ's flesh, derived from Jesus' hearers in John 6 (in Capernaum).

Charles V, Holy Roman emperor (1500-1558)   Ruled from 1519 until 1556, when his brother Ferdinand took over. He presided at the diets in Worms (1521) and Augsburg (1530, 1547-1548).

Chemnitz, Martin (1522-1586)   Lutheran theologian, student of Luther and Melanchthon, who contributed greatly to the composition of the Solid Declaration.

Christ, one person   The teaching of Christology that Christ's two natures (human and divine) are united in a single person.

Christ, two natures   The teaching of Christology that the one person of Christ has two natures: human and divine. Thus, Jesus Christ is both a human being, born of Mary, and God, begotten from eternity of God the Father.

Christian freedom   The ability to act in accord with God's will from one's heart and faith (and thus not from the coercion of the law).

Christology The teaching in the church having to do with who Jesus Christ is: one person in two natures (human and divine).

Christopher, duke of Württemberg (1515-1568) Lutheran prince and supporter of Brenz.

Christus solus Literally, Christ alone; often employed by Luther to emphasize that human salvation comes only from Christ and not from human cooperation or assistance.

Chrysostom, John (ca. 347-407) Bishop of Antioch and Constantinople, prolific writer and preacher, whose sermons on various books of the Bible were very influential in the Western Church beginning in the thirteenth century and throughout the Reformation.

Chytraeus, David (1531-1600) Lutheran theologian and student of Melanchthon who later taught at the University of Rostock and contributed to the text of the Solid Declaration.

communicatio idiomatum Literally, communication of attributes (or characteristics); the teaching of Christology that Christ's divine nature communicates its attributes in a real way to the human nature within the one person of Christ.

concordists The authors and signers of the Formula of Concord — Chemnitz, Andreae, Chytraeus, Musculus, Selnecker, and Körner.

corpus doctrinae Literally, body of doctrine; the basic teachings and, later, the collection of confessional documents binding on the Lutheran teachers and preachers in a particular principality.

Council of Trent (1545-1563) A series of assemblies by Roman Catholic bishops in the imperial (Italian) city of Trent, the decrees of which defined Roman Catholicism over against Reformation churches and rid the church of some practical abuses.

crypto-Calvinists. *See* Crypto-Philippists

crypto-Philippists A term for those Lutheran theologians (chiefly at the University of Wittenberg) who, under the guise of being faithful to the eucharistic theology of Melanchthon, established an understanding of the Lord's Supper that stressed almost exclusively Christ's spiritual presence and effect in the Lord's Supper. When their true position came to light, they were dismissed by Elector August of Saxony. Sometimes called crypto-Calvinists.

Donatists Followers of the North African schismatic bishop of Carthage, Donatus, later opposed by Augustine for insisting that the benefits of grace in the sacraments came only from pure clergy to pure recipients.

Eck, John (1486-1543) One of the chief Roman opponents of Luther and Melanchthon; he defended the papacy and accused the reformers of forbidding good works, among other things.

election. *See* Predestination

elector Next to the emperor, the highest princely title in the Holy Roman Empire, held by the four secular princes and three archbishops who elected the new emperor in an interregnum.

Enthusiasten ("enthusiasts") An ancient heresy of Greek monks who claimed they did not need external means of grace (the Word and sacraments), but relied instead on direct inspiration of the Holy Spirit; the term was applied by Luther and other Lutherans to anyone who denigrated the means of grace as God's way of redeeming human beings.

Epitome of the Formula of Concord The digest of the Solid Declaration, written by Andreae at the request of Lutheran princes, who wanted a more succinct version of the Solid Declaration.

Erasmus of Rotterdam (1469-1536) A Latin linguist and editor of Greek and Latin texts (especially the Greek New Testament) who clashed with Luther over the freedom of the will.

Eusebius of Emesa (ca. 300–ca. 359) A Greek bishop and writer, whose writings were sometimes later attributed to Basil of Caesarea.

Eutycheanism The heresy in Christology that held that after the incarnation the two natures of Christ (human and divine) formed a single nature (Monophysitism).

evangelicals The self-designation by most sixteenth-century Lutherans, as those who proclaim the good news (evangel), not to be confused with modern uses of the term for conservative (Reformed) Christians in the United States.

extra Calvinisticum The belief, often attributed to Calvin but held by other theologians as well, that the divinity of Christ remains outside of (Latin: *extra*) Christ's humanity as well as united with it. Thus, in the Lord's Supper, one could encounter Christ's divinity but not his humanity, which had ascended to God's right hand.

Flacius, Matthias (1520-1575) A Gnesio-Lutheran opponent of Melanchthon, especially on the issues of original sin, free will, and *adiaphora*.

foreknowledge As distinguished from predestination, God's knowledge of all events at all times and places, which, according to the Formula, God used to limit the evil and bend it toward the good.

forensic justification The Lutheran teaching about justification that held that, like in a court of law (Latin: *in foro*, hence, the original meaning of "forensic"), God pronounces sinners forgiven for the sake of Christ, which is their justification or righteousness before God.

Formula of Concord The document, published in *The Book of Concord*, that sought to forge peace in the 1570s among the various Lutheran factions. It consisted of two parts, the Epitome and the Solid Declaration.

free will (choice) The belief about the nature of human beings that insisted that they have certain freedom to choose and act. While all Lutherans held that human beings exercise some freedom in matters of this life, they disputed whether or not they possess any freedom to predispose themselves toward God's grace and salvation in Christ. The concordists insisted that they do not.

Gallus, Nicholas (1516-1570) A Gnesio-Lutheran pastor in Regensburg, who opposed Melanchthon and the so-called Leipzig Interim.

Gnesio-Lutherans Literally (from the Greek), genuine Lutherans; opponents of the Philippists who insisted on what they saw as Luther's actual positions on *adiaphora* and other topics. They included Flacius, Gallus, and von Amsdorf.

good works Everything a person of faith does that arises from faith and trust in Christ and from God's mercy alone and thus accords with God's will for humanity revealed in the Ten Commandments.

gospel, use of God uses the good news (or promise) of salvation in Christ to create faith, forgive sin, comfort the terrified, and enliven those dead in sin.

Hardenberg, Albert (1510-1574) A pastor in Bremen and friend of Melanchthon who held to a spiritual view of Christ's presence in the Lord's Supper similar to that of Calvin, and who was opposed by Lutheran theologians, including Chemnitz.

Heidelberg Catechism Written by Reformed theologians in the early 1560s after the ouster of Lutherans from the University of Heidelberg, it espoused a more spiritual understanding of Christ's presence in the Lord's Supper.

Hesshus, Tileman A student of Melanchthon and, later, Lutheran professor at the University of Heidelberg, who lost his position because of his (Lutheran) understanding of the Lord's Supper, when Melanchthon wrote a memorandum attacking his view.

Holy Roman Empire The political entity in central Europe, founded in 800 by Charlemagne as a continuation of the Roman Empire; in the sixteenth century it encompassed what is now Germany, Austria, the Netherlands, the Czech Republic, Slovakia, and parts of western Poland, northern Italy, eastern France, and, nominally, Switzerland.

indifferentia. See *Adiaphora*

Joachim II, elector of Brandenburg (1505-1571) Margrave of Brandenburg and elector from 1535, whose son, John George (1525-1598), signed *The Book of Concord.*

John Frederick, elector (duke) of Saxony (1503-1554) Elector from 1532 to 1546, until his defeat in the Smalcald War, when he was briefly imprisoned and allowed to keep only his ducal lands and title. He established the University of Jena.

John Frederick the Middler, duke of Saxony (1529-1595) Son of John Frederick and supporter of Gnesio-Lutherans.

justification The teaching of the church regarding righteousness (Latin: *iustitia*) before God and, hence, forgiveness of sins and salvation. Later Protestant theologians distinguished justification by faith alone (God's declaration of the sinner to be righteous in Christ) from sanctification (the Holy Spirit's making of the believing sinner into a righteous person through righteous living and attitudes). Luther and, to some extent, Melanchthon did not observe this distinction in their language or theology. *See also* Forensic justification

koinonia Literally (in Greek), communion or fellowship; preferred by Melanchthon (citing 1 Cor. 10:16) as the best way to describe Christ's presence in the Lord's Supper with the bread and wine.

Körner, Christopher (1518-1594) One of the signers of the Formula of Concord.

Large Catechism Luther's exposition of the Ten Commandments, Apostles' Creed, Lord's Prayer, baptism, the Lord's Supper, and confession, based on his 1528 and 1529 sermons in Wittenberg and published in 1529; included in *The Book of Concord.*

Lateran IV Council A 1215 council of the Western Church, held in

Rome, at which the doctrine of transubstantiation was approved, as was the withholding of the cup from the laity.

law, uses of Luther and, following him, Melanchthon defined two uses of the law in the 1520s — the first or civil use of the law, in which God uses the law (commandments) to maintain order in this world and restrain evil, and the second or theological use of the law, in which God uses the law to reveal sin, terrify the sinner, and put to death the old creature of unbelief in preparation for the gospel. In 1534 Melanchthon proposed a third use, which functioned to guide Christians toward what God wills (and thus rejected both antinomianism and Roman understandings of justification through faith and works of love) but which the concordists defined as the first and second use applied to Christians.

law and gospel. *See* Gospel, use of; Law, uses of

Leipzig Interim So called because it was proposed to the provincial Saxon diet meeting in Leipzig, where it was rejected by the Saxon estates gathered at Moritz's behest. It was a compromise proposal, written by Melanchthon and other Saxon theologians, to avert the worst parts of the Augsburg Interim, but it was bitterly attacked by Gnesio-Lutherans.

Loci communes theologici Literally (in Latin), theological commonplaces; it was the name for Melanchthon's famous theological textbook that covered the basic topics *(loci communes)* using the appropriate passages of Scripture and the church fathers.

Ludwig, Count Palatine and Elector (1539-1583) The count of the Rhenish Palatinate and signer of the *Book of Concord.*

Ludwig, duke of Württemberg (1554-1593) Duke from 1576 and important force behind and signer of the Formula of Concord.

Luther, Martin (1483-1546) Evangelical reformer and professor at the University of Wittenberg.

Major, George (1502-1574) Student of Luther and Melanchthon, professor at the University of Wittenberg, chief protagonist in the Majoristic Controversy.

Majoristic Controversy The theological dispute, involving Major and von Amsdorf, over the necessity of good works in salvation.

Manichaeanism A Christian heresy, based on formulations of the Persian dualistic teacher Mani (ca. 216–ca. 277), holding to a strict division of matter and spirit. In the sixteenth century people who held to a fatalistic view of predestination or to the notion that God created evil were often accused of Manichaeanism.

Marburg Colloquy A meeting in 1529 between Zwingli, Oecolampadius, Luther, and Melanchthon, called at the behest of Philip of Hesse in an attempt to solve the Lord's Supper controversy.

Marcion (d. ca. 160) A heretic who attempted to rid Christianity of any influence from the Old Testament but who, in the sixteenth century, was most often associated with the view that Christ was not fully human (born of a Jewish mother).

Maulbronn Formula An early formula of accord, written by theologians from Württemberg (especially Andreae) and one of the sources for the Solid Declaration.

Melanchthon, Philip (1497-1560) A colleague of Luther at the University of Wittenberg and author of the Augsburg Confession and its Apology. After Luther's death and in the aftermath of the Smalcald War, he became embroiled in many of the disputes that the Formula of Concord sought to solve. Most of the authors of the Solid Declaration were his students and were influenced by his method and theology.

Menius, Justus (1499-1558) A supporter of Melanchthon, and hence a Philippist; took part in the Majoristic Controversy.

Moritz, duke (elector) of Saxony (1521-1553) An elector beginning in 1548, by virtue of his defeat of John Frederick in the Smalcald War. In that war an ally of Charles V, he switched sides during the Princes' Revolt and defeated him, leading to the Peace of Augsburg.

Mörlin, Joachim (1514-1571) Lutheran preacher in various places in Germany and, while in Königsberg, opponent of Osiander.

Musculus, Andreas (1514-1581) Professor at the University of Frankfurt an der Oder and a contributor to and signer of the Formula of Concord.

Nestorianism The christological heresy traced to Nestorius (d. ca. 451), patriarch of Constantinople, who rejected the union of Christ's natures in favor of a conjunction.

Nicene Creed The most widely accepted Christian creed, first formulated at the Council of Nicea in 325 and reaffirmed and expanded to its present form at the Council of Constantinople in 381. It rejected all forms of Arianism.

Oecolampadius, John (1482-1531) Reformer in Basel, Switzerland, whose eucharistic theology, opposed by Luther, matched that of Zwingli.

original sin Often called in German the inherited sin *(Erbsünde)*, it is the term for the rebellious state of humanity outside the grace and mercy of God in Christ, shared by all human beings. Thus, the Augsburg Confession defines it as humanity's lack of trust in or fear of God.

Osiander, Andreas (1498-1552) Pastor in Nuremberg who fled to Königsberg in East Prussia after the Smalcald War, where he became professor and was immediately embroiled in controversy over the nature of justification through Christ's righteousness.

Otto, Anton (1505-?) A Gnesio-Lutheran pastor and one of the participants in debates over the nature of law and gospel.

particulae exclusivae Literally (from Latin), exclusive terms; used in the Formula of Concord for those terms in Scripture (such as "only," "alone," "without") that indicate that salvation comes exclusively from God's grace and mercy and is received exclusively by faith (not works).

Peace of Augsburg A political agreement, reached in 1555 in Augsburg, between the evangelical princes and the Roman Catholic princes, including Emperor Ferdinand, that resolved the dispute over religion in the Holy Roman Empire by recognizing a (second-class) status for the evangelical princes and their territories and allowing that (except in certain ecclesiastical lands) the one who ruled could determine the confession.

Pelagianism A heresy, named for the British monk Pelagius (ca. 350-420) and opposed by Augustine, that insisted that God's grace was limited to human abilities and the law and that salvation depended on human exertion. In the sixteenth century this term was often used to label any theology that seemed to undercut God's mercy and stressed human cooperation with God's grace in salvation.

Peter Lombard (ca. 1100-1160) A medieval theologian who assembled and organized an enormously popular textbook, called the *Sentences,* containing the opinions (Latin: *sententiae*) of biblical and patristic sources on a variety of theological questions. Many later theologians, including Thomas Aquinas and Luther, were required to lecture on this book to become doctors of theology.

Peucer, Caspar (1525-1602) Melanchthon's son-in-law and professor of medicine at the University of Wittenberg, and later leader of the crypto-Philippists.

Pfeffinger, Johann (1493-1573) A student of Melanchthon and professor at the University of Leipzig, involved in debates with von Amsdorf over the free will in the Synergistic Controversy.

Philip, landgrave of Hesse (1504-1567) One of the signers of the Augsburg Confession, who earlier had convened the Marburg Colloquy and was later defeated in the Smalcald War.

Philippists Supporters of Melanchthon and his theology who fought against the Gnesio-Lutherans from the 1550s through the early 1570s over *adiaphora,* free will, original sin, good works, law and gospel, and the Lord's Supper. *See also* Crypto-Philippists

Plato (ca. 427-347 B.C.) Greek philosopher who spawned numerous schools of thought and whose ideas experienced a renaissance in the sixteenth century, especially in the notion of grace understood as an essential spiritual power or force and in the distinction between the material and the spiritual.

Poach, Andreas (d. 1585) A pastor in Halle involved in disputes over law and gospel.

predestination For Lutherans the sovereign grace and mercy of God, who elects to salvation sinners without any merit or works.

Princes' Revolt The uprising of many imperial princes (evangelical and Roman Catholic) against Charles V in the early 1550s, orchestrated by Moritz of Saxony, that resulted in the Truce of Passau (1552) and then the Peace of Augsburg.

real presence The Lutheran teaching that Christ is truly present with (or in or under) the bread and wine in the Lord's Supper. This doctrine is not an explanation of *how* Christ is present and is not to be identified with consubstantiation (as opponents of Lutherans sometimes do) or transubstantiation.

Reformed theology The third major Christian confession arising out of the sixteenth-century Reformation (next to Roman Catholicism and Lutheranism) and associated with positions on the Lord's Supper held by Zwingli, Calvin, and Bucer. Many Reformed theologians also hold to a stricter understanding of predestination, which teaches that God elects people for both salvation and perdition.

Rhenish Palatinate An electoral principality of the Holy Roman Empire centered in Heidelberg and running along the Rhine River.

sacramentarian A derogatory term, used by Lutherans, for theologians who deny the real presence of Christ in the Lord's Supper.

Saliger, Johann (active after 1550) Preacher in Lübeck and Rostock who clashed with Chytraeus over the disposition of leftover elements from the celebration of the Lord's Supper.

Saxon-Swabian Concord The revised version of the Swabian Concord by Chemnitz and Chytraeus and source for the Solid Declaration.

Saxony Several principalities in east-central Germany, of which the most important was electoral Saxony. With the fall of Wittenberg in the Smalcald War, John Frederick lost the electoral dignity to his cousin, Moritz; at that point the universities of Wittenberg and Leipzig came to be in electoral Saxony.

Schwenckfeld, Caspar (1490-1561) A mystic and radical theologian who defended Christ's spiritual presence in the Lord's Supper and argued that, after the resurrection, Christ retained only a spiritual flesh.

Selnecker, Nicholas (1528/30-1592) A student of Melanchthon and professor in Wittenberg, who signed the Formula of Concord.

simul iustus et peccator Literally (from Latin), at the same time righteous and sinner; a term used by Luther to indicate that in justification God declares precisely sinners to be righteous. This contrasts to the teaching in medieval theology and in the Council of Trent moving a sinner through an infusion of grace and the disposition to love from a state of sin to a state of grace.

Smalcald Articles Written in 1536 by Luther and published in a slightly expanded form in 1538, these articles were to serve as the electoral Saxon position in the event their representatives were allowed to attend a council called by the pope and in anticipation of Luther's death.

Smalcald League A political alliance, involving particularly electoral Saxony and the Landgraviate of Hesse and begun in 1531, which saw defeat in the Smalcald War.

Smalcald War The war of 1546-1547 in the Holy Roman Empire, triggered in large part by religious differences between the Smalcald League and the emperor (but also involving claims to the bishopric of Naumburg and the duchy of Braunschweig-Wolfenbüttel), which ended with the total defeat of the Smalcald League.

Small Catechism Luther's brief introduction to the basics of the

Christian faith for the Christian household, explaining the Ten Commandments, the Apostles' Creed, the Lord's Prayer, the sacraments and including basic prayers and instructions for the household, first published in 1529 and revised in 1531.

sola fide Literally (from Latin), by faith alone; the catchword often used by Luther and other Lutheran theologians who insist that justification occurs not by human works or cooperation but by trusting God's promise of mercy in Christ.

sola gratia Literally (from Latin), by grace alone; the catchword used by many Lutherans and non-Lutherans to acknowledge God's activity in human salvation. However, when grace is defined not as a power or force infused by God into the human soul but as God's undeserved mercy and favor, then the phrase describes the Lutheran understanding of forensic justification.

sola Scriptura Literally (from Latin), by the Scripture alone; a catchword, seldom if ever used by Luther (who more often used the broader term "the Word alone" [*solum verbum*]) and first coined by later Lutherans (after the Formula of Concord) to connote that the central authority of doctrine is the Scripture.

Solid Declaration of the Formula of Concord The proposal for concord, written in the late 1570s chiefly by Andreae, Chytraeus, Chemnitz, and Musculus, beginning with Andreae's *Six Sermons* and including the Swabian Concord, the Saxon-Swabian Concord, the Maulbronn Formula, and finally the Torgau Book. Andreae condensed it in the Epitome.

Stancaro, Francesco (1501-1574) A professor at the University of Königsberg at the same time as Osiander, who fought over how Christ's natures affected justification.

Strigel, Viktorin (1524-1569) A student of Melanchthon and professor of philosophy at the University of Jena, who struggled with Flacius over the nature of original sin.

substance A technical term in Aristotelian philosophy describing the essence or quiddity of a thing (as opposed to its accidents or external qualities); used in the Middle Ages to explain Christ's presence in the Lord's Supper as transubstantiation.

Swabian Concord Andreae's rewriting of his original proposal for concord (the *Six Sermons*) in a form requested by north German theologians.

synergism, Synergistic Controversy The belief that the human will in some weak way cooperates with (Greek: *syn-ergos;* works with) God in human salvation; a view attributed to Pfeffinger in his dispute with von Amsdorf over the freedom of the will.

theology of the cross A central aspect of Luther's theology that held that God is revealed under the appearance of the opposite.

Thomas Aquinas (ca. 1225-1274) A scholastic theologian, particularly successful in blending Aristotelian metaphysics and Christian theology, whose work was later used by the Council of Trent as its chief theological resource.

Timann, Johann (d. 1557) Pastor in Bremen and opponent of Hardenberg in a debate over the Lord's Supper.

Torgau Book The compilation (by the eventual signers of the Formula of Concord) of various earlier proposals for concord (the Maulbronn Formula, the Swabian Concord, and the Saxon-Swabian Concord), which in reworked form became the Solid Declaration.

transubstantiation The medieval doctrine of Christ's presence in the Lord's Supper, approved at the Lateran IV Council, which held that the accidents of bread and wine remained unchanged but that the substance of the bread and wine were changed (transubstantiated) into the substance of Christ's body and blood.

Treatise on the Power and Primacy of the Pope An appendix to the Augsburg Confession, written by Melanchthon in 1537 and signed by many evangelical theologians, which attacked the authority of the papacy.

Truce of Passau A cease-fire in 1552, which ended the Princes' Revolt and led to the Peace of Augsburg.

ubiquity The Lutheran teaching that the whole person of Christ, in his divine and human natures, is fully present everywhere (Latin: *ubique*).

vocation The principle, espoused by Luther and many Lutherans, that God calls all believers to serve their neighbors in the household, at work, and in the broader world. Luther developed this over against the notion that the monastic "calling" (Latin: *vocatio*) was a higher way of life for Christians, and that taking vows placed a person in a so-called state of perfection.

Westphal, Joachim (1510/11-1574) A Gnesio-Lutheran pastor in Hamburg, who opposed Calvin's understanding of the Lord's Supper.

Wittenberg Concord An agreement, reached in 1536, between representatives of south German cities (notably Strasbourg, represented by Bucer) and the theologians of Wittenberg (notably Luther and Melanchthon, who with Bucer drafted the agreement).

Württemberg A duchy in south Germany whose capital was Stuttgart, served by Brenz and Andreae.

Zwingli, Ulrich The reformer of Zürich who opposed Luther's doctrine of Christ's real presence in the Lord's Supper.

Index